American
GOVERNMENT
EIGHTH EDITION

Using
MicroCase®
ExplorIt

Michael Corbett
Ball State University

Barbara Norrander
University of Arizona

THOMSON
™
WADSWORTH

Australia • Canada • Mexico • Singapore • Spain • United Kingdom • United States

Publisher/Executive Editor: *Clark Baxer/David Tatom*
Developmental Editor: *Stacey Sims*
Technology Project Manager: *Melinda Newfarmer*
Assistant Editor: *Heather Hogan*
Editorial Assistant: *Dianna Long*
Marketing Manager: *Janise Fry*

Production Service: *Jodi B. Gleason*
Consulting Editor: *Julie Aguilar*
Printbuyer: *Doreen Suruki*
Project Coordinator: *Rita Jaramillo*
Printer: *Patterson Printing*
Duplicator: *Sanyo*

Printed in the United States of America.
1 2 3 4 5 6 7   06 05 04 03 02

Printed by Patterson Printing
0-534-58785-2

**For more information about our products,
contact us at:
Thomson Learning Academic Resource Center
1-800-423-0563**

**For permission to use material from this text,
contact us by:
Phone: 1-800-730-2214
Fax: 1-800-731-2215
Web: www.thomsonrights.com**

Asia
Thomson Learning
60 Albert Complex, #15-01
Albert Complex
Singapore 189969

Australia
Nelson Thomson Learning
102 Dodds Street
South Street
South Melbourne, Victoria 3205
Australia

Canada
Nelson Thomson Learning
1120 Birchmount Road
Toronto, Ontario M1K 5G4
Canada

Europe/Middle East/South Africa
Thomson Learning
Berkshire House
168-173 High Holborn
London WC1 V7AA
United Kingdom

Latin America
Thomson Learning
Seneca, 53
Colonia Polanco
11560 Mexico D.F.
Mexico

Spain
Paraninfo Thomson Learning
Calle/Magallanes, 25
28015 Madrid, Spain

CONTENTS

ACKNOWLEDGMENTS

Michael Corbett and I assumed co-authorship of *American Government: Using MicroCase ExplorIt* with the seventh edition. Mike led the way in our efforts, having the expertise in creating interesting and challenging exercises in data analysis through his other publications using the MicroCase software. Sadly, Mike succumbed to cancer at the conclusion of the seventh edition, and his assistance on the current edition was greatly missed. Mike was a gifted teacher of political science, not only to his students at Ball State University, but to thousands of students nationwide through his textbooks and workbooks. He and his contributions will be sorely missed by the profession. Our hearts continue to express sympathy to his wife, Julia Corbett, professor of religious studies at Ball State, their children and grandchildren. I respectfully dedicate this and future editions to the memory of Michael Corbett.

The current edition also owes much of its format to the six editions that proceeded Mike's and my involvement in the project. Through the years, this book had many "authors" who helped to shape the topics and assignments. Further, the contributions of instructors who were willing to try something new need to be acknowledged. Because so many people who teach American government really care, the computer-based approach to "hands-on" learning incorporated in this workbook can continue to contribute to the education of succeeding cohorts of students.

David Tatom of Wadsworth Publishing should be credited for his continued support of the MicroCase series of workbooks. As always, Julie Aguilar, MicroCase Technology Program Manager, provided invaluable assistance in the handling of the data sets and the MicroCase program. Jodi Gleason was the production coordinator. Stacey Sims of Wadsworth Publishing oversaw the project. The contributions of Julie, Jodi, and Stacey were essential for the successful completion of this updated version.

I would like to acknowledge the contribution of Rodney Stark at the University of Washington, who first developed the format used in this series of introductory workbooks. His leadership in making real data analysis accessible to students has transformed the way many teach introductory social science courses. Special thanks goes to Matt Bahr, who oversaw much of the development, organization, and cleaning of the data files for this project.

I would like to thank a number of individuals and institutions who provided us with the data files upon which most of these exercises are based. The inclusion of selected variables from the American National Election Study would not have been possible without the generous help and permission of Nancy Burns and Donald R. Kinder and the National Election Studies, Institute for Social Research at the University of Michigan. I also thank the Inter-university Consortium for Political and Social Research for their permission to use the NES data. Special thanks goes to Tom W. Smith at the National Opinion Research Center for his continued direction and administration of the General Social

Survey. Many of the international variables are based on the World Values Survey, for which I must thank Ronald Inglehart at The Institute for Social Research, University of Michigan. Professor Inglehart's book *Modernization and Postmodernization: Cultural, Economic and Political Change in 43 Societies* (Princeton, 1997) provided the inspiration for a number of examples in this workbook. The Center for the American Woman and Politics at the Eagleton Institute of Politics at Rutgers University also provided very useful data.

Finally, I would like to thank the following individuals who have contributed to this edition or previous editions: Gary Aguiar, Texas A&M International University; John B. Ashby, Northern Michigan University; Lindsey Back, Morehead State University; Martha Bailey, Southern Illinois University at Edwardsville; Hal Barger, Trinity University; Devin Bent, James Madison University; John Berg, Suffolk University; Milton Boykin, The Citadel; Robert Bradley, Illinois State University; Chalmers Brumbaugh, Elon College; Jeri Cabot, College of Charleston; Sara B. Crook, Peru State College; Roy Dawes, Gettysburg College; Robert J. Duffy, Rider College; Leonard Faulk, SUNY at Fredonia; William Flanigan, University of Minnesota; Richard Fulton, Northwest Missouri State University; Tucker Gibson, Trinity University; John Hibbing, University of Nebraska–Lincoln; Laurence F. Jones, Angelo State University; Nancy Kindred, McNeil High School; Karen King, Bowling Green State University; Nancy Kral, North Harris Montgomery College District; Peter Maier, University of Wisconsin–Milwaukee; Theresa Marchant-Shapiro, Union College; Suzanne M. Marilley, Capital University; David McLaughlin, Northwest Missouri State University; Scott L. McLean, Quinnipiac College; Lawrence W. Miller, Collin County Community College; Francie Mizell, Dekalb College; William J. Murin, University of Wisconsin–Parkside; Dale A. Neuman, University of Missouri–Kansas City; G. R. Patterson, Porterville College; Kelly D. Patterson, Brigham Young University; Richard Pride, Vanderbilt University; Ron Rapoport, College of William and Mary; James Reed, College of St. Benedict; William Rosburg, Kirkwood Community College; Ralph Salmi, California State University–San Bernardino; David Schultz, University of Minnesota; Randy Siefkin, Modesto Jr. College; Valerie Simms, Northeastern University; J. Donald Smith, Cornell College; Joseph Stewart, University of New Mexico; Christopher Stream, University of Idaho; Eric Uslaner, University of Maryland–College Park; Jeff Walz, Concordia University–Wisconsin; Robert Weber, St. John's University; Matthew E. Wetstein, San Joaquin Delta College; Peter Wielhouwer, Spelman College; Harvey Williams, Christopher Newport College; Nancy Zingale, University of St. Thomas; Gary Zuk, Auburn University.

Barbara Norrander
Tucson, Arizona

PREFACE

The purpose of *American Government: Using MicroCase ExplorIt* is to let you discover many basic aspects of the American government and political system for yourself. There is nothing make-believe or "only educational" about this package. You will have access to the highest-quality data files available to professional researchers. The "facts" you discover are not someone's opinion—they accurately describe the real world.

You will browse the best and latest information available on questions such as:

◆ To what extent are Americans interested in (and informed about) politics? What kinds of people are more interested and informed?

◆ Who participates in politics? What kinds of people are more likely to vote? Are nonvoters different from voters in terms of political views?

◆ How concerned were Americans about domestic and international terrorism prior to the attacks on the World Trade Center and the Pentagon on September 11, 2001?

◆ In comparison with people in other nations, to what extent do Americans support civil liberties and civil rights? Would most Americans allow atheists or others who hold unpopular views to express those views? How many would be willing to vote for a woman for president?

◆ How do political parties function? How do Americans become party members? How are third parties handicapped in the United States?

◆ How does federalism work and why do people in some regions think it is unfair?

◆ What kinds of people are elected to Congress? Where do they get their money? Does it make any difference whether a member of Congress is a Democrat or a Republican? Are members of Congress more ideological or less ideological than the general public?

◆ What are minority presidents and how do they get elected? Why have so many presidents come from Ohio?

Discovering answers to these questions won't hurt a bit, even if you have never used a computer. The software is so easy to use that you will pick up everything you need to know in a few minutes.

What's New in the Eighth Edition

As before, the data sets are extensive, current, and from the best sources available. The eighth edition uses the 2000 General Social Survey and the 2000 National Election Study. Both data sets include an extensive list of questions, allowing students to analyze topics beyond those examined in the exercises. The congressional data set has been updated to the 107th Congress and includes information on individual votes, interest group ratings, campaign expenditures, and personal and political information on each representative. Updates have been added to the data set on the 50 states, especially new information from the 2000 Census.

With this edition, both the MicroCase program and the data sets are recorded on a single CD-ROM. This facilitates both the installation of the software and data files on your computer or running the application from the CD-ROM.

GETTING STARTED

INTRODUCTION

Political science is an empirical science. The goal of this workbook is to help you learn how to use data to explore the world of political science and how to investigate new ideas and conduct research to test these ideas.

Each exercise in this workbook has two sections. The first section discusses a particular area of American government and demonstrates how data are used to support, augment, and test the ideas proposed. It is possible to read this section without using your computer. However, all of the graphics in the text can be created on your computer by following the ExplorIt Guide, which is described later in this section. Ask your instructor whether you should follow along the first section of each exercise with a computer.

The worksheet section allows you to follow up on these ideas by doing your own research. You will use the student version of ExplorIt to complete these worksheets.

When you finish this workbook, you'll know what political scientists actually do!

SYSTEM REQUIREMENTS

- Windows 95 (or higher)
- 8 MB RAM
- CD-ROM drive
- 15 MB of hard drive space (if you want to install it)

To run the software on a Macintosh, you will need emulation software or hardware installed. For more information about emulation software or hardware, check with your local Macintosh retailer or try the Web site http://machardware.about.com/cs/pcemulation/.

NETWORK VERSIONS OF STUDENT EXPLORIT

A network version of Student ExplorIt is available at no charge to instructors who adopt this book for their course. It's worth noting that Student ExplorIt can be run directly from the CD-ROM on virtually any computer network—regardless of whether a network version of Student ExplorIt has been installed.

INSTALLING STUDENT EXPLORIT

If you will be running Student ExplorIt directly from the CD-ROM—or if you will be using a version of Student ExplorIt that is installed on a network—skip to the section "Starting Student ExplorIt."

To install Student ExplorIt to a hard drive, you will need the CD-ROM that is packaged inside the back cover of this book. Then follow these steps in order:

1. Start your computer and wait until the Windows desktop is showing on your screen.

2. Insert the CD-ROM disc into the CD-ROM drive of your computer.

3. On most computers the CD-ROM will automatically start and a Welcome menu will appear. If the CD-ROM doesn't automatically start, do the following:

   Click [Start] from the Windows desktop, click [Run], type **D:\SETUP**, and click [OK]. (If your CD-ROM drive is not the D drive, replace the letter D with the proper drive letter.)

4. To install Student ExplorIt to your hard drive, select the second option on the list: "Install Student ExplorIt to your hard drive."

5. During the installation, you will be presented with several screens, as described below. In most cases you will be required to make a selection or entry and then click [Next] to continue.

6. The Student ExplorIt program will now be installed. At the end of the installation, you will be asked if you would like a shortcut icon placed on the Windows desktop. It is recommended that you select [Yes]. You are now informed that the installation of Student ExplorIt is finished. Click the [Finish] button and you will be returned to the opening Welcome Screen. To exit completely, click the option "Exit Welcome Screen."

The first screen that appears is the **License Name** screen. (If this software has been previously installed or used, it already contains the licensing information. In such a case, a screen confirming your name will appear instead.) Here you are asked to type your name. It is important to type your name correctly, since it cannot be changed after this point. Your name will appear on all printouts, so make sure you spell it completely and correctly! Then click [Next] to continue.

A **Welcome** screen now appears. This provides some introductory information and suggests that you shut down any other programs that may be running. Click [Next] to continue.

You are next presented with a **Software License Agreement**. Read this screen and click [Yes] if you accept the terms of the software license.

The next screen has you **Choose the Destination** for the program files. You are strongly advised to use the destination directory that is shown on the screen. Click [Next] to continue.

STARTING STUDENT EXPLORIT

There are three ways to run Student ExplorIt: (1) directly from the CD-ROM, (2) from a hard drive installation, or (3) from a network installation. Each method is described below.

Starting Student ExplorIt from the CD-ROM

Unlike most Windows programs, it is possible to run Student ExplorIt directly from the CD-ROM. To do so, follow these steps:

1. Insert the CD-ROM disc into the CD-ROM drive.

2. On most computers the CD-ROM will automatically start and a sign-in screen will appear. (Note: If the CD-ROM does **not** automatically start after it is inserted, click [Start] from the

Windows desktop, click [Run], type **D:\SETUP** and click [OK]. If your CD-ROM drive is not the D drive, replace the letter D with the proper drive letter.) Enter your name in the box and press <Enter> to continue to the Welcome Screen.

3. Select the first option from the Welcome menu: **Run Student ExplorIt from the CD-ROM**. Within a few seconds Student ExplorIt will appear on your screen.

Starting Student ExplorIt from a Hard Drive Installation

If Student ExplorIt is installed to the hard drive of your computer (see earlier section "Installing Student ExplorIt"), it is **not** necessary to insert the CD-ROM. Instead, locate the Student ExplorIt "shortcut" icon on the Windows desktop, which looks something like this:

To start Student ExplorIt, position your mouse pointer over the shortcut icon and double-click (that is, click it twice in rapid succession). If you did not permit the shortcut icon to be placed on the desktop during the install process (or if the icon was accidentally deleted), you can alternatively follow these directions to start the software:

Click [Start] from the Windows desktop.

Click [Programs].

Click [MicroCase].

Click Student [ExplorIt - AM].

After a few seconds, Student ExplorIt will appear on your screen.

Starting Student ExplorIt from a Network

If the network version of Student ExplorIt has been installed to a computer network, double-click the Student ExplorIt icon that appears on the Windows desktop to start the program. (Note: Your instructor may provide additional information that is unique to your computer network.) Enter your name when prompted to view the Welcome screen.

MAIN MENU OF STUDENT EXPLORIT

Student ExplorIt is extremely easy to use. All you do is point and click your way through the program. That is, use your mouse arrow to point at the selection you want, then click the left button on the mouse.

The main menu is the starting point for everything you will do in Student ExplorIt. Look at how it works. Notice that not all options on the menu are always available. You will know which options are available at any given time by looking at the colors of the options. For example, when you first start the software, only the OPEN FILE option is immediately available. As you can see, the colors for this option are brighter than those for the other tasks shown on the screen. Also, when you move your mouse pointer over this option, it is highlighted.

EXPLORIT GUIDES

Throughout this workbook, "ExplorIt Guides" provide the basic information needed to carry out each task. Here is an example:

> ➤ *Data File:* **STATES**
> ➤ *Task:* **Mapping**
> ➤ *Variable 1:* **116) MURDER**
> ➤ *View:* **Map**

Each line of the ExplorIt Guide is actually an instruction. Let's follow the simple steps to carry out this task.

Step 1: Select a Data File

Before you can do anything in Student ExplorIt, you need to open a data file. To open a data file, click the OPEN FILE task. A list of data files will appear in a window (e.g., COLONIAL, COUNTY, GSS, etc.). If you click on a file name *once*, a description of the highlighted file is shown in the window next to this list. In the ExplorIt Guide shown above, the ➤ symbol to the left of the Data File step indicates that you should open the STATES data file. To do so, click STATES and then click the [Open] button (or just double-click STATES). The next window that appears (labeled File Settings) provides additional information about the data file, including a file description, the number of cases in the file, and the number of variables, among other things. To continue, click the [OK] button. You are now returned to the main menu of Student ExplorIt. (You won't need to repeat this step until you want to open a different data file.) Notice that you can always see which data file is currently open by looking at the file name shown on the top line of the screen.

Step 2: Select a Task

Once you open a data file, the next step is to select a program task. Six analysis tasks are offered in this version of Student ExplorIt. Not all tasks are available for each data file, because some tasks are appropriate only for certain kinds of data. Mapping, for example, is a task that applies only to ecological data, and thus cannot be used with survey data files.

In the ExplorIt Guide we're following, the ➤ symbol on the second line indicates that the MAPPING task should be selected, so click the MAPPING option with your left mouse button.

Step 3: Select a Variable

After a task is selected, you will be shown a list of the variables in the open data file. Notice that the first variable is highlighted and a description of that variable is shown in the Variable Description window at the lower right. You can move this highlight through the list of variables by using the up and down cursor keys (as well as the <Page Up> and <Page Down> keys). You can also click once on a variable name to move the highlight and update the variable description. Go ahead—move the highlight to a few other variables and read their descriptions.

If the variable you want to select is not showing in the variable window, click on the scroll bars located on the right side of the variable list window to move through the list. See the following figure:

By the way, you will find an appendix at the back of this workbook that contains a list of the variable names for key data files provided in this package.

Each task requires the selection of one or more variables, and the ExplorIt Guides indicate which variables should be selected. The ExplorIt Guide example here indicates that you should select 116) MURDER as Variable 1. On the screen, there is a box labeled Variable 1. Inside this box, there is a vertical cursor that indicates that this box is currently an active option. When you select a variable, it will be placed in this box. Before selecting a variable, be sure that the cursor is in the appropriate box. If it is not, place the cursor inside the appropriate box by clicking the box with your mouse. This is important because in some tasks the ExplorIt Guide will require more than one variable to be selected, and you want to be sure that you put each selected variable in the right place.

To select a variable, use any one of the methods shown below. (Note: If the name of a previously selected variable is in the box, use the <Delete> or <Backspace> key to remove it—or click the [Clear All] button.)

- Type the **number** of the variable and press <Enter>.

- Type the **name** of the variable and press <Enter>. Or you can type just enough of the name to distinguish it from other variables in the data—MUR would be sufficient for this example.

- Double-click the desired variable in the variable list window. This selection will then appear in the variable selection box. (If the name of a previously selected variable is in the box, the newly selected variable will replace it.)

- Highlight the desired variable in the variable list, then click the arrow that appears to the left of the variable selection box. The variable you selected will now appear in the box. (If the name of a previously selected variable is in the box, the newly selected variable will replace it.)

Once you have selected your variable (or variables), click the [OK] button to continue to the final results screen.

Step 4: Select a View

The next screen that appears shows the final results of your analysis. In most cases, the screen that first appears matches the "view" indicated in the ExplorIt Guide. In this example, you are instructed to look at the Map view—that's what is currently showing on the screen. In some instances, however, you may need to make an additional selection to produce the desired screen.

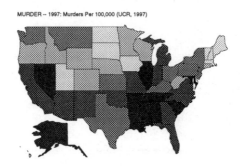

MURDER -- 1997: Murders Per 100,000 (UCR, 1997)

(OPTIONAL) Step 5: Select an Additional Display

Some ExplorIt Guides will indicate that an additional "Display" should be selected. In that case, simply click on the option indicated for that additional display. For example, this ExplorIt Guide may have included an additional line that required you to select the Legend display.

Step 6: Continuing to the Next ExplorIt Guide

Some instructions in the ExplorIt Guide may be the same for at least two examples in a row. For instance, after you display the map for murder in the example above, the following ExplorIt Guide may be given:

> Data File: **STATES**
> Task: **Mapping**
> ➤ Variable 1: **115) VIOL.CRIME**
> ➤ View: **Map**

Notice that the first two lines in the ExplorIt Guide do not have the ➤ symbol located in front of the items. That's because you already have the data file STATES open and you have already selected the MAPPING task. With the results of your first analysis showing on the screen, there is no need to return to the main menu to complete this next analysis. Instead, all you need to do is select VIOL.CRIME as your new variable. Click the [⟳] button located in the top left corner of your screen and the variable selection screen for the MAPPING task appears again. Replace the variable with 115) VIOL.CRIME and click [OK].

To repeat: You need to do only those items in the ExplorIt Guide that have the ➤ symbol in front of them. If you start from the top of the ExplorIt Guide, you're simply wasting your time.

If the ExplorIt Guide instructs you to select an entirely new task or data file, you will need to return to the main menu. To return to the main menu, simply click the [Menu] button located at the top left corner of the screen. At this point, select the new data file and/or task that is indicated in the ExplorIt Guide.

That's all there is to the basic operation of Student ExplorIt. Just follow the instructions given in the ExplorIt Guide and point and click your way through the program.

ONLINE HELP

Student ExplorIt offers extensive online help. You can obtain task-specific help by pressing <F1> at any point in the program. For example, if you are performing a scatterplot analysis, you can press <F1> to see the help for the SCATTERPLOT task.

If you prefer to browse through a list of the available help topics, select **Help** from the pull-down menu at the top of the screen and select the **Help Topics** option. At this point, you will be provided a list of topic areas. Each topic is represented by a closed-book icon. To see what information is available in a given topic area, double-click on a book to "open" it. (For this version of the software, use only the "Student ExplorIt" section of help; do not use the "Student MicroCase" section.) When you double-click on a book graphic, a list of help topics is shown. A help topic is represented by a graphic with a piece of paper with a question mark on it. Double-click on a help topic to view it.

If you have questions about Student ExplorIt, try the online help described above. If you are not very familiar with software or computers, you may want to ask a classmate or your instructor for assistance.

EXITING FROM STUDENT EXPLORIT

If you are continuing to the next section of this workbook, it is *not* necessary to exit from Student ExplorIt quite yet. But when you are finished using the program, it is very important that you properly exit the software—do not just walk away from the computer or remove your CD-ROM. To exit Student ExplorIt, return to the main menu and select the [Exit Program] button that appears on the screen.

Important: If you inserted CD-ROM before starting Student ExplorIt, remember to remove it before leaving the computer.

Part I

FOUNDATIONS

America has always been a large and very diverse place—even before it became a nation.

In 1776, at the start of the American Revolution, the 13 colonies covered 4 times the area of France and 17 times the area of England—of all European nations at that time, only Russia had a greater land area. And, although the total population of the 13 colonies was a bit less than 4 million, that was not a small population for the time. The population of England then was only slightly more than 7 million and was concentrated in an area about the size of Pennsylvania, while the American colonists were spread across an extremely diverse range of climates and terrains. Moreover, the American people themselves differed greatly from one place to another, from mountaineers and merchants to sailors and slaves.

Thus, from the very start, the physical and human features of the United States have posed political challenges. How can such a large and diverse society be governed fairly, effectively, and democratically? More than two centuries of efforts to solve these fundamental questions provide the foundations of the American government.

In the first three exercises, you will explore aspects of these foundations.

"ONE NATION": THE HISTORY AND POLITICS OF REGION

I pledge allegiance to the flag of the United States of America and to the Republic for which it stands, one Nation . . .

THE PLEDGE OF ALLEGIANCE,
FRANCIS BELLAMY, 1892

Tasks: Mapping, Historical Trends
Data Files: COLONIAL, STATES, COUNTY, HISTORY

In the beginning the "United States" were hardly united in any important sense of the word. Initially each "state" was a British colony administered independently by a governor and other officials sent from Britain. Even the perils of the Revolutionary War did not bring much unity. General George Washington often lacked troops and supplies because individual colonies often failed to keep their promises to provide them. Following the war, efforts to create a nation initially resulted in a very weak union of the 13 "states" under the provisions of the Articles of Confederation. The Articles established a national legislature having one house to which states could send up to seven delegates, but each state had only one vote. There was no president, and each state had its own courts. Real power remained in the individual states, and the national legislature was able to do very little. However, a series of political and economic crises led to growing support for a stronger central government. Eventually this resulted in the Constitutional Convention, which gathered in Philadelphia in 1787 and created the federal system that has been in operation since the Constitution was ratified by the states—Rhode Island being the last state to do so, on May 29, 1790.

All things considered, it was relatively easy to merge the original 13 colonies into a nation because they were similar in so many ways. For example, the overwhelming majority of citizens in each state were native English speakers of British ancestry (English, Scottish, Welsh, and Irish).

In a standard textbook, a statement like this might be followed by an instruction directing you to look at a printed map to show you the percentage of the population of British ancestry in each of the colonies. In fact, such a map appears on the next page of this book. But what makes this workbook different from an ordinary textbook is that *you* are able to generate a map of *any* item included in the COLONIAL, NATIONS, COUNTY, or STATES data files—whether it be a map of British ancestry in the American colonies or the unemployment rate in the 50 states today. And once a map is on your computer screen you can do a lot of other things to it, which you will discover as you proceed through this exercise.

➤ *Data File:* **COLONIAL**
➤ *Task:* **Mapping**
➤ *Variable 1:* **3) %BRITISH**
➤ *View:* **Map**

%BRITISH -- 1790: Percent of White Population of British Ancestry

If you want to reproduce this graphic on the computer screen using ExplorIt, review the instructions in the *Getting Started* section. For this example, you would open the COLONIAL data file, select the MAPPING task, and select 3) %BRITISH for Variable 1. The first view shown is the Map view. (Remember, the ➤ symbol indicates which steps you need to perform if you are doing all examples as you follow along in the text. So, in the next example, you only need to select a new view—that is, you don't need to repeat the first three steps because they were already done in this example.)

In this map of the nation in 1790, the states appear in several colors from very dark to very light. The darker a state, the higher the percentage of its citizens who were of British ancestry. The states shown in the lightest color have the lowest percentage. Now let's look at the actual percentages.

Data File: **COLONIAL**
Task: **Mapping**
Variable 1: **3) %BRITISH**
➤ *View:* **List: Rank**

RANK	CASE NAME	VALUE
1	Massachusetts	89.0
2	North Carolina	86.5
3	Virginia	84.9
4	South Carolina	84.7
5	Georgia	84.4
6	Vermont	84.3
7	Rhode Island	78.8
8	Maryland	77.9
9	Delaware	74.3
10	Maine	72.5

As indicated by the ➤ symbol, if you are continuing from the previous example, select the [List: Rank] button. The number of rows shown on your screen may be different from that shown here. Use the cursor keys and scroll bar to move through this list if necessary.

Massachusetts was the highest, with 89 percent of its population in 1790 being of British ancestry. North Carolina was number two (86.5 percent). Moving down this list we discover that Pennsylvania was the lowest, but even it had a substantial majority (54.9 percent) of British origins. Let's note that there were many colonists from other nationalities as well, such as the French, the Germans, the Swedish, and the Dutch. Further, keep in mind that there were parts of the continent that would later become part of the United States that were heavily French or Spanish (e.g., Louisiana, Florida). Keep in mind also that a substantial percentage of the population consisted of slaves, who were, of course, from Africa. However, the important point here is that the population of the original thirteen colonies was primarily from a British background and this had a great impact on the prospects of establishing a unified nation with a national identity.

Political scientists frequently refer to "variables" when they do research. For example, they might describe the percent British as an "interesting variable." A **variable** is anything that varies or takes different values among the things or units of analysis being studied. In this case these things or units are the states in 1790. And the percent British is something that varies among them. But not just any feature of states is a variable. For example, each of the states had a population. Therefore, having a population is not a variable (it does not vary). But a different number of people lived in each state, and therefore the size of each state's population is a variable: We can rank states from the smallest to the largest. Similarly, the population of each state differed (or varied) in terms of what percentage of the total was of British ancestry. Other pertinent variables include the geography and climate of these states, their histories, the percentage who belonged to churches, the size of the average farm, and the number of bars and taverns per 10,000 population—all characteristics on which the states differ are variables.

When we study individuals, we also are interested in variables: age, sex, race, weight, education, income, party affiliation, favorite TV shows, and so on—all the ways in which people differ from one another are variables.

Sometimes political scientists seek variables that reveal the greatest amount of difference. However, for the moment, our interest is in showing that there was little variation among the original states on some variables, that in these ways the states were very similar. So let's examine another such variable.

% PROT. -- 1776: Percent of Church Members Who Are Protestants

> Data File: **COLONIAL**
> Task: **Mapping**
> ➤ Variable 1: **4) % PROT.**
> ➤ View: **Map**

If you are continuing from the previous example, use the [↺] button to return to the variable selection screen. Select variable 4) % PROT. as the new Variable 1.

This map shows the percentage of all church members in each state who were Protestants in 1776.

> Data File: **COLONIAL**
> Task: **Mapping**
> Variable 1: **4) % PROT.**
> ➤ View: **List: Rank**

RANK	CASE NAME	VALUE
1	Massachusetts	100.0
1	South Carolina	100.0
1	New Hampshire	100.0
1	Rhode Island	100.0
1	North Carolina	100.0
1	Connecticut	100.0
1	Maine	100.0
1	Vermont	100.0
1	Georgia	100.0
10	Virginia	99.8

The states were even more similar in terms of religion than ethnicity. In only six states were there any Roman Catholics, and even Maryland, initially the only colony that admitted Catholics, was overwhelmingly Protestant (84.4 percent). In fact, the great majority of Americans of Irish ancestry were Irish Protestants; it was not until the 1840s that substantial numbers of Irish Catholics began to arrive.

While the overwhelming majority of the colonists were Protestants, there was substantial diversity among these Protestants—a diversity that had strong implications for the development of the new nation and its Constitution and continues to be important in American politics today. "Protestantism" in the colonies ranged from Puritans to Methodists to a rational religion based on ideas coming out of European Enlightenment. Nevertheless, the common Protestant background helped to forge a coalition of traditional and nontraditional religious groups to carry out the American Revolution.

However, the original states were extremely different in one important way—a difference that would long haunt American political history: slavery.

SLAVES -- 1790: Number of Slaves

> Data File: **COLONIAL**
> Task: **Mapping**
➤ Variable 1: **5) # SLAVES**
➤ View: **Map**

Here the variable is the number of slaves in each state as recorded by the first U.S. Census, conducted in 1790.

> Data File: **COLONIAL**
> Task: **Mapping**
> Variable 1: **5) # SLAVES**
➤ View: **List: Rank**

RANK	CASE NAME	VALUE
1	Virginia	293427
2	South Carolina	107094
3	Maryland	103036
4	North Carolina	100572
5	Georgia	29264
6	New York	21324
7	New Jersey	11423
8	Delaware	8887
9	Pennsylvania	3737
10	Connecticut	2759

Virginia had 293,427 slaves in 1790 (out of a total population of 748,308). South Carolina was second with 107,094. However, in 1790 slavery was not restricted to the southern states. In 1774 Rhode Island was the first colony to abolish slavery, but did not free those currently in bondage, requiring only that their children be born free (which is why in 1790 there were still 952 slaves in Rhode Island). In 1780 Massachusetts outlawed slavery with no exemptions, which is why no slaves were found in that state by the time of the first census (at that time Maine was part of Massachusetts). That same year

Pennsylvania abolished slavery but exempted current slaves, which is why there still were 3,737 slaves in 1790. Connecticut abolished slavery, with exemptions, in 1784. Notice that there were many slaves in New York and New Jersey in 1790. That's because these states did not outlaw slavery until 1799 and 1820, respectively. All importation of slaves into the United States was prohibited by federal law in 1808, but it would take a civil war to free the slaves already here.

As new states came into the Union, repeated battles arose as to whether slavery would be legal or prohibited in each. The first severe conflict arose in 1820 when Missouri applied for statehood as a "slave" state. Because that would have created a majority in the Senate from states permitting slavery, Missouri's admission was opposed by northern senators. The "Missouri Compromise" admitted Missouri as a slave state, but balanced its Senate membership by at the same time admitting Maine as a "free" state. The compromise also drew a line across the nation and proposed that in the future all new territory north of this line would be free and all south of it slave. This line, just south of the border between Pennsylvania and Maryland, was known as the Mason-Dixon line. The compromise did not last and, as the nation expanded westward, conflicts over slavery grew increasingly heated.

> ➤ *Data File:* **STATES**
> ➤ *Task:* **Mapping**
> ➤ *Variable 1:* **9) SLAVE/FREE**
> ➤ *View:* **Map**

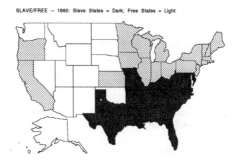

SLAVE/FREE -- 1860: Slave States = Dark; Free States = Light

The ➤ symbol on the Data File line indicates that you must return to the main menu and open a new data file—STATES.

In 1860, 15 states did not yet exist, so these states were neither slave nor free. Since these states have no data, they are the same color as the background on this map. On the ranking screen, the value of this variable for each of these states will be blank. West Virginia was part of Virginia prior to the Civil War and is shown as a slave state on this map.

Here the variable shows the split between slave and free states in 1860. Fifteen states had slavery, 19 states were free: The balance had been tipped by the admission of Kansas, Oregon, and California as free states. No wonder that the future of slavery became the dominant issue in the 1860 presidential election. There were four major candidates. First to be nominated was John Bell of Tennessee, running as the candidate of the Constitutional Union Party, which took a moderate stand on slavery. The second was Abraham Lincoln, the nominee of the new, antislavery Republican Party. That year the Democratic Party split over the issue of slavery, the southern faction adopting a platform supporting the right to own slaves while the northern faction took a much more circumspect position on the issue. The northern faction nominated Stephen A. Douglas for president, and the southern Democrats chose John C. Breckinridge of Kentucky, the current vice president. As the campaign developed and slavery became the main issue, many southern leaders made it clear that the South would secede if Lincoln won.

Data File: **STATES**
Task: **Mapping**
Variable 1: **9) SLAVE/FREE**
➤ *Variable 2:* **11) STATES1860**
➤ *Views:* **Map**

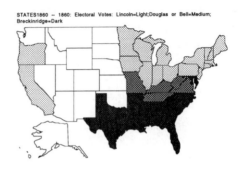

If you are continuing from the previous example, return to the variable selection screen. Keep 9) SLAVE/FREE selected as Variable 1 and select 11) STATES1860 as Variable 2.

Notice how similar these maps are. Lincoln won a close election by carrying 18 of the free states, some by very narrow margins (he won California by 711 votes out of a total of 119,868). Douglas took Missouri and part of New Jersey; Bell took Virginia, Kentucky, and Tennessee; and Breckinridge carried 11 slave states.[1]

Data File: **STATES**
Task: **Mapping**
Variable 1: **9) SLAVE/FREE**
➤ *Variable 2:* **10) UNION/CONF**
➤ *Views:* **Map**

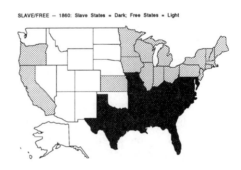

---

[1] This happened because New Jersey voters at the time cast ballots for individual electors rather than the presidential candidates. Four electors supporting Lincoln were elected, and three electors supporting Douglas were chosen.

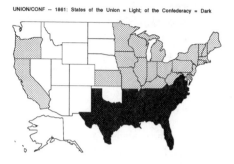

UNION/CONF -- 1861: States of the Union = Light; of the Confederacy = Dark

If you are continuing from the previous example, replace Variable 2, 11) STATES1860, with 10) UNION/CONF.

Following Lincoln's election, the South made good on its threats to secede, South Carolina being the first to do so, and the Civil War ensued. This map shows the states that remained in the Union (light colored) and those that joined the Confederate States. (West Virginia split from Virginia in opposition to the Confederacy.) By the time the war ended, 444,964 soldiers (North and South) had died to determine whether this would be two nations or one. In fact, the Civil War was the bloodiest war in American history—407,316 Americans were killed in World War II, 116,708 in World War I, 58,168 in the Vietnam War, and 293 in the Gulf War.

Although the Civil War settled the issue of slavery, it did not resolve issues concerning the position of African Americans, especially in the South, and continuing concerns about race and bitter memories of the war shaped the politics of the South for the next century.

Data File:	**STATES**
Task:	**Mapping**
Variable 1:	**9) SLAVE/FREE**
➤ *Variable 2:*	**81) STATES '20**
➤ *Views:*	**Map**

SLAVE/FREE -- 1860: Slave States = Dark; Free States = Light

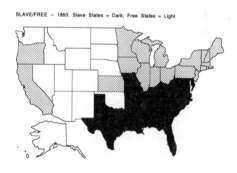

STATES '20 -- 1920: Dark States Carried by Harding (Rep.), Light States by Cox (Dem.)

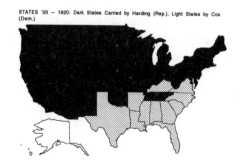

The comparison map on the preceding page shows the results of the 1920 presidential election. Warren G. Harding, Republican U.S. senator from Ohio, ran against Ohio's Democratic governor, James M. Cox. Harding won a huge victory, receiving about 62 percent of the popular votes. But he lost all of the states that had belonged to the Confederacy except Tennessee. The remaining 10 Confederate states gave all of their electoral votes to the Democratic candidate. In fact, the Republican candidate didn't even come close in these states—Harding received a minuscule 3.4 percent of the votes in South Carolina and only 14 percent in Mississippi.

Moreover, the South always gave this kind of support to Democratic candidates, holding Republicans responsible for Lincoln and the Civil War. As a result, for several generations, political commentators referred to "the Solid South," noting that every Democratic presidential candidate could count on these votes and could win by just breaking close to even elsewhere.

The Solid South began to soften during the years of the Eisenhower administration, and it appears that the 1960 presidential election was the last time that a non-southern Democratic presidential candidate could count on most of the old Solid South. The dark states on the following map are the ones carried by Kennedy, who did well in the South.

Data File: **STATES**
Task: **Mapping**
➤ Variable 1: **57) STATES '60**
➤ View: **Map**

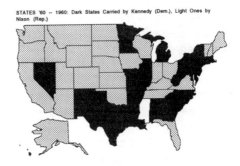
STATES '60 -- 1960: Dark States Carried by Kennedy (Dem.), Light Ones by Nixon (Rep.)

In the 1964 presidential election landslide, the Democratic candidate, Johnson, won all but six states, but five of these six states were in the South. Perhaps because Johnson steered the 1964 Civil Rights Act through Congress, he did worse in the South than in the rest of the country. Thus, the crumbling of the Solid South was evident in 1964. This crumbling continued in 1968 when the Democratic candidate, Humphrey, did worse in the South than anywhere else. The migration of southern voters to the Republican Party was not yet evident, however, because of the third-party candidacy of Alabama's George Wallace, who carried five southern states and received a substantial percentage of the votes in some other southern states.

The end of the Solid South was very evident in the 1972 election. Not only did the Republican candidate, Nixon, win by a landslide, but, as the following map shows, he did better in the South than anywhere else.

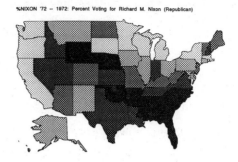

%NIXON '72 -- 1972: Percent Voting for Richard M. Nixon (Republican)

Data File: **STATES**
Task: **Mapping**
➤ Variable 1: **50) %NIXON '72**
➤ View: **Map**

Notice that the majority of the darkest colored states, where Nixon received the largest percentage of the vote in 1972, are in the South.

Data File: **STATES**
Task: **Mapping**
Variable 1: **50) %NIXON '72**
➤ View: **List: Rank**

RANK	CASE NAME	VALUE
1	Mississippi	78.2
2	Georgia	75.3
3	Oklahoma	73.7
4	Alabama	72.4
5	Florida	71.9
6	South Carolina	70.8
7	Nebraska	70.5
8	North Carolina	69.5
9	Wyoming	69.0
10	Arkansas	68.9

Additional values may be scrolled on the screen.

In a year when he carried every state except Massachusetts, it was Mississippi that gave Nixon his largest margin, followed by Georgia, Oklahoma, Alabama, Florida, and South Carolina.

Finally, the legacy of slavery was no longer the dominant feature of American regionalism. In that sense, we had moved closer to being "One Nation."

➤ Data File: **HISTORY**
➤ Task: **Historical Trends**
➤ Variables: **27) SOUTH.DEM**

● SOUTH.DEM

Percent of Southern House members who are Democrats

The ➤ symbol on the Data File line indicates that you must return to the main menu and open a new data file—HISTORY.

The percentage of southern members of the House who are Democrats has declined from over 90 percent in 1956 to only 41 percent after the 2000 elections.

While the Solid South is no more, the South is still a distinctive region.

➤ Data File: **STATES**
➤ Task: **Mapping**
➤ Variable 1: **8) THE SOUTH**
➤ View: **Map**

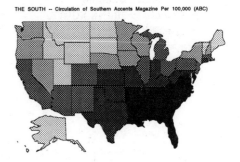

THE SOUTH -- Circulation of Southern Accents Magazine Per 100,000 (ABC)

Note that this task uses a new data file.

One way to isolate the remnants of southern allegiance is with the circulation rates of the magazine *Southern Accents*. While *Southern Accents* has subscribers in all 50 states, they are highly concentrated in the states of the Old South. Notice how similar the map of *Southern Accents* circulation is to the earlier map showing the states of the Union and the Confederacy during the Civil War.

Data File: **STATES**
Task: **Mapping**
Variable 1: **8) THE SOUTH**
➤ View: **List: Rank**

RANK	CASE NAME	VALUE
1	Georgia	385.2
2	Alabama	381.5
3	South Carolina	372.2
4	North Carolina	339.1
5	Tennessee	319.2
6	Mississippi	288.3
7	Virginia	283.7
8	Louisiana	247.2
9	Arkansas	206.1
10	Florida	197.6

Georgia has the highest circulation rate (385.2 copies per 100,000 population) closely followed by Alabama, the Carolinas, Tennessee, and Mississippi. Utah, the Dakotas, and Montana have the lowest rates.

Today, there are substantial African American populations in many states outside the South, especially in the more urban states. But the majority of African Americans still live in the South where they have become a very important political factor.

Data File: **STATES**
Task: **Mapping**
Variable 1: **8) THE SOUTH**
➤ Variable 2: **24) %AFRIC.AM**
➤ Views: **Map**

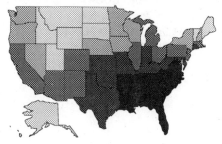

THE SOUTH -- Circulation of Southern Accents Magazine Per 100,000 (ABC)

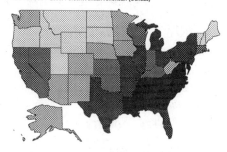

%AFRIC.AM -- 2000: Percent African American (Census)

The South is only one region.

Data File: **STATES**
Task: **Mapping**
➤ Variable 1: **3) BIG REGION**
➤ View: **Map**

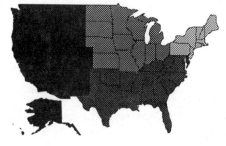

BIG REGION -- Large Regions As Defined by the Census

The Bureau of the Census defines the major American regions as the East, Midwest, South, and West. These regions are very useful for many purposes. States within a given region have certain historical and geographic similarities. But they fail to capture the real subtleties of American regionalism: that the nation consists of various regions depending on what is at issue.

Indeed, the famous analogy of the great American "melting pot" is somewhat of an exaggeration when one examines the regional variations that exist in terms of ethnicity, economics, and culture. Let's use a county-level data file to examine several race and ethnicity variables.

> ➤ *Data File:* **COUNTY**
> ➤ *Task:* **Mapping**
> ➤ *Variable 1:* **4) %BLACK**
> ➤ *View:* **Map**

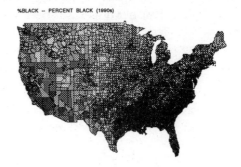

The advantage of the county-level map is that it shows more details of the variations that exist across the nation. This map provides a county-level breakdown of the percentage of African Americans. As expected, the map is similar to the state-level map shown earlier in terms of the regions where African Americans are most populous (the South).

Let's see where the largest Hispanic populations are found.

> *Data File:* **COUNTY**
> *Task:* **Mapping**
> ➤ *Variable 1:* **6) %HISPANIC2**
> ➤ *View:* **Map**

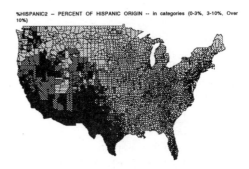

This map is very different. Here we see that people of Hispanic origin are more likely to live in the southwestern part of the United States. Counties with the darkest colors have Hispanic populations greater than 10 percent. (To examine the actual percentage for a given county, use variable %HISPANIC.)

Do American Indians tend to live in one region of the United States?

> *Data File:* **COUNTY**
> *Task:* **Mapping**
> ➤ *Variable 1:* **10) %AMER.IND2**
> ➤ *View:* **Map**

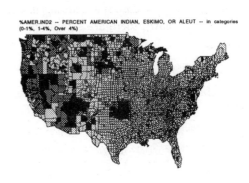

Whereas the South is widely populated by African Americans, and the Southwest has large percentages of people of Hispanic origin, American Indian populations tend to be concentrated in particular counties in Oklahoma, Arizona, and Nevada. In fact, there are many instances where a county having a high percentage of American Indians borders a county with a very low percentage of American Indians—this often reflects the location of Indian reservations.

In the worksheet section we will continue to examine regional differences in race and ethnicity. Another important way to view regional variation in America is to look at wealth and poverty rates. This time we'll analyze two maps at once.

Data File: **COUNTY**
Task: **Mapping**
➤ Variable 1: **19) %POOR**
➤ Variable 2: **20) MED.FAM$**
➤ Views: **Map**

%POOR -- PERCENT BELOW POVERTY LEVEL (1990s)

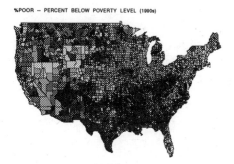

MED.FAM$ -- MEDIAN FAMILY MONEY INCOME (1990s)

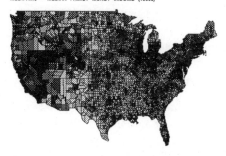

An examination of the top map reveals that the highest levels of poverty occur in the Appalachian region and throughout much of the South. Notice that the poverty rates are particularly low in the Northeast and in portions of the Midwest. If you examine the ranked list for this map, you'll discover there are 130 counties in which at least one-third of the population live below the official poverty rate. By contrast, there are dozens of counties in which less than 5 percent of the population live below the poverty level. Clearly, there are significant differences in the United States in terms of wealth and poverty.

The bottom map displays the median family income for each county. Not surprisingly, this map is nearly the opposite of the top map. For instance, notice that the dark areas in the top map tend to be colored lightly in the bottom map, and vice versa.

Let's compare two more maps: one that shows the percentage of earnings that come from farming and the other that shows the percentage of earnings that come from manufacturing.

Data File: **COUNTY**

Task: **Mapping**

➤ Variable 1: **21) FARM %**

➤ Variable 2: **22) MANUFACT%**

➤ Views: **Map**

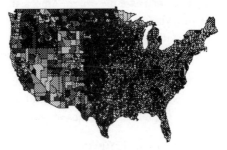

FARM % -- FARM SHARE (%) OF TOTAL EARNINGS (1990s)

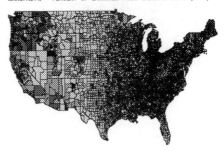

MANUFACT% -- PERCENT OF EARNINGS FROM MANUFACTURING (1990s)

The distinctions between the farming and manufacturing regions of the United States are clear. People living in the central part of the country are more likely to rely on farming for income than are those living in the East. Likewise, people living in the East are more likely to be employed in manufacturing.

At the beginning of this exercise, we saw that it was the similarities of the early colonies that helped pave the way to nationhood. By the middle of the 19th century, it was regional differences among states that led to the Civil War. Today, there continue to be substantial social, cultural, and economic differences across the regions of the nation. But do these regional differences have political implications as they did in the past? Although these differences are unlikely to lead to civil war, they surely affect the way people vote, the laws and policies that are enacted at the state and local levels, the decisions that are made in courts, and so on.

For instance, it is likely that states with high percentages of families on public aid will be more concerned with issues that relate to social programs. Voters in states where family incomes are relatively high might be more responsive to political candidates who propose lower taxes on investment earnings. States with large percentages of people who speak a language other than English may be more concerned with laws relating to bilingual education and immigration. States with higher crime rates will be more concerned about crime-related issues. Indeed, regionalism is an important factor in American politics and it will be referred to often throughout this workbook.

Your turn.

WORKSHEET

NAME: _____

COURSE: _____

DATE: _____

REVIEW QUESTIONS

Based on the first part of this exercise, answer True or False to the following items:

a. The early colonies were relatively easy to merge into a nation because they were similar in many ways.   T   F

b. The original colonies were more similar in terms of religion than they were in ancestry.   T   F

c. While the overwhelming majority of the colonists were Protestants, there was a substantial diversity among these Protestants.   T   F

d. Following the Civil War, most African Americans quickly moved to the northern states that belonged to the Union.   T   F

e. The 1960 presidential election was the last time that a non-southern Democratic candidate could count on the votes of most of the old Solid South.   T   F

f. Following the Civil War, a Republican presidential candidate was not successful in the South until 1972.   T   F

g. The percentage of southern members of the House of Representatives who are Democrats has steadily declined over the past 40 years.   T   F

h. Today, the South is quite similar to other regions in terms of culture and population characteristics.   T   F

EXPLORIT QUESTIONS

> **You will need to use the ExplorIt software for the remainder of the questions. Make sure you have already gone through the *Getting Started* section that is located prior to the first exercise. If you have any difficulties using the software to obtain the appropriate information, or if you want to learn additional features of the MAPPING task, use the on-line help (F1).**

1. In 1860 there were 15 "slave states"—states that had *not* outlawed slavery. However, not all of these states seceded from the Union. Let's see if we can determine why some seceded and others did not.

In this analysis we'll include only the 15 slave states.

> ➤ *Data File:* **STATES**
> ➤ *Task:* **Mapping**
> ➤ *Variable 1:* **89) UN/CONF SL**
> ➤ *View:* **Map**

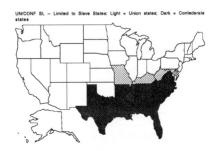

UN/CONF SL -- Limited to Slave States; Light = Union states; Dark = Confederate states

To create this map using ExplorIt, open the STATES data file, select the MAPPING task, and select 89) UN/CONF SL as Variable 1. The map on your screen should match the preceding map.

Now let's look at the rankings of states.

> ➤ *View:* **List: Rank**

Since you have already selected the appropriate data file, task, and variable, you only need to select [List: Rank] as the view.

a. List the four slave states that did not secede (exclude West Virginia): _____

_____

_____

_____

b. Look at the map again. Where are these states located relative to the Union and Confederate states? (Circle the number of the most appropriate answer.)

1. in the newest states forming in the West
2. in the deepest parts of the South
3. directly along the border between the Union and Confederate states

2. Only states with a serious commitment to slavery would be likely to take such drastic action as joining the Confederacy. Let's look at the actual extent of slavery in each state. (West Virginia is shown with missing data since it did not exist prior to the Civil War.)

> *Data File:* **STATES**
> *Task:* **Mapping**
> ➤ *Variable 1:* **90) %SLAV ST**
> ➤ *View:* **List: Rank**

Note that you only need to select a new variable, 90) %SLAV ST, and the appropriate view.

a. In the table below, list the states from high to low in percent slave and give the actual percentage. After you have finished, place a check mark to the left of each of the four states that did **not** secede.

✔	Name of State	Percentage
_____	_____	_____
_____	_____	_____
_____	_____	_____
_____	_____	_____
_____	_____	_____
_____	_____	_____
_____	_____	_____
_____	_____	_____
_____	_____	_____
_____	_____	_____
_____	_____	_____
_____	_____	_____
_____	_____	_____
_____	_____	_____
_____	_____	_____

Based on the above table, answer True or False to the following items:

b. Only states with more than 20 percent of their population as slaves joined the Confederacy.   T   F

c. If Tennessee had had a smaller percentage of slaves, it would have been more likely to stay with the Union.   T   F

d. The percentage of slaves in the population seems to determine whether a state joined the Confederacy.   T   F

3. a. Questions 1 and 2 suggest two factors that might have affected the likelihood of secession. What are these?

1. _____

2. _____

b. Of the eleven states of the Confederacy, which two states would seem to have
been most likely to have stayed with the Union based on this information?   _____

_____

4. In 1928 the Republican candidate, Herbert Hoover, easily won the presidential election. The mapping
of the variable STATES '28 shows the states that Hoover won (the dark states) and the ones he lost
(the light states).

> Data File: **STATES**
> Task: **Mapping**
> ➤ Variable 1: **76) STATES '28**
> ➤ View: **Map**

a. The eight states that didn't support Hoover were scattered throughout the nation.   T   F

In 1932 Franklin Delano Roosevelt, a Democrat, defeated Herbert Hoover, the incumbent president,
in a landslide. FDR lost the popular vote in only six states.

> Data File: **STATES**
> Task: **Mapping**
> ➤ Variable 1: **74) STATES '32**
> ➤ View: **Map**

b. The states that didn't support Roosevelt were scattered throughout the nation.   T   F

Let's look at the percentage of the vote FDR received in each state.

> Data File: **STATES**
> Task: **Mapping**
> ➤ Variable 1: **75) FDR '32**
> ➤ View: **List: Rank**

c. What state gave FDR the highest percentage?   _____

d. What percentage did FDR get in that state?   _____%

e. What state gave FDR the lowest percentage?   _____

f. What percentage did FDR get in that state?   _____%

g. List the rank of each of the following southern states:

**In finding the ranks for specific states, you may want to use the [List: Alpha] option—this
shows the states in alphabetical order.**

STATE	RANK
ALABAMA	_____
ARKANSAS	_____
GEORGIA	_____
LOUISIANA	_____
MISSISSIPPI	_____
NORTH CAROLINA	_____
SOUTH CAROLINA	_____

5. Twenty years later, in 1952, Dwight David Eisenhower, commander of the Allied forces during World War II, ran against Adlai Stevenson and gave the Republicans a lopsided victory, losing the popular vote in only nine states.

> Data File: **STATES**
> Task: **Mapping**
> ➤ Variable 1: **62) %IKE '52**
> ➤ View: **List: Rank**

a. What state gave Eisenhower the highest percentage?   _____

b. What percentage did Eisenhower get in that state?   _____%

c. What state gave Eisenhower the lowest percentage?   _____

d. What percentage did Eisenhower get in that state?   _____%

e. List the *rank* of each of the following southern states:

STATE	RANK
ALABAMA	_____
ARKANSAS	_____
GEORGIA	_____
LOUISIANA	_____
MISSISSIPPI	_____
NORTH CAROLINA	_____
SOUTH CAROLINA	_____

6. Another 20 years and another landslide. In 1972 Richard M. Nixon, a Republican, won in 49 of the 50 states, losing only one state to George McGovern of South Dakota. (In 1974, under threat of impeachment, Nixon became the first president to resign from office.)

> Data File: **STATES**
> Task: **Mapping**
> ➤ Variable 1: **50) %NIXON '72**
> ➤ View: **List: Rank**

a. What state gave Nixon the highest percentage?   _____

b. What percentage did Nixon get in that state?   _____%

c. What state gave Nixon the lowest percentage?   _____

d. What percentage did Nixon get in that state?   _____%

e. List the *rank* of each of the following southern states:

STATE	RANK
ALABAMA	_____
ARKANSAS	_____
GEORGIA	_____
LOUISIANA	_____
MISSISSIPPI	_____
NORTH CAROLINA	_____
SOUTH CAROLINA	_____

7. In 1996 President Clinton, a southerner from Arkansas, won reelection. How well did this Democratic candidate do in the southern states we have been examining?

> Data File: **STATES**
> Task: **Mapping**
> ➤ Variable 1: **93) %CLINTON96**
> ➤ View: **List: Alpha**

a. List the *rank* of each of the following southern states. (Note that two states can have the same rank because they have the same value with the variable.)

STATE	RANK
ALABAMA	_____
ARKANSAS	_____
GEORGIA	_____

STATE	RANK
LOUISIANA	_____
MISSISSIPPI	_____
NORTH CAROLINA	_____
SOUTH CAROLINA	_____

    b. Do these results suggest that the South is still solidly Democratic if the Democratic nominee is a native southerner?   Yes   No

8.   Questions 4 through 7 show how the pattern of voting in the South shifted from 1928 to 1996. Using the information from these questions, answer True or False to the following items:

    a. In the first half of this century, Republican candidates for president could pretty much concede the South to the Democrats.   T   F

    b. Even today, Democratic presidential candidates can concentrate on campaigning outside the South because the southern vote is pretty much guaranteed.   T   F

    c. In 1960 John F. Kennedy, the Democratic candidate, planned on carrying the southern states and focused his major campaigning in the most populous states outside the South. Would you advise this strategy for the Democratic candidate in the next presidential election? Why or why not?

9.   In the preliminary part of this exercise, the COUNTY data file was used to examine regionalism in the United States. Let's pursue this a bit more.

> ➤ *Data File:* **COUNTY**
> ➤ *Task:* **Mapping**
> ➤ *Variable 1:* **17) %FOREIGN2**
> ➤ *View:* **Map**

The variable %FOREIGN2 shows the percentage of people in each county who were born outside the United States. This variable has been coded so that counties having less than 4 percent of people who were foreign born will appear as a light color and counties with over 4 percent are shaded dark.

Which of the following states or regions have comparatively high percentages of people who are foreign born? (Check all that apply.)

_____ Southwest (Texas, New Mexico, Arizona, etc.)

_____ New York City and surrounding areas (from Connecticut to New Jersey)

_____ Midwest (Ohio, Indiana, Missouri)

_____ South (Alabama, Mississippi, Georgia)

_____ Florida

_____ California

10. Now map the percentage of people who speak a non-English language at home.

> Data File: **COUNTY**
> Task: **Mapping**
> ➤ Variable 1: **18) %NON-ENGL**
> ➤ View: **Map**

a. Which of the following states or regions have comparatively high percentages of people who speak a non-English language at home? (Check all that apply.)

_____ Southwest (Texas, New Mexico, Arizona, etc.)

_____ New York City and surrounding areas (from Connecticut to New Jersey)

_____ Midwest (Ohio, Indiana, Missouri)

_____ South (Alabama, Mississippi, Georgia)

_____ Florida

_____ California

➤ View: **List: Rank**

b. How many of the 3,141 counties have populations in which at least 10 percent of the people speak a language other than English at home?   _____

c. What county has the highest percentage?   _____

d. What is the percentage for this county?   _____%

e. Examine the top 15 counties on this list. Which state are they mostly from?   _____

f. Do areas that have high percentages of people who were foreign born also tend to have the highest percentages of people who speak a non-English language at home?   Yes   No

g. Describe two political issues that may be particularly important in states or regions that have high percentages of people who are foreign born or who speak a non-English language at home.

11. The "Sunbelt" refers to those warm-winter states that stretch from South Carolina on the southern Atlantic shore around the Gulf of Mexico and then up the Pacific Coast. Over the last two decades, migration has had a major impact on the social and political landscape of these states. Let's examine this.

> ➤ *Data File:* **STATES**
> ➤ *Task:* **Mapping**
> ➤ *Variable 1:* **6) SUNBELT**
> ➤ *Variable 2:* **165) POP GROW2**
> ➤ *Views:* **Map**

Compare the two maps to answer the following questions:

a. These maps, while not identical, are similar.   T   F

b. Population growth is more rapid in the Sunbelt than in other regions.   T   F

12. Now compare the Sunbelt states to the rate of new home construction.

> *Data File:* **STATES**
> *Task:* **Mapping**
> *Variable 1:* **6) SUNBELT**
> ➤ *Variable 2:* **29) NEW HOMES**
> ➤ *Views:* **Map**

a. These maps, while not identical, are similar.   T   F

b. Describe two political issues that may be of particular importance to states or regions that are experiencing high levels of population growth and new home construction.

13. Regionalism has existed on some of the most intensely debated issues in American politics: the slavery issue and issues of racial equality. In current politics, abortion is an issue many people feel intensely about. In the GSS file that you will use later, there is a question which asks people whether a woman should be able to obtain a legal abortion if she is married and does not want any more children. When the responses of people are broken down by region, the percentages of those who would allow an abortion in these circumstances are: 34 percent in the South, 39 percent in the Midwest, 47 percent in the East, and 50 percent in the West. On the basis of these results, which of the following statements is the most accurate?

    a.   There is no regionalism to this abortion issue.

    b.   Regionalism exists for the abortion issue, but the regional pattern is not likely to be as strong as the regional patterns of attitudes concerning slavery were before the Civil War.

    c.   The regional patterns concerning this abortion issue appear to be just as strong as the regional patterns concerning slavery probably were before the Civil War.

FEDERALISM: "A MORE PERFECT UNION"

*We the People of the United States, in Order to form a
more perfect Union, establish Justice, insure domestic
Tranquility, provide for the common defence, promote
the general Welfare, and secure the Blessings of
Liberty to ourselves and our Posterity, do ordain and
establish this Constitution for the United States of
America.*

PREAMBLE TO THE CONSTITUTION,
SEPTEMBER 17, 1787

Tasks: Mapping, Scatterplot
Data File: STATES

From the start, Americans had two basic concerns about the structure of their government. First,
they wished to retain as much local authority as possible—each state had its particular
concerns, interests, and local culture that it wished to protect. Second, they wished to have sufficient centralized authority so as to regulate relations among the states and provide for the common
interests—defense, for example. The first attempt failed—the Articles of Confederation maximized the
independence of the states, but failed to provide sufficient central authority. So, the Constitutional
Convention tried a different approach. The result was called **federalism**, a system of government
wherein two or more levels of government have formal authority over the same geographic area and
the same citizens. That is, unlike most European nations, which concentrate nearly all power in a
central government, a great deal of power was reserved for local governments—state, county, and city.
But, unlike the previous confederation, the federal government was given substantial powers to
enforce laws and policies nationwide. These powers were specifically spelled out in the Constitution. In
addition, the Bill of Rights, the first ten amendments to the Constitution that were adopted at the end
of 1791, further specified limits on the powers of governments and noted:

Amendment X

*The powers not delegated to the United States by the Constitution, nor prohibited by it to the
States, are reserved to the States respectively, or to the people.*

Despite these provisions, the federal and local governments exist in a state of mutual tension, pulling
and pushing for greater control. During the two centuries since the federal government was created, it
has gained a great deal more power than was intended by those who drew up the Constitution and the
power of the individual states has been curtailed.

In addition, the balance between the federal and local governments differs greatly from place to place. This is especially obvious when we examine the percentage of land in each state that the federal government owns.

> ➤ *Data File:* **STATES**
> ➤ *Task:* **Mapping**
> ➤ *Variable 1:* **17) %FED LAND**
> ➤ *View:* **Map**

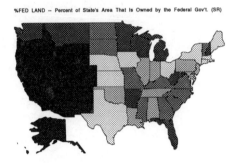

%FED LAND -- Percent of State's Area That Is Owned by the Federal Gov't. (SR)

If you want to reproduce this graphic on the computer screen using ExplorIt, review the instructions in the *Getting Started* section. For this example, you would open the STATES data file, select the MAPPING task, and select 17) %FED LAND for Variable 1. The first view shown is the Map view. (Remember, the ➤ symbol indicates which steps you need to perform if you are doing all examples as you follow along in the text. So, in the next example, you only need to select a new view—that is, you don't need to repeat the first three steps because they were already done in this example.)

On this map, the darker a state, the larger the proportion of its area that consists of federally owned land.

Data File: **STATES**
Task: **Mapping**
Variable 1: **17) %FED LAND**
➤ *View:* **List: Rank**

RANK	CASE NAME	VALUE
1	Nevada	82.74
2	Alaska	67.87
3	Utah	63.80
4	Idaho	61.72
5	Oregon	52.42
6	Wyoming	48.79
7	Arizona	47.10
8	California	44.45
9	Colorado	36.20
10	New Mexico	33.09

Nevada is highest: 82.7 percent of Nevada's land doesn't belong to Nevada at all, but to the federal government. That is, most of the area of the state is controlled by Congress and by federal agencies, and the residents of the state have very little say about how the land is used or regulated. In fact, the federal government can prohibit Nevadans from even entering parts of the state, as it often did from areas used for testing nuclear weapons. Alaska is second with two-thirds of its land under federal ownership. Utah (63.8 percent) is a very close third. Even in California, close to half (44.5 percent) of all land is federally owned. However, in many states Congress has little or no say in local land use because the amount of federal ownership is trivial: less than 1 percent in Connecticut, Rhode Island, New York, Maine, Kansas, and Iowa. For the 50 states, the average percentage of land owned by the federal government is 15 percent.

Data File: **STATES**
Task: **Mapping**
Variable 1: **17) %FED LAND**
➤ Variable 2: **7) THE WEST**
➤ Views: **Map**

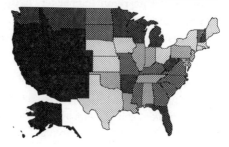

%FED LAND -- Percent of State's Area That Is Owned by the Federal Gov't. (SR)

r = 0.770**

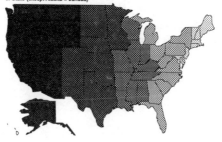

THE WEST -- Degree of Longitude West of Prime Meridian In Westernmost Point of State (except Alaska = Juneau)

If you are continuing from the previous example, return to the variable selection screen for the MAPPING task. Then select variable 7) THE WEST as Variable 2.

As is quite obvious, federal ownership of land is a very western phenomenon. As the last states to enter the Union, the western states always have faced a maximum amount of federal interference as Congress, controlled by the more populous eastern states, makes decisions based on easterners' preferences, not necessarily those of westerners. For example, Congress decides whether to permit western ranchers to graze their herds on federal land. Perhaps even more important, the eastern states have prevented the sale of federal lands in the West, defining much of it as protected wilderness areas. Many westerners complain that Congress never decides to turn large tracts of the East back into wilderness areas. These western resentments often show up rather clearly in elections and have been referred to as the "sagebrush revolt."

A source of friction inherent in federalism is over tax revenues, the proportion taken by the federal government versus the amount left to each state. This issue has been especially heated in recent times because the federal government often has initiated programs and then required each state to provide the funds. A similar friction persists at more local levels since each state is a mini-federal system wherein the state competes with local governments such as counties and cities for authority and funds.

Until the 16th Amendment to the Constitution was ratified in 1913, tax competition between the federal and state governments was minimized since each had its own separate sources. Until the 20th century, virtually all federal revenues came from customs duties on imports from abroad and from excise taxes on alcohol and tobacco, while state and local revenues came mainly from property taxes. There were neither federal nor state income taxes. During the Civil War the federal government imposed an income tax (with a minimum rate of 3 percent and a maximum rate of 5 percent). This tax was cancelled after the end of the war. In 1894 President Grover Cleveland, the newly elected

Democrat, pushed an income tax law through Congress. It was held to be unconstitutional by the Supreme Court, thus requiring backers of the tax to amend the Constitution (the 16th Amendment) in order to tax incomes. Begun in 1913, the federal income tax rates soon rose far beyond the "maximum limits" promised when the amendment was adopted.

The income tax facilitated a massive shift in governmental power because it provided the federal government with such an immense source of revenue. Thus, in 1900, prior to the income tax, state and local governments spent about twice as much per year as did the federal government. Today the federal government collects and spends about $2 to every $1 spent by state and local governments. And the income tax is the largest source of federal revenue. This is true despite the fact that in the latter part of the 20th century many states (now numbering 41) began collecting income taxes too.

Data File: **STATES**
Task: **Mapping**
➤ Variable 1: **20) INCOME TAX**
➤ View: **Map**

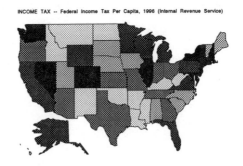

INCOME TAX -- Federal Income Tax Per Capita, 1996 (Internal Revenue Service)

Not surprisingly, the average resident in some states pays far more in federal income taxes than does the average resident in some other states.

Data File: **STATES**
Task: **Mapping**
Variable 1: **20) INCOME TAX**
➤ View: **List: Rank**

RANK	CASE NAME	VALUE
1	Connecticut	4517
2	New Jersey	3719
3	Massachusetts	3459
4	Nevada	3392
5	New York	3166
6	Illinois	3118
7	New Hampshire	3042
8	Maryland	2967
9	Washington	2893
10	Colorado	2890

People in Connecticut pay the most federal income tax (an average of $4,517 per person), followed by residents of New Jersey ($3,719). People in Mississippi pay the least ($1,487), only one-third of what people in Connecticut pay. Now let's examine family incomes in the states.

FAMILY$ -- 2000: Median Family Income (2000 Inflation-Adjusted Dollars)
(Census: C2SS)

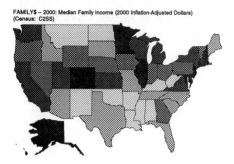

RANK	CASE NAME	VALUE
1	New Jersey	65182
2	Connecticut	64369
3	Maryland	62437
4	Massachusetts	61560
5	Alaska	60124
6	New Hampshire	58470
7	Hawaii	58159
8	Minnesota	57847
9	Colorado	55756
10	Illinois	55198

No surprise. Connecticut and New Jersey also are among the states with the highest median family incomes and Mississippi is among the lowest here too.

Obviously, per capita income tax payments reflect income. States where people earn the most are states where people pay the most income tax. That is confirmed by this map of median family income, which closely resembles the map of per capita income taxes. And that statement raises this issue: How much alike must two maps be in order for them to be "alike"?

In Exercise 1 you were asked to compare many maps of the United States and to say which ones were very similar and which ones were very different. You no doubt found it easy to notice when two maps were very much alike. But, as you examined maps that were less alike, you must have found it more difficult to say how much alike they were.

As it turns out, there is a simple method for determining precisely how much alike are any two maps. It was invented about 100 years ago in England by Karl Pearson. Once you see how he did it, you will find it easy to apply.

Let's begin with these two maps of income taxes and family income.

To see Pearson's method, we can draw a horizontal line across the bottom of a piece of paper. We will let this line represent the map of median family income. So, at the left end of this line we will write 34,465, which indicates West Virginia, the state with the lowest income. At the right end of the line we will write 65,182 to represent New Jersey as the state with the highest income.

34,465   65,182

Now we can draw a vertical line up the left side of the paper. This line will represent the map of per capita income tax. At the bottom of this line we will write 1,487 to represent Mississippi, the state with the lowest income tax. At the top we will write 4,517 to represent Connecticut, the state with the highest income tax.

Now that we have a line with an appropriate scale to represent each map, the next thing we need to do is refer to the distributions for each map in order to learn the value for each state and then locate it on each line according to its score. Let's start with New Jersey. Since it is the state with the highest median income, we can easily find its place on the horizontal line. We will make a small mark at 65,182 to locate New Jersey. Next, New Jersey has a per capita federal income tax of $3,719. So, we make a mark on the vertical line about where we think that 3,719 would be. This point will be roughly three-fourths up the vertical line. Now we draw a line up from the mark for New Jersey on the horizontal line and draw another out from the mark for New Jersey on the vertical line. Where these two lines meet (or intersect), we draw a dot. This dot represents the combined map locations of New Jersey—it represents both the per capita income tax and the median family income for this state.

Now let's locate Connecticut. To find Connecticut on the horizontal line (also known as the X-axis), estimate where 64,369 is located and make a mark at that spot. Connecticut's tax rate is easy to find because it is the highest: 4,517. So, make a mark at 4,517 on the vertical line (also known as the Y-axis). Now we draw a line up from the horizontal line and draw another line across from the mark on the vertical line. Where these two lines intersect, we put a dot to represent Connecticut for both per capita income tax and median family income.

When we have followed this procedure for each state, we will have 50 dots located within the space defined by the vertical and horizontal lines representing the two maps. What we have done is to create a **scatterplot**. Fortunately, you don't have to go to all this trouble. ExplorIt will do it for you.

Data File: **STATES**
➤ Task: **Scatterplot**
➤ Dependent Variable: **20) INCOME TAX**
➤ Independent Variable: **13) FAMILY$**

Notice that the SCATTERPLOT task requires two variables.

Special feature: When the scatterplot is showing, you may obtain information on any dot by clicking on it. A little box will appear around the dot, and the values of 13) FAMILY $ (or the X-axis variable) and of 20) INCOME TAX (or the Y-axis variable) will be shown.

Each of these dots is a state.

Once Pearson had created a scatterplot, his next step was to calculate what he called the **regression line**.

Data File: **STATES**
Task: **Scatterplot**
Dependent Variable: **20) INCOME TAX**
Independent Variable: **13) FAMILY$**
➤ View: **Reg. Line**

To show the regression line, select the [Reg. Line] option from the menu.

The regression line represents the best effort to draw a straight line that connects all of the dots. It is unnecessary for you to know how to calculate the location of the regression line—the program does it for you.

To see how the regression line would look if the maps were identical, all you need to do is examine the scatterplot for identical maps. So, if you create a scatterplot using FAMILY$ as both the dependent and independent variables, you will be comparing identical maps and the dots representing states will all be on the regression line like a string of beads.

However, since the maps for income tax and income are only very similar, but not identical, most of the dots are scattered near, but not on, the regression line. Pearson's method for calculating how much alike are any two maps or lists is easy, once the regression line has been drawn. What it amounts to is measuring the distance out from the regression line to every dot.

Data File: **STATES**
Task: **Scatterplot**
Dependent Variable: **20) INCOME TAX**
Independent Variable: **13) FAMILY$**
➤ View: **Reg. Line/Residuals**

To show the residuals, select the [Residuals] option from the menu.

See all the little lines. If you added them all together, you would have a sum of the deviation of the dots from the regression line. The smaller this sum, the more alike are the two maps. For example, when the maps are identical and all the dots are on the regression line, the sum of the deviations is 0.

In order to make it simple to interpret results, Pearson invented a procedure to convert the sums into a number he called the **correlation coefficient**. The correlation coefficient varies from 0.0 to 1.0. When maps are identical, the correlation coefficient will be 1.0. When they are completely unalike, the correlation coefficient will be 0.0. Thus, the closer the correlation coefficient is to 1.0, the more alike the two maps or lists. Pearson used the letter r as the symbol for his correlation coefficient.

Look at the lower left of the screen above and you will see r = 0.837. This indicates that the maps are extremely similar. (The meaning of the asterisks will be explained a bit later.)

Correlation coefficients can be either positive or negative. This correlation is positive: Where incomes are higher, people pay higher income taxes. That is, as one rises so does the other—they tend to occur in unison. But when we examine a new scatterplot, the whole picture changes radically.

Data File: **STATES**
Task: **Scatterplot**
➤ Dependent Variable: **12) MOBILE HOM**
➤ Independent Variable: **20) INCOME TAX**
➤ View: **Reg. Line**

Here we see that where per capita income tax payments are lower, the higher the percentage who live in mobile homes. Notice that in this case the regression line slopes downward from left to right, rather than upward. That always indicates a negative correlation. And notice that a minus sign now precedes the correlation coefficient: r = −0.608.

The point of calculating correlation coefficients is not simply to say how alike or unalike two maps are. Indeed, the point of comparing two maps usually is not motivated by artistic concerns, but is done in search of links, or connections, between variables. In Exercise 1 you looked for links between regions and potential political issues. Moreover, only when such links exist can we propose that there is a causal relationship between them. Thus, implicit in our first two uses of the scatterplot technique was the assumption that one variable might be the cause of the other.

No one would really think it is just an accident that there is an extremely high correlation between income and income taxes. Rather, it seems likely that one is a cause of the other—that people must pay high income taxes because they have high incomes. In similar fashion, it seems likely that income tax rates are lower where more people live in mobile homes because people living in mobile homes tend to have lower incomes. In fact, we can check that out.

Data File:	**STATES**
Task:	**Scatterplot**
Dependent Variable:	**12) MOBILE HOM**
➤ Independent Variable:	**13) FAMILY$**
➤ View:	**Reg. Line**

Once again we find a strong, negative correlation (r = –0.772). This tells us that where median family income is lower, more people live in mobile homes.

Whenever social scientists become interested in a variable, the first thing they generally ask is what causes it to vary. And the first test of any proposed answer to such a question is to demonstrate the existence of a correlation between the variable to be explained and its proposed cause. In this instance we have demonstrated that income may be a cause of the kind of housing people have since the two variables are highly correlated. By itself correlation does not establish that a causal relationship exists. But without a correlation, there can be no causal relationship between two variables.

That helps explain the distinction between independent and dependent variables. In the SCATTERPLOT task, the software first asks for the dependent variable and then asks for the independent variable. If we think something might be the cause of something else, then we say that the cause is the independent variable and that the consequence (or the thing being caused) is the dependent variable. Put another way, the dependent variable *depends on* the independent variable.

Now, suppose someone suggests that the prevalence of mobile homes has as much to do with climate as with income—that mobile homes are concentrated in the Sunbelt because of the mild weather. To test that suggestion we create another scatterplot.

Data File:	**STATES**
Task:	**Scatterplot**
Dependent Variable:	**12) MOBILE HOM**
➤ Independent Variable:	**6) SUNBELT**
➤ View:	**Reg. Line**

This is what a scatterplot looks like when two variables are not correlated. The dots are scattered all over, and the regression line is nearly flat. However, the value of r is not zero (r = 0.149). So, how can we say these two variables aren't correlated? We can say it because the odds are very high that this correlation is nothing but a random accident.

In Exercise 3 you will learn how political scientists calculate the odds as to whether or not a correlation is random. Here it is sufficient to know that many correlations are so small, we treat them *as if they were zero*. And the software automatically does that calculation for you and gives you the results. If you look back at the correlation between income and income tax, you will see that there are two asterisks following the value of r (r = 0.837**). Two asterisks means that there is less than 1 chance in 100 that this correlation is a random accident. One asterisk means that the odds against a correlation being random are 20 to 1. Whenever there are no asterisks following a correlation, the odds are too high that it could be random.[1] That's how we know that the correlation between mobile homes and the Sunbelt is too small to matter—there are no asterisks. *Treat all correlations without asterisks as zero correlations.*

Keep in mind, however, that correlation and causation are not the same thing. It is true that without correlation there can be no causation. But correlations often occur between two variables without one being a cause of the other. And we often are interested in correlations between two variables even when we don't think one causes the other. For example, we might wonder if states having a lot of federal land also have a lot of unattached men—that is, households lacking an adult female resident.

To see if these two variables are correlated, we will go back to the MAPPING function.

      Data File: **STATES**
    ➤ *Task:* **Mapping**
  ➤ *Variable 1:* **17) %FED LAND**
  ➤ *Variable 2:* **30) MALE HOMES**
      ➤ *Views:* **Map**

%FED LAND -- Percent of State's Area That Is Owned by the Federal Gov't. (SR)

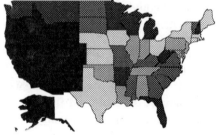

r = 0.475**

MALE HOMES -- 2000: Percent of Households that are Male Headed, No Spouse Present

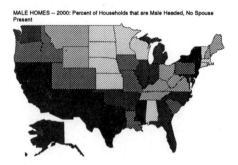

---

[1] As you'll find in the next exercise, statistical significance in survey data helps us to assess whether or not a relationship exists in the population from which the survey sample was drawn. In ecological data sets, such as the 50 states, statistical significance helps us determine whether the existing relationship is a result of chance factors.

Part I: Foundations

The maps do look much alike as both variables are highest in the West. Pearson's r (r = 0.475**) is already calculated for you when two maps are displayed at once. The scatterplot shows how correlations are calculated, but the software does it whenever you compare maps too. The two asterisks show that this is a strong correlation. But it does not show that one variable is causing the other. An over-supply of all-male households is not the cause of large federal land holdings, and federal land does not prevent marriage. Both variables are simply higher in the West.

Your turn.

WORKSHEET

NAME: _____

COURSE: _____

DATE: _____

EXERCISE

2

REVIEW QUESTIONS

Based on the first part of this exercise, answer True or False to the following items:

a. The federal government owns more than 50 percent of the land in several western states. T F

b. If the correlation coefficient between two variables is large, it means that one variable is the cause of the other. T F

c. The correlation coefficient shown when two maps are on the screen is interpreted differently than the correlation coefficient that appears in the scatterplot task. T F

d. A negative correlation coefficient confirms that two variables are not associated with one another. T F

e. When a correlation coefficient is not followed by any asterisks, we treat it as a zero correlation. T F

f. States where people have high median family incomes tend to be the same states where people pay the most income taxes. T F

EXPLORIT QUESTIONS

If you have any difficulties using the software to obtain the appropriate information, or if you want to learn additional features of the MAPPING or SCATTERPLOT tasks, refer to the online help.

1. Let's compare the unemployment rate in states with the per capita expenditures by state.

> ➤ *Data File:* **STATES**
> ➤ *Task:* **Mapping**
> ➤ *Variable 1:* **150) UNEMPLOY**
> ➤ *Variable 2:* **107) STA EX/CAP**
> ➤ *View:* **Map**

In this particular situation, it would be quite difficult to examine the maps visually and determine whether there is a pattern. Fortunately, we can simply use the Pearson correlation coefficient.

a. Write in the value of the Pearson correlation coefficient. $r =$ _____

b. Is the relationship statistically significant? Yes No

Exercise 2: Federalism: "A More Perfect Union" 39

c. Is the relationship positive or negative?   Positive   Negative

d. Based on these results, could we conclude that increases in state
   spending lead to higher unemployment?   Yes   No

e. Briefly explain your answer below.

2. Under the federalism system of government, states have substantial autonomy in how they spend tax
    dollars. Are states responsive to the unique needs of their populations, or do states tend to spend
    money similar to one another? Let's first look at a mapping of the violent crime rate, and then we will
    compare this with a mapping of the money that states spend on corrections.

                    Data File: **STATES**
                         Task: **Mapping**
            ➤ Variable 1: **115) VIOL.CRIME**
                    ➤ View: **Map**

    a. This map shows the violent crime rate for the 50 states. While there is no absolutely clear-
       cut pattern here, which of the following statements is most accurate concerning the states
       with the highest crime rates? (Circle the number of the most appropriate answer.)

       1.   Many of the states with higher crime rates are in the Midwest.
       2.   Many of the states with higher crime rates are coastal states, especially in the South
            and Southwest.
       3.   Most of the states with higher crime rates are in the Northeast.

    b. If states with higher violent crime rates also have higher rates of spending on correction facili-
       ties (e.g., prisons), when we compare the maps for these two variables they should be

       1.   similar to each other.
       2.   opposite of each other.
       3.   neither similar nor opposite.
       4.   We can't predict what the maps will look like.

    c. If states with higher violent crime rates have lower rates of spending on corrections, then
       these maps should be

       1.   similar to each other.
       2.   opposite of each other.
       3.   neither similar nor opposite.
       4.   We can't predict what the maps will look like.

3. Let's look at both maps so that we can see if the violent crime rate has any effect on how much a state spends on corrections.

> *Data File:* **STATES**
> *Task:* **Mapping**
> *Variable 1:* **115) VIOL.CRIME**
> ➤ *Variable 2:* **112) CORR$/CAP**
> ➤ *Views:* **Map**

These maps are

   a.   similar to each other.

   b.   opposite of each other.

   c.   neither similar nor opposite.

4. Sometimes it is difficult to determine how alike two maps are simply by looking at them. Let's use the SCATTERPLOT task to examine these same variables.

> *Data File* **STATES**
> ➤ *Task:* **Scatterplot**
> ➤ *Dependent Variable:* **112) CORR$/CAP**
> ➤ *Independent Variable:* **115) VIOL.CRIME**
> ➤ *View:* **Reg. Line**

Note that the SCATTERPLOT task requires you to choose two variables. Make sure your screen matches the scatterplot shown above.

  a. The states that have the highest rates of spending on corrections should appear as dots at the

    1.   right of the scatterplot.

    2.   left of the scatterplot.

    3.   top of the scatterplot.

    4.   bottom of the scatterplot.

    5.   We cannot tell where these dots should be.

  b. The states that appear as dots at the right of the scatterplot represent those that have the

    1.   highest violent crime rates.

    2.   lowest violent crime rates.

    3.   highest rates of spending on corrections.

    4.   lowest rates of spending on corrections.

    5.   The location of the dots is not related to the value of the cases on either variable.

Special feature: When the scatterplot is showing, you may obtain the information on any dot by clicking on it. A little box will appear around the dot, and the values of 112) CORR$/CAP (or the Y-axis variable) and of 115) VIOL.CRIME (or the X-axis variable) will be shown. The information also shows the value of the correlation coefficient with the highlighted case removed. Ignore this new value of the correlation coefficient.

c. Identify the case that is highest on CORR$/CAP: _____

d. What is its value on CORR$/CAP (Y)?   _____

e. What is its value on VIOL.CRIME (X)?   _____

f. Identify the case that is highest on VIOL.CRIME: _____

g. What is its value on VIOL.CRIME (X)?   _____

h. What is its value on CORR$/CAP (Y)?   _____

i. What is the correlation coefficient (r) for this scatterplot?   _____

j. Is it statistically significant?   Yes   No

k. The results indicate that states with higher violent crime rates spend higher
   proportions of money on corrections.   T   F

5. Another way of examining the connection between the crime problem and the government's response to this problem is to check the connection between the violent crime rate and the number of police officers in the state and local governments. We could hypothesize that states with higher rates of violent crime would have more police officers (per 10,000 population).

> Data File: **STATES**
> Task: **Scatterplot**
> ➤ Dependent Variable: **128) POLICE**
> ➤ Independent Variable: **115) VIOL.CRIME**
> ➤ View: **Reg. Line**

a. Write in the Pearson correlation (r) for this relationship.   r = _____

b. Is the relationship statistically significant?   Yes   No

c. In general, states that have higher crime rates have more police officers
   per 10,000 population.   T   F

d. Which state has the highest number of police officers per 10,000 population?   _____

6. In the preliminary part of this exercise, you saw that people in some states pay much higher levels of income taxes than people in other states. Perhaps the high levels of income taxes are offset by lower levels of other taxes, such as property taxes. Let's take a look.

> Data File: **STATES**
> ➤ Task: **Mapping**
> ➤ Variable 1: **114) PROP. TAX**
> ➤ Variable 2: **20) INCOME TAX**
> ➤ View: **Map**

    a. Write in the Pearson correlation (r) for this relationship.   r = _____

    b. Is the relationship statistically significant?   Yes   No

    c. States with high income taxes tend to have low levels of property taxes.   T   F

    d. States in the Northeast (e.g., New York, New Jersey, Connecticut) tend to have high levels of both income taxes and property taxes.   T   F

    e. Most states in the South tend to have relatively low levels of both income taxes and property taxes.   T   F

    f. Based on the discussion provided in the preliminary part of this exercise, what might be the reason that people in some states pay higher property taxes than people in other states?

7. The variable 106) %HI EDUC $ represents the percentage of state and local spending that goes to higher education. The variable 21) STATE DEBT indicates the amount of per capita debt that states have, while 110) WELF$/CAP is the amount of per capita spending by states on welfare. Finally, as you saw above, the variable 112) CORR$/CAP is the per capita spending on corrections.

Do the following analyses and fill in the information requested.

> Data File: **STATES**
> ➤ Task: **Scatterplot**
> ➤ Dependent Variable: **110) WELF$/CAP**
> ➤ Independent Variable: **106) %HI EDUC $**
> ➤ View: **Reg. Line**

a. Write in the Pearson correlation (r) for this relationship.   r = _____

b. Is the relationship statistically significant?   Yes   No

c. States that spend higher amounts on education tend to spend _____ on welfare (circle answer).   Less More

> Data File: **STATES**
> Task: **Scatterplot**
> ➤ Dependent Variable: **112) CORR$/CAP**
> ➤ Independent Variable: **106) %HI EDUC $**
> ➤ View: **Reg. Line**

d. Write in the Pearson correlation (r) for this relationship.   r = _____

e. Is the relationship statistically significant?   Yes   No

f. States that spend higher amounts on education tend to spend _____ on corrections (circle answer).   Less More

> Data File: **STATES**
> Task: **Scatterplot**
> ➤ Dependent Variable: **21) STATE DEBT**
> ➤ Independent Variable: **110) WELF$/CAP**
> ➤ View: **Reg. Line**

g. Write in the Pearson correlation (r) for this relationship.   r = _____

h. Is the relationship statistically significant?   Yes   No

i. States that spend higher amounts on welfare tend to have _____ levels of state debt (circle answer).   Higher Lower

> Data File: **STATES**
> Task: **Scatterplot**
> Dependent Variable: **21) STATE DEBT**
> ➤ Independent Variable: **112) CORR$/CAP**
> ➤ View: **Reg. Line**

j. Write in the Pearson correlation (r) for this relationship.   r = _____

k. Is the relationship statistically significant?   Yes   No

l. States that spend higher amounts on corrections tend to have _____ levels of state debt (circle answer).   Higher Lower

Data File: **STATES**
Task: **Scatterplot**
Dependent Variable: **21) STATE DEBT**
➤ Independent Variable: **106) %HI EDUC $**
➤ View: **Reg. Line**

m. Write in the Pearson correlation (r) for this relationship. r = _____

n. Is the relationship statistically significant? Yes   No

o. States that spend higher proportions of their budgets on education tend to have _____ levels of state debt (circle answer). Higher   Lower

8. One basis of inequality in the balance between the federal government and the states concerns the fact that the federal government does not treat all states the same when it comes to spending its money or giving grants to state and local governments.

Data File: **STATES**
➤ Task: **Mapping**
➤ Variable 1: **16) FED$ RATIO**
➤ View: **List: Rank**

a. How many states receive more money back from the federal government than they pay in? _____

b. Which states receive exactly the same amount back from the federal government as they pay in?

_____

_____

9. Let's see if we can determine what might affect this exchange ratio. We read and hear a great deal about the problems of big cities. Perhaps the more urban states have a better exchange ratio with the federal government than the less urban states.

Data File: **STATES**
➤ Task: **Scatterplot**
➤ Dependent Variable: **16) FED$ RATIO**
➤ Independent Variable: **4) URBAN00**
➤ View: **Reg. Line**

a. The dot representing the state with the most favorable exchange ratio will be at the

1. top of the scatterplot.
2. bottom of the scatterplot.
3. left of the scatterplot.
4. right of the scatterplot.

  b. The dot representing the most urban state will be at the

     1.   top of the scatterplot.

     2.   bottom of the scatterplot.

     3.   left of the scatterplot.

     4.   right of the scatterplot.

  c. Which state has the most favorable exchange?   _____

  d. What is its exchange ratio?   _____

  e. What percentage of this state lives in urban areas?   _____%

  f. Which state is the most urban?   _____

  g. What is its exchange ratio?   _____

  h. What percentage of this state lives in urban areas?   _____%

  i. What is the value of r, the correlation coefficient?   r = _____

  j. Is it significant?   Yes   No

  k. Do these results support the idea that the more urban states get a better
     exchange rate than the less urban states?   Yes   No

10. Perhaps the "wealth" of a state affects its exchange ratio.

                Data File: **STATES**

                     Task: **Scatterplot**

      Dependent Variable: **16) FED$ RATIO**

  ➤ *Independent Variable:*   **13) FAMILY$**

             ➤ *View:*   **Reg. Line**

  a. Write in the Pearson correlation (r) for this relationship.   r = _____

  b. Is the relationship statistically significant?   Yes   No

  c. The higher the median family income, the lower the exchange ratio.   T   F

11. Median income is one indicator of the wealth of a state—the *higher* the median income, the wealthier
the state. We could also use poverty as an indicator of the wealth of a state—the *lower* the poverty
rate, the wealthier the state.

                Data File: **STATES**

                     Task: **Scatterplot**

      Dependent Variable: **16) FED$ RATIO**

  ➤ *Independent Variable:*   **15) % POOR**

             ➤ *View:*   **Reg. Line**

a. Write in the Pearson correlation (r) for this relationship.   r = _____

b. Is the relationship statistically significant?   Yes   No

c. The higher the poverty rate, the lower the exchange ratio.   T   F

12. Those who favor a strong federal government argue that the federal government can play the role of Robin Hood, taking from the rich states and giving to the poor states and thus compensating for inequalities in resources across the states. Do the results in Questions 10 and 11 support the idea that the federal government is, in fact, doing this? Be sure to cite the evidence for your conclusion.

"OF THE PEOPLE": AN INTERESTED AND INFORMED PUBLIC

> *. . . government of the people, by the people, for the people . . .*
>
> ABRAHAM LINCOLN,
> GETTYSBURG ADDRESS,
> NOV. 19, 1863

Tasks: Mapping, Univariate, Cross-Tabulation, Auto-Analyzer
Data Files: NATIONS, NES

While not everyone would agree completely on the details of what we can loosely call democratic theory, there are certain ideas that most democratic theorists would agree on. Most would agree, for example, that a democratic government must be responsive to the will of the people and that it must act in accord with at least some definition of the public good. On the other side of this coin, democratic theory also makes certain assumptions about the citizen. In order for the government to represent the people, citizens must take an interest in public affairs and be adequately informed about them. (Democratic theory also assumes that citizens participate in politics, and we will return to political participation in Exercise 8.) Let's begin with interest in politics.

> ➤ *Data File:* **NATIONS**
> ➤ *Task:* **Mapping**
> ➤ *Variable 1:* **3) P.INTEREST**
> ➤ *View:* **Map**

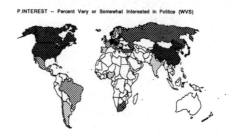

P.INTEREST -- Percent Very or Somewhat Interested in Politics (WVS)

This map is based on public opinion polls conducted in 40 nations from 1991 through 1993. The same questions (translated into the local language) were asked in each poll. Here we see the percentage of people in each country who responded that they were very or somewhat interested in politics when asked "How interested would you say you are in politics?"

Data File: **NATIONS**

Task: **Mapping**

Variable 1: **3) P.INTEREST**

➤ View: **List: Rank**

RANK	CASE NAME	VALUE
1	Latvia	79
2	Czech Republic	75
3	Germany	74
4	South Korea	73
4	Bulgaria	73
4	Lithuania	73
7	Norway	72
8	Switzerland	66
9	Japan	62
9	Netherlands	62
9	China	62

People in Latvia were most apt to say that they were "very" or "somewhat" interested in politics, closely followed by the Czechs and the Germans. The Japanese (62 percent) and Chinese (62 percent) were slightly more interested in politics than were Americans, who were tied with Slovaks and Estonians at 59 percent, while 58 percent of Canadians were very or somewhat interested in politics. In contrast, in many nations, including Mexico, Italy, and India, only about a third of survey participants were interested in politics and in Romania only 18 percent were interested.

Data File: **NATIONS**

Task: **Mapping**

➤ Variable 1: **4) TALK POL.**

➤ View: **Map**

TALK POL. -- Percent Who Often Talk about Politics with Their Friends (WVS)

This map shows variations across nations in the percentage who answered "often" to the question "When you get together with your friends, would you say you discuss political matters frequently, occasionally, or never?"

Data File: **NATIONS**

Task: **Mapping**

Variable 1: **4) TALK POL.**

➤ View: **List: Rank**

RANK	CASE NAME	VALUE
1	Latvia	47
2	Lithuania	45
3	Bulgaria	42
3	Estonia	42
5	Czech Republic	33
5	Belarus	33
5	Germany	33
8	Russia	31
9	Slovak Republic	30
10	Argentina	28

Again, Latvians rank highest, at 47 percent, in talking about politics. Indeed, people in the nations of Eastern Europe, once part of the Soviet bloc, do the most talking about politics. Only 14 percent of Americans frequently talk politics, and only 6 percent of the Japanese do.

➤ *Data File:* **NES**
➤ *Task:* **Univariate**
➤ *Primary Variable:* **20) INTEREST?**
➤ *View:* **Pie**

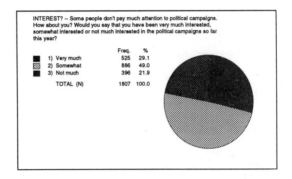

Note that this task uses a new data file.

Here are the results of a national survey of American adults conducted during the 2000 election. This opinion survey, known as the *National Election Study*, is conducted every two years during the national election campaigns by the Institute for Social Research of the University of Michigan. During the interview, each respondent was asked about his or her interest in the political campaigns. Twenty-nine percent of the interviewees indicated a high level of interest; the rest had less interest.

You probably take opinion polling for granted—you have been encountering survey findings in the news media as long as you can remember. Nevertheless, you may have wondered how it is possible to assess the distribution of political opinions among more than 280 million Americans, 150 million Russians, or more than 1 billion Chinese on the basis of interviews conducted with only 1,000 to 2,000 people. The answer is to be found in the **laws of probability**.

Just as a sophisticated gambler can calculate the odds involved in a particular bet, so too political scientists know how to calculate the odds that findings based on a sample of the population yield an accurate portrait of that population. And just as gamblers assume that they are participating in a random game (that the deck has not been stacked or the dice loaded), so too the odds on a sample being accurate depend on the sample being selected at random from the population.

Thus, the first principle of accurate polling is that people are selected by using **random sampling**. For example, interviewers conducting telephone polls often use random dialing software to place their calls. This produces a random sample of all telephones (including those with unlisted numbers) and therefore a random sample of households (except for the 1 percent having no phone). The most careful pollsters then randomly sample a person in each selected household.

If the sample is selected at random, we can use the laws of probability to calculate the odds that what we find accurately reflects the population from which the sample was drawn. These odds are determined by two factors: the size of the sample and the size of observed differences within the sample.

First of all, the sample must be **sufficiently large**. Obviously, we couldn't use a sample of two people as the basis for describing the American population—there is a very high probability that they both would be white. For this reason, survey studies include enough cases so that they can accurately reflect the population in terms of variations in such characteristics as age, sex, education, religion, and the like. The accuracy of a random sample is a function of its size: the larger the sample, the more accurate it is. Oddly enough, accuracy depends only on the size of the sample, not on the size of the sample relative to the size of the population from which the sample is drawn. Thus, a sample of 1,000 persons will yield an equally accurate description of the populations of Fargo, North Dakota, New York City, or the whole United States.

Good survey samples include at least 1,000 persons. The National Election Survey we are using in this exercise is based on 1,807 Americans, and therefore the results are very accurate.

Often, news reports of surveys of public opinion consist of the percentages in favor of or against something—usually something controversial. Unfortunately, too often these "surveys" are not based on randomly selected samples (as when people are invited to register their opinions by dialing an 800 number) or are based on samples that are far too small to be accurate.

The data we have examined thus far report the distribution of opinions of entire populations, for example, how interested are Russians, Canadians, or Americans in politics. However, often we wish *to compare* the opinions of various *groups* within the population. For example, are Americans more or less interested in politics depending on their region?

Data File:	**NES**
➤ Task:	**Cross-tabulation**
➤ Row Variable:	**20) INTEREST?**
➤ Column Variable:	**1) REGION**
➤ View:	**Table**
➤ Display:	**Column %**

INTEREST?   by   REGION
Cramer's V: 0.037

INTEREST?	REGION				
	East	Midwest	South	West	TOTAL
Very much	97	120	206	102	525
	30.7%	26.7%	31.4%	26.6%	29.1%
Somewhat	148	230	310	198	886
	46.8%	51.1%	47.2%	51.6%	49.0%
Not much	71	100	141	84	396
	22.5%	22.2%	21.5%	21.9%	21.9%
TOTAL	316	450	657	384	1807
	100.0%	100.0%	100.0%	100.0%	

To construct this table, return to the main menu and select the CROSS-TABULATION task, then select 20) INTEREST? as the row variable and 1) REGION as the column variable. When the table is showing, select the [Column %] option.

Here, region, as defined by the Bureau of the Census, is divided into four areas. The table reveals that people living in the South (31.4 percent) are more apt than people in other regions to say they are highly interested in politics. People in the West are least apt to be interested (26.6 percent) with Easterners (30.7 percent) and Midwesterners (26.7 percent) falling in between.

Here, however, we must deal with a second limitation on the accuracy of survey results, one that has to do with the **magnitude of the difference** observed in the table. Simply put, if the difference between the percentaged results is high (e.g., 80 percent of Southerners are very interested in political campaigns, compared to 30 percent of Westerners), then the odds that a difference actually exists in the full population are very good. But if the percentaged differences are small (31 percent of Southerners are very interested in political campaigns, compared to 27 percent of Westerners), then there is an increased chance that these differences are simply due to randomness, rather than some actual difference in the population. Think about it this way. Suppose you have a bag containing 1,000 marbles. If after drawing out 100 of the marbles you find that 90 are black and 10 are white, you can be pretty confident in stating that there are many more black marbles remaining in the bag than white marbles. However, if you draw out 55 black marbles and 45 white marbles, you will be less confident in stating that there are more black marbles than white marbles remaining in the bag. Thus, in addition to the overall size of the sample, *the size of the difference within the sample* must be considered. The larger the difference that is observed, the greater the probability that it is representative of the population.

These two limits apply because samples are based on the principle of random selection, and therefore they are subject to some degree of *random fluctuation*. That is, for purely random reasons there can be small differences between the sample and the population. Thus, whenever we examine cross-tabulations such as the one shown above, political scientists always must ask whether what they are seeing is a real difference—one that would turn up if the entire population were examined—or only a random fluctuation, which does not reflect a true difference in the population.

The small size of the regional differences observed above (on a sample this size) will always make an experienced analyst suspicious that it is merely the result of random fluctuations. Fortunately, there is a simple technique for calculating the odds that a given difference is real or random. This calculation is called a **test of statistical significance**. Differences observed in samples are said to be statistically significant when the odds against random results are high enough. There is no mathematical way to determine just how high is high enough. But, through the years, social scientists have settled on the rule of thumb that they will ignore all differences (or correlations) unless the odds are at least 20 to 1 against their being random. Put another way, social scientists reject all findings when the probability they are random is greater than .05, or 5 in 100. What this level of significance means is that if 100 random samples were drawn independently from the same population, a difference this large would not turn up more than 5 times, purely by chance.

There are two ways to see what the level of significance is for this table. If you want to know the exact probability of whether the results may be due to random fluctuations, you need to switch to the statistics view.

Data File:	**NES**
Task:	**Cross-tabulation**
Row Variable:	**20) INTEREST?**
Column Variable:	**1) REGION**
View:	**Table**
➤ Display:	**Statistics (Summary)**

INTEREST?   by   REGION

Nominal Statistics

Chi-Square: 4.986	(DF =	6; Prob. = 0.546)			
V:	0.037	C:	0.052		
Lambda:	0.000	Lambda:	0.000	Lambda:	0.000
(DV=1)		(DV=20)			

Ordinal Statistics

Gamma:	0.003	Tau-b:	0.002	Tau-c:	0.002
s.error	0.030	s.error	0.020	s.error	0.021
Dyx:	0.002	Dxy:	0.003		
s.error	0.019	s.error	0.022		
Prob. =	0.909				

Ignore everything on this screen except for the first two lines of text. At the end of the first line you'll see "Prob. = 0.546." This value indicates that the odds these results are simply due to randomness are 546 in 1,000 (or about 5 in 10). Since social scientists require that these odds be less than 1 in 20 (.05), we know that the slight regional differences between those who were highly interested in the campaign might be due to random fluctuations.

There is another number on this screen that you'll find useful when doing cross-tabulation analysis. In the second row, locate the value "V = 0.037." The V stands for Cramer's V, which is a correlation coefficient developed for cross-tabulations. Cramer's V is similar to Pearson's r (see Exercise 2) in that its value varies from 0 to 1. If the relationship between these two variables was perfect (that is, if all people in the South indicated they were very interested in the political campaign while all people in the West indicated they were not interested in the political campaign), then this would be a value of 1. However, unlike Pearson's r, V does not indicate whether the relationship is positive or negative—the kind of relationship must be inferred from the table itself. Also, it should be noted that survey data produce much lower correlations than do data based on aggregates such as states or nations. For our purposes, let's use the following guidelines to assess the strength of Cramer's V.

- If V is between .00 and .10, the relationship is very weak or nonexistent.

- If V is between .10 and .25, the relationship is moderate.

- If V is over .25, the relationship is strong.

For this table, V is only .037. Thus, there is virtually no strength to this relationship and it is not important.

It's important to understand that Cramer's V assesses the strength of the relationship shown in the table, not the odds that the results are statistically significant. Don't confuse Cramer's V with the probability value—they provide different information.

Here's something else to remember. Sometimes in large surveys like the NES, you'll see differences in tables of only 2 to 3 percentage points, yet they are statistically significant. Even if this difference does exist in the entire population, it's generally not worthy of note. Whenever you examine cross-tabulations in this book, always look at the actual difference in percentage points. If the difference is less than 5 or 10 percentage points, ask yourself whether it's substantively significant.

Hence, when doing cross-tabulation analysis, you should follow these steps. First, look at the table to see if the observed differences are worth noting. If the categories you are comparing differ by fewer than 5 to 10 percentage points, the analysis may not be worth pursuing. Second, if you are testing a hypothesis, be sure that the percentages differ in the predicted direction. For instance, if you predict that men are more likely than women to be interested in politics, then the differences in the table should support this. Assuming you make it through the first two steps, the third step is to look at the actual strength of the relationship by examining the correlation coefficient (V). Finally, determine whether the results are statistically significant. It's in this final step that you apply the .05 rule described earlier.

The CROSS-TABULATION task in ExplorIt makes this process even easier by placing all the information needed on one screen. Return to the [Column %] option to view the table again. Notice that the value of V appears at the top of this screen too. If these results were statistically significant at the .05 level, one asterisk would appear after this value. If these results were significant at the .01 level (making the odds 1 in 100), two asterisks would appear. Since there are no asterisks following the V value, we know that these regional differences are too small to be statistically significant.

The following chart sums up the process of "Assessing a Relationship Between Variables in a Cross-Tabulation." If you need guidelines, just follow the steps in this chart.

ASSESSING A RELATIONSHIP BETWEEN VARIABLES IN A CROSS-TABULATION

Step 1: Determine whether the observed differences are worth noting. Example: Are the differences in political interest between men and women big enough to be important?

| The differences are only a few percentage points. | The differences are at least 5–10 percentage points. |

| The relationship is not important. | The relationship might be important. |

Step 2: If testing a hypothesis, check whether the results are in the hypothesized direction. For example, if you hypothesized that men would have higher political interest than women, are the results in accord with this?

Step 3: Examine the strength of the relationship by looking at the correlation coefficient, Cramer's V.

Step 4: Determine whether the results are statistically significant.

| The significance level is .05 or less —there is at least one asterisk next to Cramer's V. | The significance level is greater than .05—there is no asterisk next to Cramer's V. |

| The relationship is statistically significant. We decide that there is a real relationship between the variables in the population from which the sample was selected. | The relationship is not statistically significant. We decide that there is no real relationship between the variables in the population. |

Let's examine another example.

Data File: **NES**
Task: **Cross-tabulation**
Row Variable: **20) INTEREST?**
➤ Column Variable: **5) AGE**
➤ View: **Table**
➤ Display: **Column %**

INTEREST? by AGE
Cramer's V: 0.155 **

		AGE						TOTAL
		Under 30	30 to 39	40 to 49	50 to 64	65 & over	Missing	
INTEREST?	Very much	39	87	108	164	126	1	524
		14.0%	22.3%	27.8%	38.7%	40.0%		29.1%
	Somewhat	156	199	195	197	133	6	880
		55.9%	50.9%	50.1%	46.5%	42.2%		48.9%
	Not much	84	105	86	63	56	2	394
		30.1%	26.9%	22.1%	14.9%	17.8%		21.9%
	TOTAL	279	391	389	424	315	9	1798
		100.0%	100.0%	100.0%	100.0%	100.0%		

Reading and comparing across the values for the first *row*, we discover that older people are more interested in politics than are younger people. Cramer's V is 0.155**, which is moderate in size. The two asterisks indicate that the odds are less than 1 in 100 that these age differences are random. We can have a lot of confidence that in this instance age really matters.

Does one's education level affect the level of interest he or she has in politics?

Data File: **NES**
Task: **Cross-tabulation**
Row Variable: **20) INTEREST?**
➤ Column Variable: **4) EDUCATION**
➤ View: **Table**
➤ Display: **Column %**

INTEREST? by EDUCATION
Cramer's V: 0.175 **

		EDUCATION					TOTAL
		Not HS grd	HS grad	Some col	Coll.grad.	Missing	
INTEREST?	Very much	31	107	151	234	2	523
		17.2%	20.6%	27.7%	42.1%		29.1%
	Somewhat	86	259	286	254	1	885
		47.8%	49.9%	52.5%	45.7%		49.2%
	Not much	63	153	108	68	4	392
		35.0%	29.5%	19.8%	12.2%		21.8%
	TOTAL	180	519	545	556	7	1800
		100.0%	100.0%	100.0%	100.0%		

We easily can see in the table that more educated people are more likely to be interested in politics. Once again the relationship is moderate (V = 0.175**) and the results are statistically significant at the .01 level, as indicated by the two asterisks. Let's examine another key demographic: gender.

Data File: **NES**
Task: **Cross-tabulation**
Row Variable: **20) INTEREST?**
➤ Column Variable: **3) SEX**
➤ View: **Table**
➤ Display: **Column %**

INTEREST? by SEX
Cramer's V: 0.056

		SEX		TOTAL
		Male	Female	
INTEREST?	Very much	252	273	525
		31.9%	26.8%	29.1%
	Somewhat	375	511	886
		47.5%	50.2%	49.0%
	Not much	163	233	396
		20.6%	22.9%	21.9%
	TOTAL	790	1017	1807
		100.0%	100.0%	

The table shows that men (31.9 percent) are more apt to be interested in political campaigns than are women (26.8 percent). Notice, however, there is only a 5-percentage-point difference between men and women. This small difference does not have much substantive significance—even if the results are statistically significant. In this situation, both men and women lack interest in politics and the difference between them is so small that it is not important. In this particular example, the summary statistics reiterate the weak relationship: Cramer's V is very slight (0.056), and the results are not statistically significant.

Part I: Foundations

When political scientists study a particular behavior or attitude, they first examine the overall distribution (such as a pie chart) of that attitude. For example, one of the first things we looked at in this exercise was the percentage of Americans who indicate they are very interested in the campaign, what percentage have some interest, and so on. Next, political scientists look at the relationship between that variable and various demographic variables, such as age, education, gender, and so on. We did the same thing in this exercise using the technique of cross-tabulation to see how interest in politics is distributed in the population. This type of preliminary analysis provides a snapshot of the population with regard to the variable of interest.

For the next two examples, let's use the AUTO-ANALYZER task that is available on the main menu.

<table>
<tr><td>Data File: NES</td><td></td></tr>
<tr><td>➤ Task: Auto-Analyzer</td><td></td></tr>
<tr><td>➤ Variable: 20) INTEREST?</td><td></td></tr>
<tr><td>➤ View: Univariate</td><td></td></tr>
</table>

	PERCENT
Very much	29.1%
Somewhat	49.0%
Not much	21.9%

Among all respondents, 29.1% of the sample are very much interested in following the political campaigns this year.

To obtain these results, return to the main menu and select the AUTO-ANALYZER task. Then select 20) INTEREST? as your analyzer variable and click [OK].

The first result that Auto-Analyzer provides is the *univariate* distribution for the variable you selected. As you can see, the percentages are the same as what we found earlier using the UNIVARIATE task from the main menu. As the textual summary indicates, among all respondents, 29.1 percent of the sample expressed very much interest in the political campaigns.

Data File: **NES**
Task: **Auto-Analyzer**
Variable: **20) INTEREST?**
➤ View: **Race**

	RACE	
	White	African American
Very much	29.9%	26.9%
Somewhat	48.4%	53.4%
Not much	21.8%	19.7%

Blacks and whites are about equally likely to be very much interested in following the political campaigns this year.

If continuing from the previous example, simply click the button [Race] to see the results.

These results are identical to what you would obtain if you cross-tabulated the variable INTEREST? with RACE. The only difference is that it is not necessary for you to percentage the table and a summary of the table is provided. As shown by the description, African Americans and white Americans are equally likely to be very much interested in the political campaign. The small differences are not statistically significant.[1]

---

[1] In some cases, the significance of V on the table and the significance given in Auto-Analyzer may be slightly different. The statistic V is used in the CROSS-TABULATION task and is based on chi-square, which summarizes the entire table. Auto-Analyzer relies on column-by-column comparisons in an attempt to uncover patterns of interest. In other words, these two tasks focus on slightly different aspects of the results.

In the worksheets, you'll have a chance to explore several attitudes using the AUTO-ANALYZER task. You will also find this task useful in doing exploratory analysis for papers or projects you may work on for this and other classes.

Your turn.

WORKSHEET

NAME:

COURSE:

DATE:

EXERCISE
3

REVIEW QUESTIONS

Based on the first part of this exercise, answer True or False to the following items:

a. When compared to other countries, people from the former Soviet bloc have very little interest in politics.   T   F

b. One of the most reliable polling methods is to establish an 800 phone number where people can register their opinions on a particular issue.   T   F

c. Cramer's V is similar to Pearson's r in that both are correlation coefficients.   T   F

d. The probability (significance) level assesses the strength of the relationship, while V indicates the odds that the results are due to random fluctuations.   T   F

e. Older people tend to have greater interest in politics than do younger people.   T   F

f. Cramer's V does not indicate whether a relationship is positive or negative. The kind of relationship must be inferred from the table itself.   T   F

g. A relationship between two variables can be *statistically significant* without being strong enough to be *substantively significant*.   T   F

h. In order for us to decide that a relationship is statistically significant, we want the significance level to be greater than .05.   T   F

EXPLORIT QUESTIONS

1. Let's look at some other variables that might affect interest in politics. First of all, we might hypothesize that political interest will be higher among those people who disagree with the idea that politics is too complicated.

> ➤ *Data File:* **NES**
> ➤ *Task:* **Cross-tabulation**
> ➤ *Row Variable:* **20) INTEREST?**
> ➤ *Column Variable:* **95) COMPLICATE**
> ➤ *View:* **Table**
> ➤ *Display:* **Column %**

Open the NES data file and select the CROSS-TABULATION task. Select 20) INTEREST? as the row variable and select 95) COMPLICATE as the column variable. When the table appears, select the [Column %] option.

Copy the first row of the percentaged table:

95) COMPLICATE

	AGREE	**NEITHER**	**DISAGREE**
a. % VERY MUCH	_____%	_____%	_____%

b. What is the value of Cramer's V for this table? V = _____

c. Is V statistically significant? Yes No

d. Are the results in the predicted direction? That is, was political interest higher among those who disagree with the idea that politics is too complicated? Yes No

2. Let's see whether political interest is related to political ideology.

>
> Data File: **NES**
> Task: **Cross-tabulation**
> Row Variable: **20) INTEREST?**
> ➤ Column Variable: **17) IDEOLOGY**
> ➤ View: **Table**
> ➤ Display: **Column %**

Copy the first row of the percentaged table:

17) IDEOLOGY

	LIBERAL	**MODERATE**	**CONSERVATIVE**
a. % VERY MUCH	_____%	_____%	_____%

b. What is the value of Cramer's V for this table? V = _____

c. Is V statistically significant? Yes No

d. Which of the three groups was the least interested in politics? (Circle the number of the most appropriate answer.)

1. Liberals
2. Moderates
3. Conservatives

e. Give a reason why this particular group might be less interested in politics than the other two groups are.

3. Turning to the matter of political information, let's use the AUTO-ANALYZER task to look at the distribution of 21) INFORMED?.

>   *Data File:* **NES**
>   ➤ *Task:* **Auto-Analyzer**
>   ➤ *Variable:* **21) INFORMED?**
>   ➤ *View:* **Univariate**

> **With the NES file open, select the AUTO-ANALYZER task, then select 21) INFORMED? as the analyzer variable.**

The first table shows the distribution of this attitude in the entire sample.

> Write the summary of this univariate distribution that appears below the table:

_____

_____

4. Let's now look at the effect of some demographic characteristics on the person's level of information. In addition to looking at whether the results are statistically significant, you must look at the actual percentages to determine which differences are important.

> **The AUTO-ANALYZER task has eleven demographic characteristics, each represented by a separate option. By selecting one of these demographic options, you see not only the table showing the relationship between the analyzer variable and the selected demographic variable, but also a brief summary of the relationship.**

>   *Data File:* **NES**
>   *Task:* **Auto-Analyzer**
>   *Variable:* **21) INFORMED?**
>   ➤ *View:* **Region**

Answer True or False to the following items:

a. Those in the Midwest are the most informed.   T   F

b. The regional difference on this variable is not statistically significant.   T   F

c. There is little difference between the East and the West.   T   F

>   ➤ *View:* **Education**

d. The higher a person's education, the better informed the person.   T   F

e. This suggests that education may help create an informed electorate.   T   F

➤ *View:* **Sex**

f. Males and females are equally well informed.   T   F

g. Females are better informed than males.   T   F

h. Males are better informed than females, and the difference is statistically significant. T   F

➤ *View:* **Income**

i. The higher the income, the more likely the individual is to be well informed.   T   F

j. Those with the highest income are the least informed.   T   F

➤ *View:* **Age**

k. Younger people are less informed about politics.   T   F

l. Those over 65 are the most informed.   T   F

5. a. Based on the information in Question 4, describe the characteristics of the person who is most likely to be well informed.

    b. Describe the characteristics of the person who is least likely to be well informed.

6. Notice, however, that this AUTO-ANALYZER option is available only for basic demographic variables. In order to look at the effect of other variables on this attitude, you must use the CROSS-TABULATION task. Let's look at the effect of news orientation on how informed the individual is.

> Data File: **NES**
> ➤ Task: **Cross-tabulation**
> ➤ Row Variable: **21) INFORMED?**
> ➤ Column Variable: **24) NEWS TYPE**
> ➤ View: **Table**
> ➤ Display: **Column %**

   a. The relationship between political information and type of news orientation is not statistically significant.   T   F

   b. Those who use both television and newspaper are the best informed.   T   F

   c. Those who use the newspaper are more informed than those who use television.   T   F

   d. Those who use both television and newspaper are not much more informed than those who use the newspaper only.   T   F

7. Not all research is simply descriptive. Frequently, political scientists analyze data to test hypotheses. For example, most of us would hypothesize a link between an individual's interest and level of information: Those who are more interested will be better informed. We can use cross-tabulation to test this hypothesis.

> Data File: **NES**
> Task: **Cross-tabulation**
> Row Variable: **21) INFORMED?**
> ➤ Column Variable: **20) INTEREST?**
> ➤ View: **Table**
> ➤ Display: **Column %**

Copy the first row of the percentaged table:

20) INTEREST?

	VERY MUCH	SOMEWHAT	NOT MUCH
a. %HIGH	_____%	_____%	_____%

   b. What is the value of V for this table?   V = _____

   c. Is V statistically significant?   Yes   No

   d. This table supports our hypothesis that those who are more interested will be better informed.   T   F

8. Use the AUTO-ANALYZER task to determine what kinds of people are more likely to know the names of candidates for congressional elections. On the basis of this analysis, answer the questions below.

> *Data File:* **NES**
> ➤ *Task:* **Auto-Analyzer**
> ➤ *Variable:* **29) KNOW HOUSE**

a. What percentage of the respondents said they could name the
    congressional candidates? _____%

b. Females are more likely to know the names of congressional candidates than
    males are.   T   F

c. The differences here between Democrats, Independents,and Republicans are
    not statistically significant.   T   F

d. Jews are more likely to know the names of the congressional
    candidates than Catholics are.   T   F

e. Lower-income people are more likely to know the names of congressional
    candidates than higher-income people are.   T   F

Part II

FREEDOM: CIVIL LIBERTIES AND CIVIL RIGHTS

Exercise 4   **Civil Liberties: Free Speech**

Exercise 5   **Civil Rights: Equality**

When people speak of the United States as a "free country," they have two basic kinds of freedom in mind. The first kind of freedom consists of what are called **civil liberties**. These include freedom of speech, press, religion, assembly, and petition. The Bill of Rights guarantees these freedoms from infringement by the government or by citizen-groups. If a mob shouts down a speaker, they are denying his or her civil liberties. If the government forbids an unpopular group from expressing their views, that too is a violation of their civil liberties.

The second kind of freedom consists of **civil rights**. These include all the rights of democratic citizenship including voting, equal treatment before the law, an equal share of public benefits, and equal access to public facilities. When African Americans were excluded from voting and from jury duty, and denied access to park benches in the South, they were being denied their civil rights.

In the next two exercises, you will examine public opinion about civil liberties and civil rights.

CIVIL LIBERTIES: FREE SPEECH

*Congress shall make no law respecting an establish-
ment of religion, or prohibiting the free exercise thereof;
or abridging the freedom of speech, or of the press; or
the right of the people peaceably to assemble, and to
petition the Government for a redress of grievances.*

FIRST AMENDMENT TO
THE CONSTITUTION,
RATIFIED IN 1791

Tasks: Mapping, Univariate, Cross-Tabulation, Scatterplot, Historical Trends, Auto-Analyzer
Data Files: NATIONS, GSS, HISTORY

The Bill of Rights was written and adopted because there was widespread public concern that, because these civil liberties were not specifically guaranteed by the Constitution, future governments might fail to uphold them. Many amendments making up the Bill of Rights are concerned with keeping the government from committing abuses such as failing to hold a speedy trial or forcing people to testify against themselves in court. But the five freedoms mentioned in the First Amendment (shown above) concern freedom of expression. The first-mentioned freedom in the First Amendment concerns an establishment of religion and the free exercise of religion. Sometimes the religious freedom clauses (known as the Establishment Clause and the Free Exercise Clause) in the First Amendment are referred to as the "First Freedom" because they were listed first. James Madison, the "Father of the Constitution," was certainly very concerned with religious freedom. He and Jefferson had fought a series of battles in Virginia to protect religious liberty and to prevent the state from favoring one religion over another. Throughout history, many of the battles concerning freedom of expression have been fought over issues of religious liberty.

The other four freedoms in the First Amendment are concerned primarily with enabling people to influence and change the government. The Constitution itself provides the means by which it can be amended. But, without the freedom to speak, write, assemble, or petition, the people would lack the political means to amend the Constitution, influence officials, affect public policy, or successfully vote "the rascals" out of office. Of course, the rights of free speech and a free press extend far beyond direct applications to politics, but these remain the most basic aspects of freedom.

➤ *Data File:* **NATIONS**
　➤ *Task:* **Mapping**
➤ *Variable 1:* **6) PETITION?**
　➤ *View:* **Map**

PETITION? -- Percent Who Have Signed a Political Petition (WVS)

This map shows how people in many nations responded when asked whether they had ever signed a political petition.

Data File: **NATIONS**
Task: **Mapping**
Variable 1: **6) PETITION?**
➤ *View:* **List: Rank**

RANK	CASE NAME	VALUE
1	Canada	77
2	Great Britain	75
3	Sweden	72
4	United States	71
5	Latvia	65
6	Switzerland	63
7	Japan	62
8	Norway	61
9	Germany	60
10	Lithuania	58

More than 7 out of 10 people in Canada, Great Britain, Sweden, and the United States have used their freedom to petition their government. But in many countries few have signed petitions: 14 percent in Turkey and Poland and only 5 percent in Nigeria. Keep in mind that nations with high levels of political freedom are very overrepresented among these nations—public opinion polling is itself an aspect of political expression and therefore is discouraged or controlled in some nations (which is one reason this question was not asked in the Chinese survey).

Regardless of what constitutions say about civil liberties, however, a major factor always is the extent to which the citizens are committed to maintaining these rights. Thus, for example, if enough Americans became disgusted with free speech, they would have the right to repeal the First Amendment and substitute laws limiting free speech. Moreover, in actual practice the extent to which people do have free speech depends to some extent on the degree to which other Americans respect that right. "Freedom of speech" is not really a freedom unless people feel free to use it. If a person holds unpopular opinions, other people might resist allowing that person to present his or her views—or they might retaliate against the person for presenting unpopular views. So, let's explore public commitment to free speech.

➤ *Data File:* **GSS**
➤ *Task:* **Univariate**
➤ *Primary Variable:* **36) ATHEIST SP**
➤ *View:* **Pie**

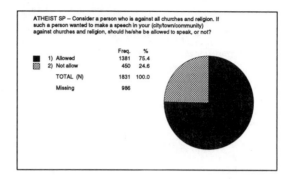

ATHEIST SP -- Consider a person who is against all churches and religion. If such a person wanted to make a speech in your (city/town/community) against churches and religion, should he/she be allowed to speak, or not?

		Freq.	%
■	1) Allowed	1381	75.4
▨	2) Not allow	450	24.6
	TOTAL (N)	1831	100.0
	Missing	986	

The 2000 General Social Surveys asks: "Consider a person who is against all churches and religion. If such a person wanted to make a speech in your (city/town/community) against churches and religion, should he/she be allowed to speak, or not?"

Here we see that 75 percent of those polled would allow an atheist to make a speech. The GSS has been asking Americans this question since 1972, when about 67 percent said the speech should be allowed. But the history of this question goes back to a famous survey by Samuel Stouffer in 1954 during the "McCarthy era" when only 37 percent would allow the speech.[1]

Let's see if this attitude toward freedom of speech is the same in all regions.

Data File: **GSS**
➤ *Task:* **Cross-tabulation**
➤ *Row Variable:* **36) ATHEIST SP**
➤ *Column Variable:* **20) REGION**
➤ *View:* **Table**
➤ *Display:* **Column %**

ATHEIST SP by REGION
Cramer's V: 0.116 **

		REGION				
		East	Midwest	South	West	TOTAL
ATHEIST SP	Allowed	282	321	464	314	1381
		79.0%	73.1%	70.5%	83.3%	75.4%
	Not allow	75	118	194	63	450
		21.0%	26.9%	29.5%	16.7%	24.6%
	Missing	211	231	348	196	986
	TOTAL	357	439	658	377	1831
		100.0%	100.0%	100.0%	100.0%	

Westerners are most likely (83.3 percent) to allow an atheist to speak, and Southerners are least likely (70.5 percent). The difference is statistically significant (V = 0.116**). Perhaps this regional difference is more about dislike of atheists than about general attitudes about freedom of speech. One way to find out is to see if the regional differences persist on a different aspect of free speech. What about freedom to give racist speeches?

---

[1] Samuel Stouffer, *Communism, Conformity, and Civil Liberties* (New York: Doubleday, 1955).

Data File: **GSS**
➤ Task: **Univariate**
➤ Primary Variable: **37) RACIST SP**
➤ View: **Pie**

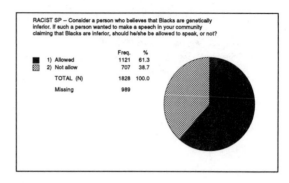

RACIST SP -- Consider a person who believes that Blacks are genetically inferior. If such a person wanted to make a speech in your community claiming that Blacks are inferior, should he/she be allowed to speak, or not?

		Freq.	%
■	1) Allowed	1121	61.3
▨	2) Not allow	707	38.7
	TOTAL (N)	1828	100.0
	Missing	989	

Overall, Americans are less willing to give free speech to "a person who believes that Blacks are genetically inferior," but here too the majority is in favor of allowing the person to speak.

Data File: **GSS**
➤ Task: **Cross-tabulation**
➤ Row Variable: **37) RACIST SP**
➤ Column Variable: **20) REGION**
➤ View: **Table**
➤ Display: **Column %**

RACIST SP   by   REGION
Cramer's V: 0.017

	REGION				
		East	Midwest	South	West	TOTAL
Allowed	223	265	402	231	1121
	62.5%	60.1%	61.8%	60.9%	61.3%
Not allow	134	176	249	148	707
	37.5%	39.9%	38.2%	39.1%	38.7%
Missing	211	229	355	194	989
TOTAL	357	441	651	379	1828
	100.0%	100.0%	100.0%	100.0%	

This time Easterners are most likely (62.5 percent) to support free speech and Midwesterners are least likely (60.1 percent). However, the difference is not statistically significant (V = 0.017).

Let's look at a third test of support for free speech.

Data File: **GSS**
➤ Task: **Univariate**
➤ Primary Variable: **38) COMMUN.SP**
➤ View: **Pie**

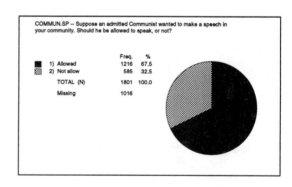

COMMUN.SP -- Suppose an admitted Communist wanted to make a speech in your community. Should he be allowed to speak, or not?

		Freq.	%
■	1) Allowed	1216	67.5
▨	2) Not allow	585	32.5
	TOTAL (N)	1801	100.0
	Missing	1016	

Overall, Americans are about equally likely to give free speech to "an admitted Communist" as to a racist.

Data File:	**GSS**
➤ Task:	**Cross-tabulation**
➤ Row Variable:	**38) COMMUN.SP**
➤ Column Variable:	**20) REGION**
➤ View:	**Table**
➤ Display:	**Column %**

COMMUN.SP   by   REGION
Cramer's V: 0.100 **

		REGION				
		East	Midwest	South	West	TOTAL
C O M M U N . S P	Allowed	234	290	409	283	1216
		66.5%	67.0%	63.4%	76.3%	67.5%
	Not allow	118	143	236	88	585
		33.5%	33.0%	36.6%	23.7%	32.5%
	Missing	216	237	361	202	1016
	TOTAL	352	433	645	371	1801
		100.0%	100.0%	100.0%	100.0%	

Once again, Southerners are least likely to support free speech. Since V = 0.100**, the difference is statistically significant.

The consistency of these findings reflects the fact that each of these three questions really measures the same thing: support for free speech. When political scientists use multiple measures of something, they often combine the results into a single measure called an attitude index or scale.

An **attitude index** measures an attitude on the basis of answers to several questions believed to be measures of the same general attitude. The logic involved is the same logic teachers use when they construct an examination. For example, when teachers give a test made up of true/false or multiple-choice questions, they don't just ask one or two questions. They ask many. They do so because they know that even the best-prepared students can miss any given question and that the worst students could get any particular answer right. So, teachers give tests asking a lot of questions in order to get a more accurate measure of what students have learned.

Just as individual scores on a test are calculated on the basis of the number of correct (or incorrect) answers, attitude indexes "add up" values assigned to some set of questions. In this instance we have three questions measuring support for free speech. Suppose we give each respondent a point for every question to which he or she answered "not allowed" and no points for "allowed" answers. Thus, people who would extend freedom of speech in all three instances would score 0 and those who would deny free speech in all three instances would score 3. To simplify the index slightly, we will combine people with scores of 1 and 2 to make a single category (moderate support for free speech) so that there will be only three rather than four categories.

Data File:	**GSS**
➤ Task:	**Univariate**
➤ Primary Variable:	**39) FR.SPEECH**
➤ View:	**Pie**

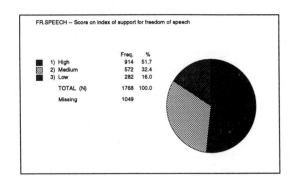

FR.SPEECH -- Score on index of support for freedom of speech

		Freq.	%
■	1) High	914	51.7
▨	2) Medium	572	32.4
■	3) Low	282	16.0
	TOTAL (N)	1768	100.0
	Missing	1049	

All things considered, Americans have considerable respect for freedom of speech—more than half (51.7 percent) would extend free speech in all three instances. On the other hand, these results suggest that almost half of the American citizenry would deny freedom of speech to some people. Let's examine the results by region again.

Data File: **GSS**
➤ Task: **Cross-tabulation**
➤ Row Variable: **39) FR.SPEECH**
➤ Column Variable: **20) REGION**
➤ View: **Table**
➤ Display: **Column %**

FR.SPEECH by REGION
Cramer's V: 0.076 **

		REGION				
		East	Midwest	South	West	TOTAL
FR.SPEECH	High	181	215	319	199	914
		53.1%	50.5%	50.4%	54.1%	51.7%
	Medium	114	136	189	133	572
		33.4%	31.9%	29.9%	36.1%	32.4%
	Low	46	75	125	36	282
		13.5%	17.6%	19.7%	9.8%	16.0%
	Missing	227	244	373	205	1049
	TOTAL	341	426	633	368	1768
		100.0%	100.0%	100.0%	100.0%	

We see only a small amount of regional variation, with less support in the South and Midwest and more support in the East and West.

➤ Data File: **NATIONS**
➤ Task: **Mapping**
➤ Variable 1: **19) CIVIL LIBS**
➤ View: **Map**

CIVIL LIBS -- Index of Civil Liberties, Higher = Greater Liberty (FITW, 1997)

Using the same logic as used to construct the index of support for free speech, each year an American organization known as Freedom House scores every nation (including the tiny ones) on an index of civil liberties. Those nations that sustain the maximum amount of civil liberties are scored 7, and the scores go as low as 1 for nations in which people do not have civil liberties.

Data File: **NATIONS**
Task: **Mapping**
Variable 1: **19) CIVIL LIBS**
➤ View: **List: Rank**

RANK	CASE NAME	VALUE
1	Finland	7
1	Luxembourg	7
1	Canada	7
1	Malta	7
1	Belize	7
1	Barbados	7
1	Denmark	7
1	Ireland	7
1	Portugal	7
1	Switzerland	7

Here we see that a number of nations including the United States and Canada were scored 7 in civil liberties. At the bottom of the ranking, we find that 18 countries were scored 1.

Data File: **NATIONS**
Task: **Mapping**
Variable 1: **19) CIVIL LIBS**
➤ Variable 2: **6) PETITION?**
➤ Views: **Map**

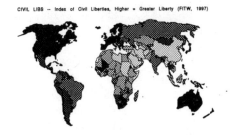

CIVIL LIBS -- Index of Civil Liberties, Higher = Greater Liberty (FITW, 1997)

r = 0.569**

PETITION? -- Percent Who Have Signed a Political Petition (WVS)

As would be expected, there is a very high correlation (r = 0.569**) between scores on the civil liberties index and the percentage in each nation who said they had signed a petition.

Sometimes it is argued that allowing freedom of expression to the people of a country allows them to express their frustrations and that this will prevent pressure from building up that might lead to rebellion. Let's cross-tabulate the civil liberties index by the percentage in nations that agreed their society must be changed radically by revolutionary action.

Data File: **NATIONS**
Task: **Mapping**
Variable 1: **19) CIVIL LIBS**
➤ Variable 2: **9) REVOLUTION**
➤ Views: **Map**

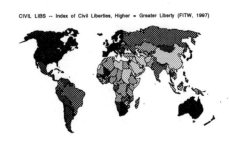

CIVIL LIBS -- Index of Civil Liberties, Higher = Greater Liberty (FITW, 1997)

r = –0.392**

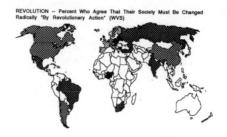

REVOLUTION -- Percent Who Agree That Their Society Must Be Changed Radically "By Revolutionary Action" (WVS)

We see that there is a statistically significant negative relationship (r = –0.392**) between civil liberties in nations and the extent to which people in those nations say that a revolution is needed. This supports the idea that having civil liberties reduces pressures for a rebellion.

Your turn.

WORKSHEET

NAME:

COURSE:

DATE:

EXERCISE

4

REVIEW QUESTIONS

Based on the first part of this exercise, answer True or False to the following items:

a. Civil rights include such things as the right to assemble and to petition the
government.   T   F

b. Most Americans would deny free speech to an atheist.   T   F

c. In the United States, no regional differences exist in support of racist speech.   T   F

d. Support for civil liberties is higher in Canada than in the United States.   T   F

e. Freedom of speech is one of the first things guaranteed in the Constitution. T   F

f. One freedom denied to Americans by their Constitution is the freedom to
eliminate civil liberties.   T   F

g. The basic freedom of expression rights are contained in the First Amendment
to the U.S. Constitution.   T   F

h. People in nations that have more civil liberties are more likely to think that a
revolution is needed in their nation.   T   F

EXPLORIT QUESTIONS

1.   We've found that nations differ in the extent to which civil liberties are supported. Let's see which
     characteristics of nations may have an effect on this variable. Perhaps the level of democracy?

> *Data File:* **NATIONS**
> *Task:* **Mapping**
> *Variable 1:* **19) CIVIL LIBS**
> *Variable 2:* **18) DEMOCRACY**
> *Views:* **Map**

a. What is the value of r for these comparison maps? $r = \_\_\_\_\_$

b. Is it statistically significant?   Yes   No

Exercise 4: Civil Liberties: Free Speech   75

   c. Which statement best summarizes the relationship between these variables? (Circle the number of the most appropriate answer.)

     1.   The more democratic the country, the better its civil liberties rating.

     2.   The less democratic the country, the better its civil liberties rating.

     3.   Democracy and civil liberties appear to be unrelated.

2.   Let's examine the effect of education on support of civil liberties. In the NATIONS data file, we will use the estimated education level that citizens of a country are expected to achieve as a measure of education.

>   Data File: **NATIONS**
>   ➤ Task: **Scatterplot**
> ➤ Dependent Variable: **19) CIVIL LIBS**
> ➤ Independent Variable: **40) EDUC EXPTD**
>   ➤ View: **Reg. Line**

   a. Write in the Pearson correlation (r) for this relationship.   r = _____

   b. Is the relationship statistically significant?   Yes   No

Answer True or False to the following items:

   c. There is no relationship between the education level of the populace and the rating on civil liberties.   T   F

   d. Countries with higher education levels tend to score higher on the civil liberties index.   T   F

   e. These results suggest that there may be a causal relationship between education and civil liberties.   T   F

3.   Let's look at educational level and attitude toward free speech over time in the United States.

>   ➤ Data File: **HISTORY**
>   ➤ Task: **Historical Trends**
> ➤ Variables: **28) CIVLIB INX**
>   **7) %COLLEGE**

Open the HISTORY data file and select the HISTORICAL TRENDS task. Select 28) CIVLIB INX and 7) %COLLEGE as your trend variables.

Because the GSS was not started until the 1970s, comparable data in the index are not available prior to 1970.

   a. What is the description of 28) CIVLIB INX?

_____

_____

    b. What is the description of 7) %COLLEGE?

_____

_____

    c. Over the past 20 years, the percentage opposing free speech has increased
       dramatically in the United States.   T   F

    d. The percentage of the population who have graduated from college and the
       tolerance for free speech have both increased over the past two decades.   T   F

    e. This graph suggests that an individual's education might affect his or her attitude
       toward free speech.   T   F

4.   We can also look at the effect of education on support of free speech using survey data.

> ➤ *Data File:*   **GSS**
> ➤ *Task:*   **Cross-tabulation**
> ➤ *Row Variable:*   **39) FR.SPEECH**
> ➤ *Column Variable:*   **3) EDUCATION**
> ➤ *View:*   **Table**
> ➤ *Display:*   **Column %**

Copy the first row of the percentaged table.

	NOT HS GRD	HS GRD	SOME COLL.	COLL GRAD
a. % SCORING HIGH	_____%	_____%	_____%	_____%

    b. What is the value of V for this table?   V = _____

    c. Is V statistically significant?   Yes   No

    d. The higher one's educational attainment, the less likely one is to endorse
       the right of free speech.   T   F

    e. Each additional level of education seems to increase tolerance of free speech.   T   F

5.   Let's see what other characteristics may affect support for free speech.

> *Data File:*   **GSS**
> ➤ *Task:*   **Auto-Analyzer**
> ➤ *Variable:*   **39) FR.SPEECH**
> ➤ *View:*   **Age**

    First select the AUTO-ANALYZER task and select 39) FR.SPEECH as the analyzer variable.
    Then select the option corresponding to age.

Carefully review the results for this analysis and then answer True or False to the following items:

    a. About 55 percent of those under age 30 scored high on freedom of speech.   T   F

    b. The age group of 65 and over has the highest percentage who scored high on freedom of speech.   T   F

    c. Among those younger than 65, the four age categories are fairly similar in their support for freedom of speech.   T   F

6.   Continue to use the AUTO-ANALYZER task and 39) FR.SPEECH to look at the effects of sex, political party, and religion on support of free speech. Carefully look at the tables and summaries for each item. Based on these results and the results of Question 5, describe the person most likely to endorse the right of free speech.

7.   Frequently one person's freedom of speech interferes with another person's perceived rights. For example, does the right to freedom of speech include the right to use racial slurs, the right to call for the radical overthrow of the government, and the right to distribute pornography?

>   Data File: **GSS**
> ➤   Task: **Univariate**
> ➤ Primary Variable: **66) PORN.LAW?**
> ➤   View: **Pie**

What percentage responded that

    a. there should be laws against the distribution of pornography, whatever the age?   _____%

    b. there should be laws against the distribution of pornography to persons under age 18?   _____%

    c. there should be no laws forbidding the distribution of pornography?   _____%

8. Let's see how a person's attitude toward free speech affects his or her attitude toward the distribution of pornography.

        Data File: **GSS**
        ➤ Task: **Cross-tabulation**
        ➤ Row Variable: **66) PORN.LAW?**
        ➤ Column Variable: **39) FR.SPEECH**
        ➤ View: **Table**
        ➤ Display: **Column %**

    Fill in the percentages for the first row of this cross-tabulation—the percentages of persons who would outlaw all pornography.

	HIGH	**MEDIUM**	**LOW**
a. %YES:ALL	_____%	_____%	_____%

    b. What is the value of Cramer's V for this table?   V = _____

    c. Is V statistically significant?   Yes   No

    d. Which of the following statements most accurately summarizes the relationship between support for freedom of speech and support for outlawing all pornography? (Circle the number of the most appropriate answer.)

        1. Those who support freedom of speech do not support outlawing pornography.
        2. Those who support freedom of speech also support outlawing pornography.
        3. There is no relationship between support for freedom of speech and support for outlawing pornography.

9. Until the 1960s, public schools typically began the day with Bible readings and a prayer. In 1962, these school-sponsored religious activities were ruled to be unconstitutional by the Supreme Court. Today, the issue of school prayer is argued as a freedom of expression issue by both those who oppose it and those who favor it. How do attitudes on this issue relate to support for freedom of speech?

        Data File: **GSS**
        Task: **Cross-tabulation**
        ➤ Row Variable: **45) SCH.PRAY**
        ➤ Column Variable: **39) FR.SPEECH**
        ➤ View: **Table**
        ➤ Display: **Column %**

    Fill in the percentages for the first row of this cross-tabulation—the percentages of persons who do not favor school prayer.

	HIGH	**MEDIUM**	**LOW**
a. % NO PRAYER	_____%	_____%	_____%

Exercise 4: Civil Liberties: Free Speech

b. What is the value of Cramer's V for this table?   V = _____

c. Is V statistically significant?   Yes   No

d. Which of the following statements most accurately summarizes the relationship between support for school prayer and support for freedom of speech? (Circle the number of the most appropriate answer.)

    1.   Those who support freedom of speech do not support school prayer.

    2.   Those who support freedom of speech also support school prayer.

    3.   There is no relationship between support for freedom of speech and support for school prayer.

10. It has been apparent throughout this analysis that some Americans support freedom of speech more than others. But are those who support freedom of speech in particular situations simply supporting it because they tend to agree with the views of the particular group/person being discussed? To take a particular example, are those who would allow a speech by a racist simply more likely to be racists themselves? Let's test this idea using the question of whether interracial marriage should be outlawed as a measure of whether one holds racist ideas or not.

Data File:	**GSS**
Task:	**Cross-tabulation**
➤ Row Variable:	**37) RACIST SP**
➤ Column Variable:	**46) INTERMAR.?**
➤ View:	**Table**
➤ Display:	**Column %**

Fill in the percentages for the first row of this cross-tabulation—the percentages of persons who would allow a speech by a racist.

	YES	NO
a. % ALLOWED	_____%	_____%

b. What is the value of Cramer's V for this table?   V = _____

c. Is V statistically significant?   Yes   No

d. Which of the following statements most accurately summarizes the relationship between willingness to allow a speech by a racist and opposition to laws against interracial marriage? (Circle the number of the most appropriate answer.)

    1.   Those who took the racist position (the YES position—favor laws against interracial marriage) are more likely to allow a speech by a racist.

    2.   Those who took the nonracist position (the NO position—oppose laws against interracial marriage) are more likely to allow a speech by a racist.

    3.   There is no relationship between willingness to allow a speech by a racist and opposition to laws against interracial marriage.

CIVIL RIGHTS: EQUALITY

*We hold these truths to be self-evident: That all men
are created equal; that they are endowed by their
Creator with certain unalienable rights; that among
these are life, liberty, and the pursuit of happiness. . . .*

THE DECLARATION OF
INDEPENDENCE,
JULY 4, 1776

Tasks: Mapping, Univariate, Cross-Tabulation, Historical Trends, Scatterplot, Auto-Analyzer
Data Files: NATIONS, GSS, STATES, HISTORY, NES

These shining phrases announced the intention of the American colonists to cast off British rule and assert their "unalienable rights." Unfortunately, as the authors frankly stated, equality did not entirely apply to women ("all men"), and, as they failed to mention, these rights applied not at all to the hundreds of thousands of slaves—many slave-owners were among those who signed the Declaration. Nor did they apply to those inhabitants of America who already were here when Europeans arrived to "discover" the New World.

The struggle to include "all" within the boundaries of equality has gone on since the founding of the nation, and, although civil rights are far more extensive and secure than they were even a few years ago, the politics of "inclusion" and "exclusion" remain a central feature of our time. At a literalist level, one might have thought that the matter of equality would have been solved by the Fourteenth Amendment which, among other things, defines citizenship as "all persons born or naturalized in the United States, and subject to the jurisdiction thereof" and prohibits the states from denying any citizen within their jurisdiction the equal protection of the laws. This, of course, was not sufficient. For example, it took the Nineteenth Amendment to give women even the right to vote. The quest for equality has resulted in a variety of civil rights movements as African Americans, women, ethnic and racial minorities, sexual minorities, and others have sought equal treatment.

Nevertheless, Americans too often mistakenly regard our conflicts over civil rights as unique. In fact, conflicts based on racial, ethnic, and cultural prejudices probably are as old as the human race and exist to some degree in all societies.

> *Data File:* **NATIONS**
> *Task:* **Mapping**
> *Variable 1:* **11) ANTI-RACE**
> *View:* **Map**

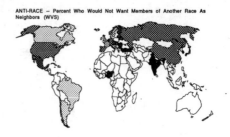

ANTI-RACE -- Percent Who Would Not Want Members of Another Race As Neighbors (WVS)

Here we see the percentage of people in each of 41 nations who indicated that they would not want to have "people of a different race as neighbors."

Data File: **NATIONS**
Task: **Mapping**
Variable 1: **11) ANTI-RACE**
> *View:* **List: Rank**

RANK	CASE NAME	VALUE
1	South Korea	58
2	India	44
3	Slovenia	40
4	Bulgaria	39
5	Turkey	34
5	Nigeria	34
5	Slovak Republic	34
8	Czech Republic	28
8	Romania	28
10	Finland	25

The majority of South Koreans don't want people of a different race as neighbors, nor would 44 percent of the populace in India and 40 percent in Slovenia. In contrast, only 10 percent of Americans feel this way and only 5 percent of Canadians.

Data File: **NATIONS**
Task: **Mapping**
Variable 1: **11) ANTI-RACE**
> *Variable 2:* **12) ANTI-FORGN**
> *Views:* **List: Rank**

RANK	CASE NAME	VALUE
1	South Korea	58
2	India	44
3	Slovenia	40
4	Bulgaria	39
5	Turkey	34

RANK	CASE NAME	VALUE
1	South Korea	53
2	India	48
3	Slovenia	40
4	Czech Republic	34
4	Bulgaria	34

Select the [List: Rank] option on both the upper and lower maps.

The upper box of rankings contains information on Variable 1; the lower box of rankings contains information on the comparison variable.

South Koreans (53 percent) are also least receptive to having "foreigners" as neighbors, and again India (48 percent) is second. Only 10 percent of Americans object to foreigners as neighbors, and people in Switzerland and Argentina are least likely to object.

There is a huge correlation (0.899**) between not wanting neighbors who are of another race and not wanting neighbors who are foreigners. This reveals that prejudice and discrimination tend to be unidimensional phenomena—people tend to reject or accept everyone or no one. Let's pursue this idea.

Data File: **NATIONS**
Task: **Mapping**
Variable 1: **11) ANTI-RACE**
➤ Variable 2: **13) ANTI-JEW**
➤ Views: **List: Rank**

RANK	CASE NAME	VALUE
1	South Korea	58
2	India	44
3	Slovenia	40
4	Bulgaria	39
5	Turkey	34

RANK	CASE NAME	VALUE
1	India	86
2	Turkey	59
3	Slovenia	37
4	Nigeria	34
5	Bulgaria	30

If you are continuing from the previous example, return to the variable selection screen, then select 13) ANTI-JEW as the new Variable 2.

The lower table shows the percentages in each nation who don't want Jews in their neighborhood. Indians (86 percent) overwhelmingly take this view as do the majority of Turks (59 percent). About a third of Slovenians, Nigerians, and Bulgarians don't want Jews in their neighborhood. Few Canadians (6 percent) or Americans (5 percent) take this view. But here too the correlation with objecting to persons of another race is very high (0.790**), giving further confirmation to the unidimensional nature of prejudice and the willingness to deny civil rights.

Data File: **NATIONS**
Task: **Mapping**
Variable 1: **11) ANTI-RACE**
➤ Variable 2: **14) ANTI-GAY**
➤ Views: **List: Rank**

RANK	CASE NAME	VALUE
1	South Korea	58
2	India	44
3	Slovenia	40
4	Bulgaria	39
5	Turkey	34

RANK	CASE NAME	VALUE
1	Turkey	92
2	India	91
3	Lithuania	87
4	Russia	82
5	Belarus	79

Finally, we see very strong objections in many nations to having homosexual neighbors: 92 percent in Turkey, 91 percent in India, 82 percent in Russia, 73 percent in Nigeria, 69 percent in Japan, 38 percent in the United States, 30 percent in Canada—amazingly, South Koreans, who are most opposed to living near foreigners or members of another race, are not opposed to homosexual neighbors (4 percent).

Of course, no one objects to having women living in the neighborhood, so that can't be used as a measure of civil rights for women. But the following is a measure of gender equality.

Data File: **NATIONS**
Task: **Mapping**
Variable 1: **11) ANTI-RACE**
➤ Variable 2: **15) %FEM LEGIS**
➤ Views: **List: Rank**

RANK	CASE NAME	VALUE
1	South Korea	58
2	India	44
3	Slovenia	40
4	Bulgaria	39
5	Turkey	34

RANK	CASE NAME	VALUE
1	Sweden	40.4
1	Norway	36.4
3	Finland	33.5
4	Denmark	33.0
5	New Zealand	29.2

This variable shows the percentage of seats in national parliaments that are held by women. Sweden (40.4 percent) is highest, the United States is relatively low with 11.2 percent, whereas in Kuwait and the United Arab Emirates none of the seats are held by women. This variable also is significantly correlated with objecting to having neighbors of another race. In this instance, of course, the correlation is negative—nations where racial prejudice is higher tend to have a lower percentage of females in the legislature.

That the battery of questions about prejudice shown above asked about willingness to have people who are different from them as neighbors reveals a universal aspect of civil rights which is based on an inherent contradiction concerning freedom: that one person's freedom can be another person's fetters. In this case, the freedom of one racial group to live in their own neighborhood curtails the freedom of others to live where they want.

Of course, for generations Americans had the freedom to exclude others from their neighborhoods, clubs, schools, buses, playgrounds, teams, beaches, hotels, theaters, restaurants, and similar settings. The most severe restrictions were imposed by whites on blacks and other nonwhites, but considerable limits also were imposed on Jews, Catholics, and various ethnic groups.

A major consequence of the civil rights movement during the 1950s and 1960s was to curtail this freedom in exchange for the freedom of others to freely associate. That is, equality was used as the standard against which to balance individual freedoms, and efforts by a group to be separated from others (to maintain *segregation*) were outlawed in many aspects of social life, including real estate.

> *Data File:* **HISTORY**
> > *Task:* **Historical Trends**
> *Variables:* **66) RACE SEG**

Percent who agree that whites have a right to keep African Americans out of their neighborhoods

During the 1940s, an overwhelming majority of Americans favored separate neighborhoods for African Americans. In 1972, four out of ten Americans thought that it was acceptable for whites to exclude African Americans from their neighborhoods. By 1994, this had dropped to one in ten.

Civil rights advocates in the 1970s and 1980s pushed for the creation of affirmative action programs designed to compensate for past discrimination against minority groups. During this period, government, colleges and universities, businesses, and other groups adopted affirmative action programs to encourage the advancement of members of minority groups.

These programs have also encountered the basic contradiction: Enhancing the rights of one group may restrict the rights of another group. In 1978, the Supreme Court ruled on *Regents of the University of California v. Bakke*, one of the first cases questioning the constitutionality of such programs. Mr. Bakke, a white male, had been denied admission to medical school, while less qualified students had been admitted under a special minority program. The lawyers for Mr. Bakke alleged that the special admissions program was, in effect, reverse discrimination—it excluded Bakke on the basis of his race. The Supreme Court agreed that the special admissions program violated the Equal Protection Clause of the Fourteenth Amendment. In recent years, voter initiatives prohibiting such programs have been placed on the ballot in several states.

Let's see how Americans feel about preferential treatment of African Americans to make up for past discrimination.

> *Data File:* **NES**
> > *Task:* **Univariate**
> *Primary Variable:* **57) AFFIRM.ACT**
> > *View:* **Pie**

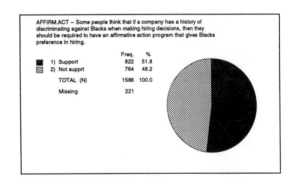

When asked about a company with a record of past discrimination, half of all Americans approve of affirmative action.

Data File: **NES**
➤ Task: **Cross-tabulation**
➤ Row Variable: **57) AFFIRM.ACT**
➤ Column Variable: **7) RACE**
➤ View: **Table**
➤ Display: **Column %**

AFFIRM.ACT   by   RACE
Cramer's V: 0.249 **

		RACE			
		White	African-Am	Missing	TOTAL
AFFIRM.ACT	Support	567	158	97	725
		46.3%	82.7%		51.2%
	Not supprt	658	33	73	691
		53.7%	17.3%		48.8%
	Missing	168	17	36	221
	TOTAL	1225	191	206	1416
		100.0%	100.0%		

African Americans overwhelmingly support affirmative action programs for companies with a record of discrimination, while white Americans are almost evenly split between support and opposition.

The issue of civil rights is quite complex, and Americans show divergent levels of support depending on which aspect of civil rights is contained in a survey question. For example, let's look at Americans' perceptions about the likelihood of reverse discrimination.

➤ Data File: **GSS**
➤ Task: **Univariate**
➤ Primary Variable: **103) REV.DISCRM**
➤ View: **Pie**

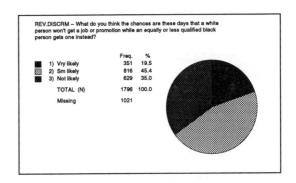

REV.DISCRM -- What do you think the chances are these days that a white person won't get a job or promotion while an equally or less qualified black person gets one instead?

		Freq.	%
■	1) Vry likely	351	19.5
▨	2) Sm likely	816	45.4
▨	3) Not likely	629	35.0
	TOTAL (N)	1796	100.0
	Missing	1021	

About one in five Americans believes that reverse discrimination is very likely to occur, and another two in five believe that it is somewhat likely to occur.

Earlier we saw that a good measure of gender equality could be based on the percentage of women in political office. Let's take a closer look.

Data File: **GSS**
Task: **Univariate**
➤ Primary Variable: **59) MEN BETTER**
➤ View: **Pie**

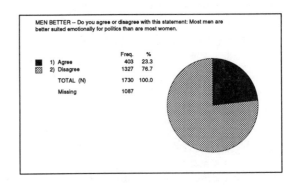

MEN BETTER -- Do you agree or disagree with this statement: Most men are better suited emotionally for politics than are most women.

		Freq.	%
■	1) Agree	403	23.3
▨	2) Disagree	1327	76.7
	TOTAL (N)	1730	100.0
	Missing	1087	

Three-quarters of Americans believe that women are equally as well suited for politics as men are.

Finally, let's consider whether Americans are willing to vote for a woman to be president of the United States. In recent years, more than 90 percent of Americans say they would vote for a woman for president. That wasn't always so. When this question was asked in the 1930s, only about one-third of Americans would vote for a woman for president. Let's look at the trend.

➤ *Data File:* **HISTORY**
  ➤ *Task:* **Historical Trends**
➤ *Variables:* **29) %FEM PRES**

Percent who would vote for woman for president (survey data)

Your turn.

REVIEW QUESTIONS

Based on the first part of this exercise, answer True or False to the following items:

a. All changes in civil rights increase the freedom of everyone.   T   F

b. Most Americans reject preferential treatment of African Americans to make up for
   past discrimination.   T   F

c. People in nonwhite nations are far less apt to be prejudiced against other
   races than are people in most white nations.   T   F

d. Public opinion on civil rights varies by what aspect of the issue is contained in
   the survey question.   T   F

e. Only about 75 percent of Americans say they would vote for a woman for
   president.   T   F

f. In the past 30 years, there has been a large change in attitudes toward racially
   segregated housing.   T   F

EXPLORIT QUESTIONS

1. Let's see if there is any connection between extent of civil liberty in nations and the attitudes of the
    populace to other groups.

    ➤ Data File: **NATIONS**
    ➤ Task: **Scatterplot**
    ➤ Dependent Variable: **11) ANTI-RACE**
    ➤ Independent Variable: **19) CIVIL LIBS**
    ➤ View: **Reg. Line**

    Answer True or False to the following items:

    a. There is a negative, but not significant, correlation between the civil liberties score
       and the tolerance for other races.   T   F

    b. The nation with the least tolerance for civil liberties is China. (Hint: Use your mouse
       to click the appropriate dot on the scatterplot.)   T   F

Exercise 5: Civil Rights: Equality

2. In Exercise 4, we found that the educational level of the population was strongly related to the degree of civil liberty in the country. Let's see if education has any effect on attitudes toward civil rights.

> Data File: **NATIONS**
> Task: **Scatterplot**
> Dependent Variable: **11) ANTI-RACE**
> ➤ Independent Variable: **40) EDUC EXPTD**
> ➤ View: **Reg. Line**

    a. As the level of education of the populace increases, the level of anti-race attitudes significantly decreases.   T   F

    b. As the level of education of the populace increases, the level of anti-race attitudes increases, but the effect is not significant.   T   F

> Data File: **NATIONS**
> Task: **Scatterplot**
> ➤ Dependent Variable: **13) ANTI-JEW**
> ➤ Independent Variable: **40) EDUC EXPTD**
> ➤ View: **Reg. Line**

    c. Which of the following statements best describes this relationship? (Circle the number of the most appropriate answer.)

      1. The higher the level of education, the lower the level of anti-Jewish attitudes, often referred to as anti-Semitism.

      2. The lower the level of education, the lower the level of anti-Semitism.

      3. The relationship between the level of education of the population and the level of anti-Semitism is not statistically significant.

> Data File: **NATIONS**
> Task: **Scatterplot**
> ➤ Dependent Variable: **14) ANTI-GAY**
> ➤ Independent Variable: **40) EDUC EXPTD**
> ➤ View: **Reg. Line**

    d. Nations that have higher education are less anti-gay.   T   F

    e. This relationship is strong and statistically significant.   T   F

3. Let's take a closer look at the question concerning women's suitability for politics.

> ➤ Data File: **GSS**
> ➤ Task: **Univariate**
> ➤ Primary Variable: **59) MEN BETTER**
> ➤ View: **Pie**

    a. What is the question wording for 59) MEN BETTER?

_____

_____

_____

    b. What percentage *disagreed* with this statement?   _____%

4.   Let's see whether men and women have different attitudes about the role of women in politics.

> Data File: **GSS**
> ➤ Task: **Cross-tabulation**
> ➤ Row Variable: **59) MEN BETTER**
> ➤ Column Variable: **6) SEX**
> ➤ View: **Table**
> ➤ Display: **Column %**

Copy the second row of the percentaged table.

	MALE	FEMALE
a. % DISAGREE	_____%	_____%

    b. What is the value of V for this table?   V = _____

    c. Is V statistically significant?   Yes   No

    d. Women are less likely to agree that men are better qualified to be in politics.   T   F

5.   Using MEN BETTER to indicate attitudes about the role of women in politics, let's use Auto-Analyzer to see how such attitudes are related to the demographic characteristics of people.

> Data File: **GSS**
> ➤ Task: **Auto-Analyzer**
> ➤ Variable: **59) MEN BETTER**
> ➤ View: **Religion**

    a. Conservative Protestants are the most supportive of equality for women in politics.   T   F

    b. Those with no religion are the least supportive of equality for women in politics.   T   F

> ➤ View: **Region**

c. Southerners are the least supportive of equality for women in politics.   T   F

d. Midwesterners are the most supportive of equality for women in politics.   T   F

➤ *View:* **Age**

e. People 65 and over are the least supportive of equality for women in politics.   T   F

➤ *View:* **Education**

f. The higher the education of people, the more likely they are to support equality for women in politics.   T   F

➤ *View:* **Income**

g. People with higher incomes are less supportive of equality for women in politics.   T   F

➤ *View:* **Race**

h. Whites support equality for women in politics more than African Americans do.   T   F

6. In Exercise 4 we examined civil *liberties* attitudes, and now we are examining civil *rights* attitudes in this exercise. How are civil liberties attitudes related to civil rights attitudes? Let's continue using MEN BETTER as a measurement of civil rights attitudes (specifically, attitudes toward equality for women in politics) and see how it is related to a civil liberties measure, support for freedom of speech as indicated by the FR.SPEECH variable.

> *Data File:* **GSS**
> ➤ *Task:* **Cross-tabulation**
> ➤ *Row Variable:* **59) MEN BETTER**
> ➤ *Column Variable:* **39) FR.SPEECH**
> ➤ *View:* **Table**
> ➤ *Display:* **Column %**

Fill in the *Disagree* row of percentages below.

39) FR.SPEECH	HIGH	MEDIUM	LOW
a. %DISAGREE	_____%	_____%	_____%

b. What is the value of Cramer's V for this table?   V = _____

c. Is V statistically significant?   Yes   No

d. On the basis of these results, which of the following is the most appropriate conclusion concerning the relationship between civil liberties attitudes and civil rights attitudes? (Circle the number of the most appropriate answer.)

1. People who support civil liberties the most are also likely to support civil rights the most.

2. People who support civil liberties the most are the least likely to support civil rights.

3. There is no connection between civil liberties attitudes and civil rights attitudes.

7. Let's look at changes over time in willingness to vote for an African American or a woman for president.

> ➤ *Data File:* **HISTORY**
> ➤ *Task:* **Historical Trends**
> ➤ *Variables:* **32) % BLK PRES**
> **29) %FEM PRES**

Which of the following statements best summarizes this graph?

a. The percentage who would vote for a woman for president and the percentage who would vote for an African American for president have generally increased over time.

b. The percentage who would vote for a woman for president has generally increased, but the percentage who would vote for an African American for president has decreased.

c. The percentage who would vote for a woman for president and the percentage who would vote for an African American for president have generally decreased over time.

d. The percentage who would vote for a woman for president has generally decreased, but the percentage who would vote for an African American for president has increased.

8. Another way to look at the attitude toward women in politics is to examine the proportion of females in the state legislatures.

> ➤ *Data File:* **STATES**
> ➤ *Task:* **Mapping**
> ➤ *Variable 1:* **32) %FEMALE LG**
> ➤ *View:* **List: Rank**

a. List the two states with the highest percentage of women in the legislature.

RANK	STATE	PERCENT
HIGHEST	_____	_____%
SECOND HIGHEST	_____	_____%

b. List the two states with the lowest percentage.

RANK	STATE	PERCENT
LOWEST	_____	_____%
SECOND LOWEST	_____	_____%

c. Women comprise less than 50 percent of the legislature in every state.　　T　F

d. Women comprise less than 20 percent of the legislature in most southern states.　　T　F

9. The variable 31) N.R./NAT. is the circulation of *National Review*, a conservative magazine, divided by the circulation of *Nation*, a liberal magazine, and it provides a measure of how politically conservative a state is. (The higher the resulting proportion, the more conservative the state is likely to be.)

> Data File: **STATES**
> Task: **Mapping**
> Variable 1: **32) %FEMALE LG**
> ➤ Variable 2: **31) N.R./NAT.**

a. What is the value of r, the correlation coefficient?　　r = _____

b. Is it statistically significant?　　Yes　No

c. The more conservative the state, the smaller the percentage of women in the legislature.　　T　F

d. By this measure, southern states are among the most conservative.　　T　F

10. The variable CONSER provides another way to measure the conservatism of states. Using this measure, let's again examine the relationship between conservatism in states and the percentage of women in state legislatures.

> Data File: **STATES**
> Task: **Mapping**
> Variable 1: **32) %FEMALE LG**
> ➤ Variable 2: **170) CONSER**
> ➤ View: **Map**

a. What is the value of r?　　r = _____

b. Is it statistically significant?　　Yes　No

c. Using this measure of conservatism in states, the relationship between conservatism and percentage of women in the legislature is about the same as it was in the previous analysis.　　T　F

11. Let's see how the education level of states is related to the percentage of state legislators who are women.

> Data File: **STATES**
> Task: **Mapping**
> Variable 1: **32) %FEMALE LG**
> ➤ Variable 2: **125) %COLLEGE**
> ➤ View: **Map**

a. What is the value of r?   r = _____

b. Is it statistically significant?   Yes   No

c. States with a higher percentage of college graduates tend to have a higher percentage of state legislators who are women.   T   F

Part III

GOVERNMENT AND THE INDIVIDUAL

The basis of political freedom is simple to identify and very difficult to maintain: We the People. But who are the people? Are they everyone? Or only everyone who cares? Or are they only those who try to influence political decisions? What is consent? Do elections provide an adequate measure of it? Or should elected officials simply vote according to the polls? If not, how should they represent us? How shall governments distinguish between the abiding interests of the people and our momentary enthusiasms? As we shall see, there are no clear or final answers to these questions. But only as we constantly apply them to our political realities, can we sustain a free society.

PUBLIC OPINION AND
POLITICAL SOCIALIZATION

*About things on which the public thinks long it
commonly attains to think right.*

SAMUEL JOHNSON, 1778

> *Tasks:* Univariate, Cross-Tabulation, Mapping
> *Data Files:* GSS, STATES

The opinion poll (or survey) has become an essential part of our political life offering constant reflections of the opinions, interests, anxieties, and antagonisms of the American public. Yet, not so many years ago there were no polls and no one could really know how the public felt about anything. The first reliable pre-election polls of voters were conducted in 1936 by George Gallup, founder of the Gallup Poll, and by his rival Elmo Roper, founder of the Roper Poll. Then, as now, the polls often revealed surprises—if it were easy to gauge public opinion, no one would pay the large sums needed to conduct a trustworthy survey.

In Exercise 3 you learned that public opinion polls work because they are based on *random samples* of sufficient size. However, even when the results are based on large, random samples, they can be very misleading. Consequently, some of the "surprises" revealed by surveys don't really mean what they appear to mean.

Suppose we want to know how Americans feel about legal abortions.

> ➤ *Data File:* **GSS**
> ➤ *Task:* **Univariate**
> ➤ *Primary Variable:* **61) ABORT.HLTH**
> ➤ *View:* **Pie**

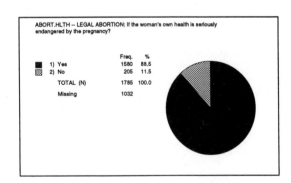

Someone might look at these results and report that nearly all Americans (88.5 percent) favor allowing abortions to be legal. Clearly, it is true that about 9 Americans out of 10 favor allowing abortions when a woman's own health is seriously endangered by the pregnancy. (Notice that the question was not asked of all respondents; thus, data are missing on the attitudes of 1,032 persons. This does not weaken our confidence in the results because random techniques were used not only to select the total sample but also to decide which members of the sample were asked this question.)

However, before we rush to report the huge public support for abortion, notice that the question is not about abortion in general, but about abortions for a very specific reason. Perhaps Americans line up rather differently when the reason for an abortion is less compelling than to save the woman's life?

Data File: **GSS**
Task: **Univariate**
➤ *Primary Variable:* **60) ABORT.WANT**
➤ *View:* **Pie**

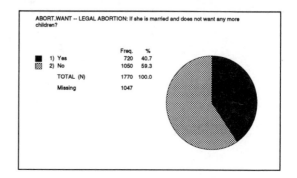

Based on these results alone, someone might report that most Americans (59.3 percent) oppose abortion. Here, again, abortion opinions are linked to a very specific circumstance, a married woman who does not want any more children. So, what do Americans think about abortion in general?

Data File: **GSS**
Task: **Univariate**
➤ *Primary Variable:* **62) ABORT ANY**
➤ *View:* **Pie**

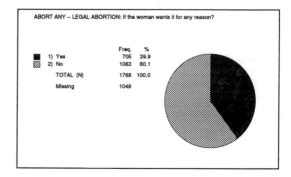

When asked whether abortions ought to be legal "if the woman wants it for any reason," most Americans (60.1 percent) disapprove.

So, in response to the question "Do Americans favor or oppose abortion?" the most accurate answer is "It depends."

That public opinion would vary greatly across these three questions may seem obvious. But even far more subtle differences can cause large shifts in how people answer.

Data File: **GSS**
Task: **Univariate**
➤ Primary Variable: **30) WELFARE $**
➤ View: **Pie**

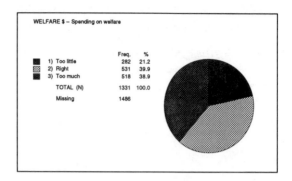

Here we see public opposition to welfare. Only 21.2 percent think the government is spending too little money on welfare, while one-third (38.9 percent) think the government is spending too much. Results like these have stimulated many accusations that Americans lack compassion, that they don't care what happens to poor people.

Data File: **GSS**
Task: **Univariate**
➤ Primary Variable: **33) POOR $**
➤ View: **Pie**

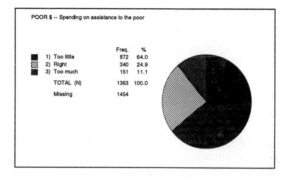

But if that's so, what are we to make of this result? When asked about spending on assistance to the poor rather than spending on welfare, more than half (64.0 percent) of Americans responded that the government is spending too little! Only about 1 in 10 thought current spending is too high. How would you explain these "conflicting" results?

Suppose that rather than asking why people give such different answers to these two questions, we asked a far more basic question: *How do people come to hold any of the opinions and beliefs that they do?*

There are, of course, many answers to that question because many factors influence our opinions. However, there is a very general and basic difference between people in the way they assess political issues. Some people form their political opinions issue by issue, and surveys reveal very little consistency among their opinions. That is, some people take a very liberal position on one issue, a very conservative position on another, and a moderate position on a third. However, when we identify liberal and conservative positions on issues, we are assuming that there exist consistent sets of political opinions. Such sets are called **political ideologies**.

Unlike people who form their opinions issue by issue, others have acquired and developed a general frame of reference, an ideology, against which to judge specific issues as they arise. In American politics the labels "liberal," "moderate," and "conservative" identify the major ideologies.

Exercise 6: Public Opinion and Political Socialization   101

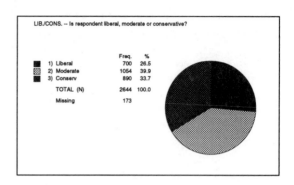

Data File: **GSS**
Task: **Univariate**
➤ Primary Variable: **23) LIB./CONS.**
➤ View: **Pie**

Today, liberals (26.5 percent) are outnumbered by conservatives (33.7 percent) and by moderates (39.9 percent). Now let's see how ideology influences attitudes about abortion.

Data File: **GSS**
➤ Task: **Cross-tabulation**
➤ Row Variable: **60) ABORT.WANT**
➤ Column Variable: **23) LIB./CONS.**
➤ View: **Table**
➤ Display: **Column %**

ABORT WANT by LIB./CONS.
Cramer's V: 0.215 **

		LIB./CONS.				
		Liberal	Moderate	Conserv	Missing	TOTAL
ABORT.WANT	Yes	257	272	165	26	694
		57.0%	40.7%	29.6%		41.4%
	No	194	396	392	68	982
		43.0%	59.3%	70.4%		58.6%
	Missing	249	386	333	79	1047
	TOTAL	451	668	557	173	1676
		100.0%	100.0%	100.0%		

Very strongly! Liberals are far more likely than conservatives to approve of abortions being legal for married women who don't want any more children. Put another way, if a person says he or she is liberal the odds are about 3 to 2 that he or she will approve of abortions in this circumstance, whereas for those who say they are conservatives the odds are about 2 to 1 in the other direction. And, of course, differences this great in a sample this large are highly significant.

Notice, however, that many Americans hold views on this issue that are not a reflection of their ideology. That is, many liberals oppose abortion in this circumstance, while many conservatives support it. Thus, political scientists acknowledge that ideology plays only a limited role in American politics—and probably a far more limited role than it does in some other nations. In addition, ideology plays a more important role on some issues than on others.

But where do people get their political opinions, especially their political ideologies? The answer is, of course, that we learn them from others and from experience. And this learning process often is referred to as political socialization.

Political socialization is the complex process by which individuals become aware of politics, learn political facts, and form their political views. Although political socialization helps to explain how people acquire their opinions on *specific* issues, it is especially useful for examining how people acquire a general perspective or political ideology. Political scientists take a special interest in political socialization, paying particular attention to **agents of socialization**, the primary sources of political socialization.

Our political socialization begins early as our families are the initial agents of our socialization. Considerable research shows that people tend to resemble their parents in terms of their political ideologies and interest. This is especially true of party preferences. Democrats tend to raise Democrats, while the children of Republicans tend to grow up as Republicans.

But, although childhood influences may be an important source of political socialization, they are soon reinforced or countermanded by other primary agents of socialization: school, church, work, region, and community. In addition to these, our political outlooks are greatly shaped by our life experiences. Here's an example:

Data File: **GSS**
Task: **Cross-tabulation**
➤ Row Variable: **23) LIB./CONS.**
➤ Column Variable: **12) EVER UNEMP**
➤ View: **Table**
➤ Display: **Column %**

LIB./CONS.   by   EVER UNEMP
Cramer's V: 0.102 **

		\multicolumn{4}{c}{EVER UNEMP}
		Yes	No	Missing	TOTAL
LIB./CONS.	Liberal	156	300	244	456
		29.5%	25.1%		26.5%
	Moderate	228	441	385	669
		43.1%	36.9%		38.8%
	Conserv	145	454	291	599
		27.4%	38.0%		34.7%
	Missing	32	83	58	173
	TOTAL	529	1195	978	1724
		100.0%	100.0%		

People who have been unemployed are more likely to be liberals than are those who have never been out of work, and they are less likely to be conservatives. Put another way, people who have been unemployed are about equally likely to be liberals (29.5 percent) as to be conservatives (27.4 percent), but those who never have been unemployed are far more likely to be conservatives (38.0 percent) than to be liberals (25.1 percent).

Another aspect of life experience that is apt to influence ideology is one's racial or ethnic background.

Data File: **GSS**
Task: **Cross-tabulation**
Row Variable: **23) LIB./CONS.**
➤ Column Variable: **7) RACE**
➤ View: **Table**
➤ Display: **Column %**

LIB./CONS.   by   RACE
Cramer's V: 0.075 **

		\multicolumn{4}{c}{RACE}
		White	African Am	Missing	TOTAL
LIB./CONS.	Liberal	554	108	38	662
		26.2%	27.3%		26.4%
	Moderate	810	183	61	993
		38.3%	46.3%		39.5%
	Conserv	753	104	33	857
		35.6%	26.3%		34.1%
	Missing	121	37	15	173
	TOTAL	2117	395	147	2512
		100.0%	100.0%		

Race does shape political ideologies. But the differences are smaller than many would have expected. Among Whites, conservatives modestly outnumber liberals; among African Americans, liberals (27.3 percent) modestly outnumber conservatives (26.3 percent).

Another factor shaping our political ideologies is *where* we live.

Data File: **GSS**
Task: **Cross-tabulation**
Row Variable: **23) LIB./CONS.**
➤ Column Variable: **20) REGION**
➤ View: **Table**
➤ Display: **Column %**

LIB./CONS.   by   REGION
Cramer's V: 0.089 **

		REGION				
		East	Midwest	South	West	TOTAL
LIB./CONS.	Liberal	165	163	197	175	700
		31.5%	25.6%	21.0%	31.9%	26.5%
	Moderate	220	265	383	186	1054
		42.1%	41.7%	40.9%	33.9%	39.9%
	Conserv	138	208	356	188	890
		26.4%	32.7%	38.0%	34.2%	33.7%
	Missing	45	34	70	24	173
	TOTAL	523	636	936	549	2644
		100.0%	100.0%	100.0%	100.0%	

Southerners are the least apt to identify themselves as liberals, and Westerners and Easterners are the most likely. Southerners are the most likely to say they are conservatives. Here, too, although the differences are statistically significant, they are modest.

An important agent of political socialization is the church.

Data File: **GSS**
Task: **Cross-tabulation**
Row Variable: **23) LIB./CONS.**
➤ Column Variable: **14) RELIGION**
➤ View: **Table**
➤ Display: **Column %**

LIB./CONS.   by   RELIGION
Cramer's V: 0.162 **

		RELIGION						
		Lib Prot.	Con Prot.	Catholic	Jewish	None	Missing	TOTAL
LIB./CONS.	Liberal	126	134	160	31	159	90	610
		23.0%	17.8%	25.2%	51.7%	43.0%		25.8%
	Moderate	239	307	253	20	139	96	958
		43.6%	40.7%	39.8%	33.3%	37.6%		40.5%
	Conserv	183	313	223	9	72	90	800
		33.4%	41.5%	35.1%	15.0%	19.5%		33.8%
	Missing	18	61	43	3	28	20	173
	TOTAL	548	754	636	60	370	296	2368
		100.0%	100.0%	100.0%	100.0%	100.0%		

Here we see that members of conservative Protestant denominations (Baptists or Assemblies of God, for example) are those most apt to identify themselves as political conservatives. However, they are not much more apt to do so than are members of liberal Protestant denominations (Methodists or Episcopalians, for example) or Catholics. In all three Christian groupings, conservatives outnumber liberals. But this pattern is sharply reversed among Jews and those who say they have no religious preference.

A person's gender is also an important element of socialization. Let's see if this has any effect on political views.

Data File: **GSS**
Task: **Cross-tabulation**
Row Variable: **23) LIB./CONS.**
➤ Column Variable: **6) SEX**
➤ View: **Table**
➤ Display: **Column %**

LIB./CONS.   by   SEX
Cramer's V: 0.083 **

		SEX		
		Male	Female	TOTAL
LIB./CONS.	Liberal	292	408	700
		25.0%	27.7%	26.5%
	Moderate	433	621	1054
		37.0%	42.1%	39.9%
	Conserv	445	445	890
		38.0%	30.2%	33.7%
	Missing	59	114	173
	TOTAL	1170	1474	2644
		100.0%	100.0%	

We can see that the respondent's gender has a relatively weak effect.

Let's see how stable these attitudes are.

Data File: **GSS**
Task: **Cross-tabulation**
Row Variable: **23) LIB./CONS.**
➤ Column Variable: **9) AGE**
➤ View: **Table**
➤ Display: **Column %**

LIB./CONS.   by   AGE
Cramer's V: 0.073 **

		AGE						
		Under 30	30 to 39	40 to 49	50 to 64	65 & over	Missing	TOTAL
LIB./CONS.	Liberal	141	167	159	149	83	1	699
		28.4%	29.2%	26.3%	28.2%	19.0%		26.5%
	Moderate	215	211	244	184	194	6	1048
		43.3%	37.0%	40.4%	34.8%	44.4%		39.7%
	Conserv	140	193	201	196	160	0	890
		28.2%	33.8%	33.3%	37.1%	36.6%		33.8%
	Missing	30	39	30	27	46	1	173
	TOTAL	496	571	604	529	437	8	2637
		100.0%	100.0%	100.0%	100.0%	100.0%		

The older the individual, the less likely he or she is to be liberal and the more likely to be conservative. This suggests that these political attitudes may change as a person gets older. This would be an aging effect. However, these data are not adequate to establish that a change in opinion occurs with aging. It also is possible that today's elderly were more conservative in their youth and have remained conservative throughout their lifetimes. This would be a generational effect. In order to distinguish between an aging effect and a generational effect, we would need to follow the *same respondents* over their lifetimes. A cross-sectional survey, like the General Social Survey, can tell us only that older people differ from younger people.

In the opening paragraph of this exercise, we noted that public opinion includes people's anxieties as well as their opinions on specific issues. The terrorist attacks on the World Trade Center in New York City and the Pentagon in Washington, D.C., on September 11, 2001 affected Americans in many ways. The American public rallied behind President George W. Bush, citizens displayed flags on their houses and cars to demonstrate their patriotism, and many individuals gave charitable contributions or donated blood. The terrorist attacks of 9/11 were not the only such occurrences in recent history. One hundred sixty-nine Americans died when the federal building in Oklahoma City was bombed in an incident of domestic terrorism in 1995, and international terrorism brought down Pan Am Flight 103 over Scotland in 1988, killing 270 individuals.

We can look at responses to the 2000 GSS survey to see how worried the American public was about domestic and international terrorism before 9/11.

Data File: **GSS**
➤ Task: **Univariate**
➤ Primary Variable: **98) FRTERROR**
➤ View: **Pie**

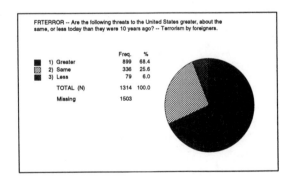

FRTERROR -- Are the following threats to the United States greater, about the same, or less today than they were 10 years ago? -- Terrorism by foreigners.

		Freq.	%
■	1) Greater	899	68.4
▨	2) Same	336	25.6
■	3) Less	79	6.0
	TOTAL (N)	1314	100.0
	Missing	1503	

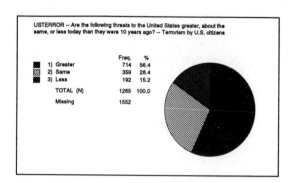

USTERROR -- Are the following threats to the United States greater, about the same, or less today than they were 10 years ago? -- Terrorism by U.S. citizens

	Freq.	%
■ 1) Greater	714	56.4
▨ 2) Same	359	28.4
■ 3) Less	192	15.2
TOTAL (N)	1265	100.0
Missing	1552	

Slightly over one-half of the American public in 2000 felt that the threat of an international terrorist attack was greater than it had been in the previous decade. About half of all Americans also were fearful of a terrorist attack by a United States citizen. Unfortunately, 9/11 and other recent events have heightened Americans' concerns over homeland security.

Your turn.

WORKSHEET

NAME:

COURSE:

DATE:

EXERCISE

6

REVIEW QUESTIONS

Based on the first part of this exercise, answer True or False to the following items:

a. Most Americans think abortions should be legally available to a woman who wants one for any reason.	T	F
b. There are more liberals than conservatives in the United States.	T	F
c. Most Americans oppose helping the poor.	T	F
d. Among Catholics, liberals outnumber conservatives.	T	F
e. The West is the region with the highest percentage of conservatives.	T	F

EXPLORIT QUESTIONS

1. Let's look at how liberals and conservatives differ on some issues.

    For each of the variables below, copy the first row of the percentaged table, give the value of V, and indicate if it is significant.

    45) SCH.PRAY

    The United States Supreme Court has ruled that no state or local government may require the reading of the Lord's Prayer or Bible verses in public schools. What are your views on this?

    > *Data File:* **GSS**
    > *Task:* **Cross-tabulation**
    > *Row Variable:* **45) SCH.PRAY**
    > *Column Variable:* **23) LIB./CONS.**
    > *View:* **Table**
    > *Display:* **Column %**

	LIBERAL	MODERATE	CONSERVATIVE
a. % NO PRAYER	_____%	_____%	_____%

Exercise 6: Public Opinion and Political Socialization

b. What is the value of V for this table?   V = _____

c. Is V statistically significant?   Yes   No

41) GUN LAW?

Would you favor or oppose a law which would require a person to obtain a police permit before he or she could buy a gun?

> Data File: **GSS**
> Task: **Cross-tabulation**
> ➤ Row Variable: **41) GUN LAW?**
> ➤ Column Variable: **23) LIB./CONS.**
> ➤ View: **Table**
> ➤ Display: **Column %**

	LIBERAL	MODERATE	CONSERVATIVE
d. % FAVOR	_____%	_____%	_____%

e. What is the value of V for this table?   V = _____

f. Is V statistically significant?   Yes   No

35) TAXES?

Do you consider the amount of federal income tax which you have to pay as too high, about right, or too low?

> Data File: **GSS**
> Task: **Cross-tabulation**
> ➤ Row Variable: **35) TAXES?**
> ➤ Column Variable: **23) LIB./CONS.**
> ➤ View: **Table**
> ➤ Display: **Column %**

	LIBERAL	MODERATE	CONSERVATIVE
g. % TOO HIGH	_____%	_____%	_____%

h. What is the value of V for this table?   V = _____

i. Is V statistically significant?   Yes   No

49) BIG BIZ?

How much confidence do you have in major companies?

> Data File: **GSS**
> Task: **Cross-tabulation**
> ➤ Row Variable: **49) BIG BIZ?**
> ➤ Column Variable: **23) LIB./CONS.**
> ➤ View: **Table**
> ➤ Display: **Column %**

	LIBERAL	MODERATE	CONSERVATIVE
j. % GREAT DEAL	_____%	_____%	_____%

k. What is the value of V for this table?   V = _____

l. Is V statistically significant?   Yes   No

58) MILITARY?

How much confidence do you have in the military?

> Data File: **GSS**
> Task: **Cross-tabulation**
> ➤ Row Variable: **58) MILITARY?**
> ➤ Column Variable: **23) LIB./CONS.**
> ➤ View: **Table**
> ➤ Display: **Column %**

	LIBERAL	MODERATE	CONSERVATIVE
m. % GREAT DEAL	_____%	_____%	_____%

n. What is the value of V for this table?   V = _____

o. Is V statistically significant?   Yes   No

40) EXECUTE?

Do you favor or oppose the death penalty for persons convicted of murder?

> *Data File:* **GSS**
> *Task:* **Cross-tabulation**
> ➤ *Row Variable:* **40) EXECUTE?**
> ➤ *Column Variable:* **23) LIB./CONS.**
> ➤ *View:* **Table**
> ➤ *Display:* **Column %**

	LIBERAL	MODERATE	CONSERVATIVE
p. % FAVOR	_____%	_____%	_____%

q. What is the value of V for this table?   V = _____

r. Is V statistically significant?   Yes   No

s. Which of these issues are *not* related to political ideology?

t. Which of these issues are related to political ideology?

Notice that on some issues, even when ideology appears to play a role, the majority of each ideological group make the *same* response.

2. Based on the results in Question 1, does ideology seem to be an important element in political views in the United States? Explain.

3. In Question 1, we saw that people's ideology influences their opinions on the death penalty. Another factor that could influence people's opinions on the death penalty is whether or not the state in which they live has a death penalty law. In recent decades, around a dozen states have not had capital punishment laws, while the majority of states have such laws. The presence of a law can produce a legitimation effect, whereby the public is more likely to adopt the position incorporated in the law. Thus, we would expect the public in states without death penalty laws to have a lower level of approval for capital punishment while Americans living in states with death penalty laws should express more approval.

    It is often difficult to test the influence of state laws on public opinion, because we rarely find public opinion polls with samples of each of the 50 states. The National Election Studies, however, in the early 1990s took such a poll. The average approval level of the death penalty in each state is listed in the STATES file, along with the existence of a capital punishment law in the prior year.

    > Data File: **STATES**
    > Task: **Mapping**
    > Variable 1:   **166) DTH OPIN**
    > Variable 2:   **167) DTH LAW**
    > View: **Map**
    > Display: **Legend**

    a. What is the Pearson's r between public approval of the death penalty
       and state laws on capital punishment?   r = _____

    b. Do these figures support the legitimation effect whereby we would expect higher
       levels of approval of capital punishment in states with death penalty laws than in
       states without such a law?   Yes   No

    c. Most other countries across the world do not have death penalty laws. Based
       on the results above, would you expect lower levels of approval for capital
       punishment in countries without death penalty laws?   Yes   No

4. Let's return to Americans' concerns over international terrorism. We might expect that whether people have children and where they live might influence their level of concern.

    > Data File: **GSS**
    > Task: **Cross-tabulation**
    > Row Variable: **98) FRTERROR**
    > Column Variable: **2) # CHILDREN**
    > View: **Table**
    > Display: **Column %**

	NONE	1 – 2	3 AND UP
a. % GREATER	_____%	_____%	_____%

    b. What is the value of V for this table?   V = _____

c. Is V statistically significant?   Yes   No

> Data File: **GSS**
> Task: **Cross-tabulation**
> Row Variable: **98) FRTERROR**
> ➤ Column Variable: **19) URBAN?**
> ➤ View: **Table**
> ➤ Display: **Column %**

	BIG CITY	SUBURBS	TOWN/VIL	RURAL
d. % GREATER	_____%	_____%	_____%	_____%

e. What is the value of V for this table?   V = _____

f. Is V statistically significant?   Yes   No

Answer True or False to the following items:

g. Parents of children were more concerned about international terrorism than those without children.   T   F

h. Those living in urban areas were more concerned about international terrorism than those living in rural areas.   T   F

THE MEDIA

Where the press is free and every[one] able to read, all is safe.

THOMAS JEFFERSON, 1816

Tasks: Mapping, Univariate, Cross-Tabulation, Historical Trends
Data Files: NATIONS, NES, GSS, HISTORY

Few Americans have ever attended a political gathering, met a candidate for national office, or observed a session of an elected body—neither Congress nor their local city council. For most Americans, politics is a media event, and in that sense they resemble the old-time cowboy comedian Will Rogers who liked to claim "All I know is what I read in the papers."

For generations, newspapers were the only important mass medium—newsmagazines are far more recent. *Time* was founded in 1923 but did not gain much circulation during its first few years of operation, and *Newsweek* did not appear until several years later. The many magazines of political opinion, such as *National Review*, *Nation*, *New Republic*, and *American Spectator*, are much more recent and have only small circulations—*National Review* is the largest but has a total circulation of less than 200,000. By the 1930s, radio competed with the print media to bring the news, to offer live broadcasts of political conventions, and to report returns on election nights. Following World War II, television soon became the dominant medium—the first political conventions were televised in 1948, and that also was the first time a computer (weighing many tons) was used on election night.

Today, Americans gain their knowledge and impressions of politics from both the print and electronic media. The same is true in most of the world.

➤ *Data File:* **NATIONS**
➤ *Task:* **Mapping**
➤ *Variable 1:* **30) NEWSPAPERS**
➤ *View:* **List: Rank**

RANK	CASE NAME	VALUE
1	Norway	607
2	Japan	576
3	Croatia	575
4	Iceland	515
5	Sweden	483
6	Finland	473
7	Austria	472
8	Switzerland	409
9	South Korea	404
10	Kuwait	401

Newspaper readership differs a lot among these nations. In Norway, 607 newspapers are circulated daily for every 1,000 persons. By comparison, newspaper readership is rather low in the United States, about one paper for every four persons. However, newspaper circulation once was much higher in the United States.

➤ Data File: **HISTORY**
  ➤ Task: **Historical Trends**
➤ Variables: **25) NEWS/100**

Newspaper circulation per 100 population in U.S.

One reason newspaper readership has declined in the United States, and probably in some other nations as well, is the prevalence of television.

➤ Data File: **NATIONS**
  ➤ Task: **Mapping**
➤ Variable 1: **31) TELEVISION**
  ➤ View: **List: Rank**

RANK	CASE NAME	VALUE
1	United States	81.73
2	Malta	73.91
3	Canada	68.26
4	Japan	68.00
5	Oman	66.78
6	France	58.89
7	Germany	55.75
8	Denmark	53.59
9	New Zealand	51.93
10	Finland	51.12

The United States leads the world in the number of television sets per 100 persons, with 81.73. Next is Malta, followed by Canada, Japan, and Oman. In contrast, there are few television sets in Nigeria (4.24) and India (4.04).

➤ Data File: **HISTORY**
  ➤ Task: **Historical Trends**
➤ Variables: **26) TV/100HH**

Number of televisions per 100 households in U.S.

The spread of television sets in the United States was amazingly rapid. In 1949 hardly anyone had a set, whereas in 1959 almost everyone did.

Of course, many people with TV sets don't watch television news.

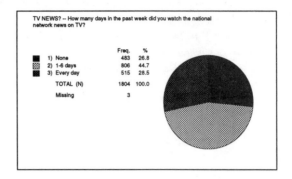

> *Data File:* **NES**
> *Task:* **Univariate**
> *Primary Variable:* **23) TV NEWS?**
> *View:* **Pie**

About a quarter of Americans say they watch TV news every day.

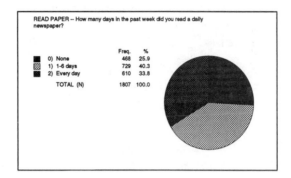

Data File: **NES**
Task: **Univariate**
> *Primary Variable:* **22) READ PAPER**
> *View:* **Pie**

About a third of Americans say they read a newspaper every day.

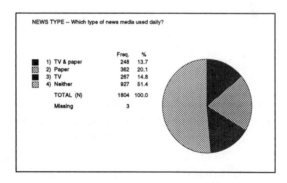

Data File: **NES**
Task: **Univariate**
> *Primary Variable:* **24) NEWS TYPE**
> *View:* **Pie**

Here the questions about watching TV news and reading newspapers have been combined to produce four basic types of persons. The first consists of those who read newspapers and watch TV news every day. They make up about 14 percent of the adult population. The second type only reads the newspapers daily, watching TV news less often. They are about 20 percent of Americans. The third type watches TV news daily but reads the paper less often. Finally, the fourth type consists of those who do not watch TV news or read a newspaper daily—about half of the public.

Does it matter if one both watches the TV news and reads the newspaper in terms of being informed about politics?

> *Data File:* **NES**
> ➤ *Task:* **Cross-tabulation**
> ➤ *Row Variable:* **21) INFORMED?**
> ➤ *Column Variable:* **24) NEWS TYPE**
> ➤ *View:* **Table**
> ➤ *Display:* **Column %**

INFORMED? by NEWS TYPE
Cramer's V: 0.147 **

		NEWS TYPE					
		TV & paper	Paper	TV	Neither	Missing	TOTAL
INFORMED?	High	138	191	118	328	0	775
		55.9%	53.1%	44.5%	35.5%		43.1%
	Average	79	107	95	304	1	585
		32.0%	29.7%	35.8%	32.9%		32.6%
	Low	30	62	52	293	2	437
		12.1%	17.2%	19.6%	31.7%		24.3%
	Missing	1	2	2	2	0	7
	TOTAL	247	360	265	925	3	1797
		100.0%	100.0%	100.0%	100.0%		

Yes! A majority of those who both read newspapers and watch TV news daily were rated as highly informed by the interviewers. However, those who rely primarily on the newspaper were equally likely to be highly informed. But those who rely on TV news were much less apt to be highly informed (44.5 percent). Not surprisingly, most of those who neither read the paper nor watch TV news daily were rated as less then highly informed.

But what about credibility? The effects of the news media depend, at least in part, on how much confidence readers and viewers place in them.

> ➤ *Data File:* **NATIONS**
> ➤ *Task:* **Mapping**
> ➤ *Variable 1:* **22) PRESS?**
> ➤ *View:* **List: Rank**

RANK	CASE NAME	VALUE
1	Nigeria	75
2	Estonia	73
3	Lithuania	67
4	South Korea	66
5	India	63
6	Latvia	60
7	South Africa	59
8	United States	56
8	China	56
10	Brazil	55

People in each nation were asked how much confidence they had in the press. Here we see the percentage who said they had at least some confidence in the press as compared with little or no confidence. Three of four people in Nigeria said they had at least some confidence in the press. The United States and China are tied, with 56 percent saying they had some confidence. Keeping in mind that this is the most generous estimate of confidence in the press, it would appear that large numbers of people simply don't trust what they read in the papers, hear on the radio, or see on TV. In Great Britain only 14 percent say they have some confidence in the press as do 18 percent in Austria.

> ➤ *Data File:* **HISTORY**
> ➤ *Task:* **Historical Trends**
> ➤ *Variables:* **37) CONF.PRESS**

Percent with great deal of confidence in the press (survey data)

Confidence in the press has been declining in the United States.

> *Data File:* **GSS**
>> *Task:* **Cross-tabulation**
> *Row Variable:* **54) PRESS?**
> *Column Variable:* **20) REGION**
>> *View:* **Table**
>> *Display:* **Column %**

PRESS? by REGION
Cramer's V: 0.056

			REGION			
		East	Midwest	South	West	TOTAL
PRESS?	Great deal	47	43	69	32	191
		12.7%	9.9%	10.6%	8.4%	10.4%
	Only some	182	220	312	165	879
		49.2%	50.7%	47.8%	43.4%	47.8%
	Hardly any	141	171	272	183	767
		38.1%	39.4%	41.7%	48.2%	41.8%
	Missing	198	236	353	193	980
	TOTAL	370	434	653	380	1837
		100.0%	100.0%	100.0%	100.0%	

There is no significant regional effect on confidence in the press.

In addition to watching TV and reading the paper, many people listen to talk shows on the radio.

> *Data File:* **NES**
>> *Task:* **Univariate**
> *Primary Variable:* **25) TALK RADIO**
>> *View:* **Pie**

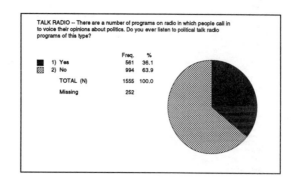

We find that a third of Americans listen to radio talk shows.

The three traditional news media sources over the past 50 years have been newspapers, TV, and radio. The Internet has now joined these traditional news sources. Many newspapers and television outlets have expanded to include Internet sites. Candidates, interest groups, and the political parties now use the Internet to bring their messages directly to the public.

Now you will have a chance to find out more about the audience for different types of media and what impact the media have on political opinions.

Your turn.

NAME:

COURSE:

DATE:

REVIEW QUESTIONS

Based on the first part of this exercise, answer True or False to the following items:

a. Because it can provide live video, TV is more effective than newspapers in communicating political information.   T   F

b. Newspaper circulation is increasing, primarily because Americans are becoming more educated.   T   F

c. A majority of Americans watch TV news every day.   T   F

d. Confidence in the press has been declining in the United States.   T   F

e. The British have less confidence in the press than do Americans.   T   F

EXPLORIT QUESTIONS

1. For the media to have any impact, someone must read, or listen to, or watch the medium. Let's see how education and age influence what and how much people read or watch.

> *Data File:* **NES**
> *Task:* **Cross-tabulation**
> *Row Variable:* **22) READ PAPER**
> *Column Variable:* **4) EDUCATION**
> *View:* **Table**
> *Display:* **Column %**

	NOT HS GRD	HS GRAD	SOME COL	COLL.GRAD.
a. % EVERY DAY (Note: this is the third row of the table.)	_____%	_____%	_____%	_____%

b. What is the value of V for this table?   V = _____

c. Is it statistically significant?   Yes   No

Data File: **NES**
Task: **Cross-tabulation**
➤ *Row Variable:* **23) TV NEWS?**
➤ *Column Variable:* **4) EDUCATION**
➤ *View:* **Table**
➤ *Display:* **Column %**

	NOT HS GRD	HS GRAD	SOME COL	COLL.GRAD.
d. % EVERY DAY (Note: this is the third row of the table.)	_____%	_____%	_____%	_____%

e. What is the value of V for this table?   V = _____

f. Is it statistically significant?   Yes   No

Data File: **NES**
Task: **Cross-tabulation**
➤ *Row Variable:* **22) READ PAPER**
➤ *Column Variable:* **5) AGE**
➤ *View:* **Table**
➤ *Display:* **Column %**

	UNDER 30	30–39	40–49	50–64	65 & OVER
g. % EVERY DAY	_____%	_____%	_____%	_____%	_____%

h. What is the value of V for this table?   V = _____

i. Is it statistically significant?   Yes   No

Data File: **NES**
Task: **Cross-tabulation**
➤ *Row Variable:* **23) TV NEWS?**
➤ *Column Variable:* **5) AGE**
➤ *View:* **Table**
➤ *Display:* **Column %**

	UNDER 30	30–39	40–49	50–64	65 & OVER
j. % EVERY DAY	_____%	_____%	_____%	_____%	_____%

k. What is the value of V for this table?   V = _____

l. Is it statistically significant?   Yes   No

Answer True or False to the following items:

    m. The higher an individual's education, the more likely he or she is to watch TV news daily.   T   F

    n. The higher an individual's education, the more likely he or she is to read the newspaper daily.   T   F

    o. Older people are more likely to read the newspaper every day than are younger people.   T   F

    p. Younger people are more likely to watch TV news daily than are older people.   T   F

2. There are several variables that provide additional information about the respondent's political knowledge. Included in these is awareness of the two major contenders for the 2000 Democratic nomination for president, Vice President Al Gore and New Jersey Senator Bill Bradley. Let's see if reading the paper or watching TV news made any difference in awareness of these two candidates.

>   Data File: **NES**
>   Task: **Cross-tabulation**
> ➤ Row Variable: **38) GORE KNOW**
> ➤ Column Variable: **22) READ PAPER**
> ➤   View: **Table**
> ➤   Display: **Column %**

    a. What is the value of V for this table?   V = _____

    b. Is it statistically significant?   Yes   No

    c. If significant, is this a moderate or weak relationship?   Moderate   Weak   Not Significant

>   Row Variable: **38) GORE KNOW**
> ➤ Column Variable: **23) TV NEWS?**
> ➤   View: **Table**
> ➤   Display: **Column %**

    d. What is the value of V for this table?   V = _____

    e. Is it statistically significant?   Yes   No

    f. If significant, is this a moderate or weak relationship?   Moderate   Weak   Not Significant

> ➤ Row Variable: **39) BRAD. KNOW**
> ➤ Column Variable: **22) READ PAPER**
> ➤   View: **Table**
> ➤   Display: **Column %**

g. What is the value of V for this table?   V = _____

h. Is it statistically significant?   Yes   No

i. If significant, is this a moderate or weak relationship?   Moderate   Weak   Not Significant

     Row Variable: **39) BRAD. KNOW**
➤ Column Variable: **23) TV NEWS?**
       ➤ View: **Table**
      ➤ Display: **Column %**

j. What is the value of V for this table?   V = _____

k. Is it statistically significant?   Yes   No

l. If significant, is this a moderate or weak relationship?   Moderate   Weak   Not Significant

m. Summarize what these results suggest about the relative impact of newspapers and TV news on the respondent's knowledge.

3. Previously we saw that those who both read newspapers and watched TV news daily were better informed about politics. Let's see how daily media usage affects the likelihood that people will talk about politics.

          Data File: **NES**
             Task: **Cross-tabulation**
  ➤ Row Variable: **71) TALK POL?**
➤ Column Variable: **24) NEWS TYPE**
         ➤ View: **Table**
      ➤ Display: **Column %**

	TV & PAPER	PAPER	TV	NEITHER
a. % YES	_____%	_____%	_____%	_____%

b. What is the value of V for this table?   V = _____

c. Is it statistically significant?   Yes   No

4. Some critics of media coverage of government contend that the media present only the negative side of the story, such as when a government program is not working. If these critics are correct, then people who frequently watch TV news and read newspapers should be less trusting of the government than other Americans. Other pundits might contend that people who are very distrustful of the government would not bother watching TV news or reading the newspaper, since these Americans would be less interested in news about a government they distrusted. Finally, a third group of scholars might speculate that since most Americans tend to distrust the government, media usage would have little to no influence on any individual's evaluation of the government. Let's see which of these three possible explanations might be correct.

> Data File: **NES**
> Task: **Cross-tabulation**
> ➤ Row Variable: **87) TRUST GOV**
> ➤ Column Variable: **24) NEWS TYPE**
> ➤ View: **Table**
> ➤ Display: **Column %**

	TV & PAPER	PAPER	TV	NEITHER
a. % SOME/NEVER	_____%	_____%	_____%	_____%

b. What is the value of V for this table?   V = _____

c. Is it statistically significant?   Yes   No

d. Which of the three contending explanations is best supported by the survey data? (Circle the number of the most appropriate answer.)

    1. Those who watch TV news and read the newspaper every day are less trusting of the government.

    2. Those who neither watch TV news nor read the newspaper every day are less trusting of the government.

    3. Media usage has little to no influence on political trust.

EXERCISE 8

POLITICAL PARTICIPATION

Politics ought to be the part-time profession of every citizen...

DWIGHT D. EISENHOWER, 1954

Tasks: Mapping, Univariate, Cross-Tabulation, Historical Trends, Auto-Analyzer
Data Files: NATIONS, NES, STATES, HISTORY

Political participation refers to the actions by ordinary citizens in pursuit of their political goals. The usual modes of participation are conventional—they are legal and regarded as appropriate. For example, voting, signing petitions, or campaigning on behalf of candidates or issues are conventional modes of political participation (at least they are in democratic nations). Sometimes, however, groups utilize unconventional means in pursuit of their goals. These are unusual modes of participation, often outside the law and in defiance of the government or social conventions—these include protests, demonstrations, even rebellions. Keep in mind too, as noted above, what are conventional means of political participation in some nations, such as free elections, are unavailable in others. However, while many people (usually the overwhelming majority) do not engage in unconventional political participation, many also fail to utilize conventional modes of participation. For example, many people don't bother to vote.

Let's begin with measures of unconventional participation.

> *Data File:* **NATIONS**
> *Task:* **Mapping**
> *Variable 1:* **8) SIT-INS**
> *View:* **List: Rank**

RANK	CASE NAME	VALUE
1	South Korea	10.7
2	Italy	9.7
3	France	7.9
4	Mexico	5.2
5	Belgium	4.3
6	Chile	4.2
7	Poland	3.8
8	Canada	3.0
9	Spain	2.9
10	Argentina	2.7

Few people in any of these nations have "occupied buildings or factories" as an act of direct political action. South Koreans are highest (10.7 percent), closely followed by the Italians (9.7 percent) and the French (7.9 percent). Two percent of Americans, Brazilians, and the Irish have done so. Only one person out of a thousand has taken part in a "sit-in" in Hungary.

Data File: **NATIONS**

Task: **Mapping**

➤ Variable 1: **39) FIGHT COPS**

➤ View: **List: Rank**

RANK	CASE NAME	VALUE
1	Slovak Republic	78.0
2	Czech Republic	77.3
3	Finland	74.9
4	Mexico	73.0
5	Latvia	71.7
6	Belarus	71.0
7	Lithuania	68.8
8	South Korea	66.6
9	Russia	61.6
10	Netherlands	60.7

In contrast, large numbers in most countries think it sometimes is justified to fight with the police—about three-fourths of those in the Slovak and the Czech Republics, Finland, and Mexico hold this view of illegal political expression. About half of Americans also think it sometimes is justified to battle the cops, as do Italians, Poles, Canadians, and the French. Small minorities expressed this opinion in Denmark, Romania, and Brazil.

Data File: **NATIONS**

Task: **Mapping**

➤ Variable 1: **5) PERSUASION**

➤ View: **List: Rank**

RANK	CASE NAME	VALUE
1	Denmark	34.0
2	Lithuania	32.6
3	Romania	31.6
4	Hungary	30.2
5	Belarus	27.5
6	Bulgaria	26.9
7	Nigeria	26.1
8	Argentina	24.2
9	Chile	23.5
10	Estonia	23.2

Turning to more conventional modes of participation, here we see the percentage in each nation who often try to persuade others to accept their political views. In no nation is this something that most people do often. Denmark is highest with 34 percent, only 16.9 percent of Americans said they did this often, and fewer than one in ten did so in Great Britain, France, India, Japan, and Finland.

Data File: **NATIONS**

Task: **Mapping**

➤ Variable 1: **38) % VOTED**

➤ View: **List: Rank**

RANK	CASE NAME	VALUE
1	Malta	98.0
2	Uruguay	96.1
3	Indonesia	92.8
4	Cambodia	88.8
5	Angola	88.3
6	Iceland	87.8
7	Italy	87.3
8	Somalia	87.1
9	Western Samoa	86.3
10	South Africa	85.5

Here we see the percentage of the population who voted in the most recent national election (although the percentages are quite stable from one election to the next). In many nations, more than 80 percent vote (98 percent in Malta). Voter turnout is about 50 percent in the United States. In the close and heated election of 2000, voter turnout was approximately 51 percent in the United States.

Much mention is made in the press about low voter turnouts in the United States, but the reasons are rather obvious. For one thing, because of the frequency of state and local elections, Americans are asked to vote far more often than are people in most nations; even so, the American voter usually faces a much longer and far more complex ballot than do most voters—far more American offices are elective, and in many nations there are no bond issues or initiatives on the ballot. A second reason is registration. Americans must register themselves to vote whereas in many other nations the government sees to it that everyone is registered. A third reason is that some nations—including Australia and Belgium—have compulsory voting laws. Citizens who fail to vote must pay a fine or are subject to a special tax. Finally, many critics believe that American voters lack motivation to vote because their choices are limited to two parties.

> Data File: **NES**
> Task: **Univariate**
> Primary Variable: **72) BUTTON**
> View: **Pie**

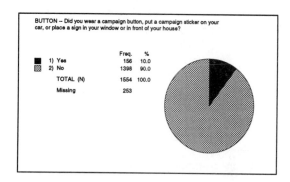

Until recently, campaign buttons, bumper stickers, and yard signs were widely used forms of American political expression. As election day neared, a substantial number of people wore buttons in support of candidates (especially presidential candidates) and automobile bumpers offered an instant education in partisan politics. But in the past several years, bumper stickers and campaign buttons are much less common. In fact, only 10 percent reported wearing a button, displaying a bumper sticker, or putting a sign in their window or yard.

Data File: **NES**
Task: **Univariate**
> Primary Variable: **73) CONTRIBUTE**
> View: **Pie**

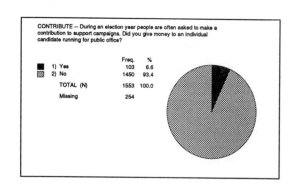

One American in 20 reported that he or she had made a campaign contribution to a candidate for political office during the previous year.

Data File: **NES**
Task: **Univariate**
➤ Primary Variable: **74) CONT$PARTY**
➤ View: **Pie**

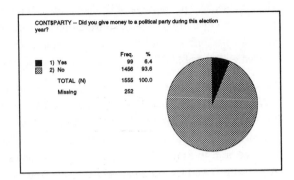

The same number of Americans had given money to a political party. How, then, does the average American participate in politics?

Data File: **NES**
Task: **Univariate**
➤ Primary Variable: **71) TALK POL?**
➤ View: **Pie**

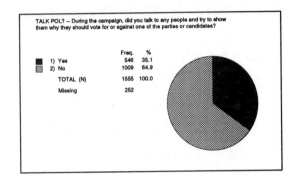

About one in three Americans tries to influence the political views of others in informal conversations.

Data File: **NES**
Task: **Univariate**
➤ Primary Variable: **26) VOTED**
➤ View: **Pie**

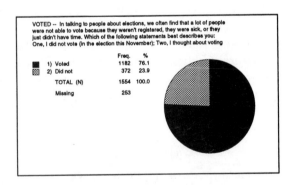

The most common and conventional form of political participation in the United States is voting. Here we see the percentage who said they voted, based on the National Election Study, conducted in 2000. The NES found that 76.1 percent claimed to have voted in the 2000 election, but in fact, only 51.3 percent voted.

There are three reasons for the overestimate. One is that some people who meant to vote and often vote, but who didn't vote this time, said they did. But an equally important reason for the overestimate is that all survey studies more accurately represent some kinds of people than others, whereas population voting statistics are based on the entire population. That is, not everyone is easily found by survey interviewers, nor is everyone willing to be interviewed. Consider the problems of finding or of gaining interviews with migrant workers, the homeless, or people in illegal occupations such as prostitution or drug dealing. In addition, institutional populations such as those in jails, prisons, college dorms, convents, or the armed forces are not included in national survey samples. The same people who are hard for pollsters to locate and to interview also are those who are least apt to vote. Finally, many people don't like to admit that they skipped an election.

Still, even poll results show that a large number of Americans don't vote, even in presidential elections. Worse yet, the proportion voting in the 20th century has never approached the level recorded in the election of 1900. Keep in mind, however, that the 20th century saw major expansions in the types and numbers of people who were eligible to vote, and this no doubt affected the percentages of the eligible voters who actually voted. In 1900, in general, only males who were age 21 and above could vote. The 19th Amendment (1920) doubled this eligibility by giving women the right to vote. But women were not in the habit of voting, and so look at what happened to the voting participation curve in 1920 and 1924—it dropped drastically. It was not until the 1928 election that voting participation began to rise again. The 26th Amendment (1971) reduced the voting age to 18 nationally—the requirement had been 21 in all but a couple of states. The drop in voting participation in the 1972 election can be attributed partly to the fact that a new age group had been added to the eligible electorate and that this age group was not in the habit of voting.

➤ *Data File:* **HISTORY**
  ➤ *Task:* **Historical Trends**
➤ *Variable:* **12) VOTER PART**

Percent of those eligible who voted for president

Not only have Americans become less likely to vote, there also are decided regional effects on voter turnouts.

➤ *Data File:* **STATES**
  ➤ *Task:* **Mapping**
➤ *Variable 1:* **198) %VOTED 00**
  ➤ *View:* **List: Rank**

RANK	CASE NAME	VALUE
1	North Dakota	70.4
2	Maine	70.1
2	Wisconsin	70.1
4	Minnesota	69.8
5	Alaska	67.7
6	Iowa	67.4
7	Missouri	66.7
8	Oregon	66.6
8	New Hampshire	66.6
10	Louisiana	65.7

North Dakota had the highest percentage of voter turnout in the 2000 presidential election, with 70.4 percent. Maine (70.1 percent) and Wisconsin (70.1 percent) were next highest. Hawaii had the lowest percentage of voter turnout (44.1 percent).

Data File: **STATES**
Task: **Mapping**
Variable 1: **198) %VOTED 00**
➤ *Variable 2:* **8) THE SOUTH**
➤ *Views:* **Map**

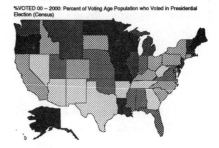

%VOTED 00 -- 2000: Percent of Voting Age Population who Voted in Presidential Election (Census)

r = –0.292*

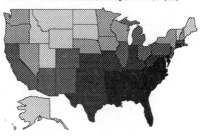

THE SOUTH -- Circulation of Southern Accents Magazine Per 100,000 (ABC)

Here we see that southern states had lower voter turnouts in the 2000 election, as indicated by the significant, negative correlation: –0.292*.

Data File: **STATES**
Task: **Mapping**
Variable 1: **198) %VOTED 00**
➤ *Variable 2:* **6) SUNBELT**
➤ *Views:* **Map**

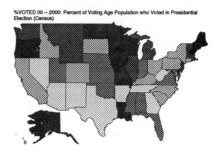

%VOTED 00 -- 2000: Percent of Voting Age Population who Voted in Presidential Election (Census)

r = –0.589**

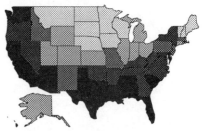

SUNBELT -- Warm Winters: Average January Low Temperature

In fact, however, low turnouts are typical in the Sunbelt, which includes states in much of the South as well as some of the West. The correlation is stronger than with the South alone: –0.589**.

Voting turnout might also be affected by the demographic characteristics of states such as the degree of urbanism, education level, and income level.

Data File: **STATES**
Task: **Mapping**
Variable 1: **198) %VOTED 00**
➤ Variable 2: **4) URBAN00**
➤ Views: **Map**

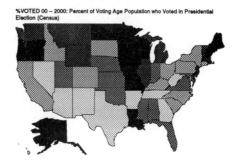

%VOTED 00 -- 2000: Percent of Voting Age Population who Voted in Presidential Election (Census)

r = –0.036

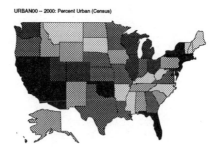

URBAN00 -- 2000: Percent Urban (Census)

Here we see that there is no relationship (r = –0.036) between urbanism and voter turnout.

Data File: **STATES**
Task: **Mapping**
Variable 1: **198) %VOTED 00**
➤ Variable 2: **126) %HIGH SCH**
➤ Views: **Map**

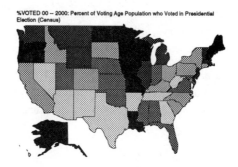

%VOTED 00 -- 2000: Percent of Voting Age Population who Voted in Presidential Election (Census)

r = 0.431**

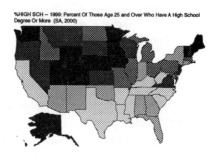

%HIGH SCH -- 1999: Percent Of Those Age 25 and Over Who Have A High School Degree Or More (SA, 2000)

Here we see that voter turnout is positively related to the percentage of the state's population that has a high school degree. The correlation coefficient r is 0.431** and it is statistically significant.

Data File: **STATES**
Task: **Mapping**
Variable 1: **198) %VOTED 00**
➤ Variable 2: **136) PER CAP$**
➤ Views: **Map**

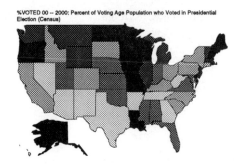

%VOTED 00 -- 2000: Percent of Voting Age Population who Voted in Presidential Election (Census)

r = 0.195

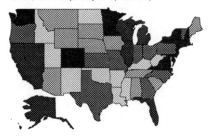

PER CAP$ -- 2000: Per Capita Money Income (Census: C2SS)

Voter turnout is not, however, related to the per capita income of states. The correlation coefficient r is only 0.195 and it is not statistically significant.

Now let's turn to survey data to examine who is most likely to vote. Remember, however, that some of the people in surveys who say they voted did not actually vote. Nevertheless, these self-reports are sufficiently accurate to serve as a basis for analyzing who votes.

In general terms, we might expect that voting participation among citizens would vary according to demographic characteristics (e.g., education, age, income), political knowledge, and attitudes toward the workings of the political system (e.g., political trust). Let's begin with a demographic variable, education.

➤ Data File: **NES**
➤ Task: **Cross-tabulation**
➤ Row Variable: **26) VOTED**
➤ Column Variable: **4) EDUCATION**
➤ View: **Table**
➤ Display: **Column %**

VOTED by EDUCATION
Cramer's V: 0.313 **

		Not HS grd	HS grad	Some col	Coll.grad.	Missing	TOTAL
VOTED	Voted	73	286	365	456	2	1180
		49.0%	66.1%	77.5%	91.8%		76.1%
	Did not	76	147	106	41	2	370
		51.0%	33.9%	22.5%	8.2%		23.9%
	Missing	31	86	74	59	3	253
	TOTAL	149	433	471	497	7	1550
		100.0%	100.0%	100.0%	100.0%		

When we examined the relationship between voter turnout and the education level of states, we found that states with higher percentages of high school graduates had higher rates of voter turnout. Here the survey results confirm the link between education level and voting participation: The higher the education level of people, the more likely they are to vote. Note that 91.8 percent of those with a college degree said they had voted—which is almost twice as high as the voting turnout among those who didn't finish high school.

Data File: **NES**

Task: **Cross-tabulation**

Row Variable: **26) VOTED**

➤ Column Variable: **1) REGION**

➤ View: **Table**

➤ Display: **Column %**

VOTED by REGION
Cramer's V: 0.093 **

		REGION				
		East	Midwest	South	West	TOTAL
VOTED	Voted	212	320	410	240	1182
		78.8%	81.6%	73.5%	71.6%	76.1%
	Did not	57	72	148	95	372
		21.2%	18.4%	26.5%	28.4%	23.9%
	Missing	47	58	99	49	253
	TOTAL	269	392	558	335	1554
		100.0%	100.0%	100.0%	100.0%	

These findings show that Southerners and Westerners are less likely to have voted.

Data File: **NES**

Task: **Cross-tabulation**

Row Variable: **26) VOTED**

➤ Column Variable: **20) INTEREST?**

➤ View: **Table**

➤ Display: **Column %**

VOTED by INTEREST?
Cramer's V: 0.385 **

		INTEREST?			
		Very much	Somewhat	Not much	TOTAL
VOTED	Voted	433	595	154	1182
		91.5%	79.5%	46.2%	76.1%
	Did not	40	153	179	372
		8.5%	20.5%	53.8%	23.9%
	Missing	52	138	63	253
	TOTAL	473	748	333	1554
		100.0%	100.0%	100.0%	

Not surprisingly, people expressing more interest in the campaign were more apt to have voted.

Data File: **NES**

Task: **Cross-tabulation**

Row Variable: **26) VOTED**

➤ Column Variable: **21) INFORMED?**

➤ View: **Table**

➤ Display: **Column %**

VOTED by INFORMED?
Cramer's V: 0.402 **

		INFORMED?				
		High	Average	Low	Missing	TOTAL
VOTED	Voted	626	389	165	2	1180
		91.0%	76.3%	46.7%		76.1%
	Did not	62	121	188	1	371
		9.0%	23.7%	53.3%		23.9%
	Missing	87	76	86	4	253
	TOTAL	688	510	353	7	1551
		100.0%	100.0%	100.0%		

And the more informed they were, the more apt people also were to have voted.

Data File: **NES**

Task: **Cross-tabulation**

Row Variable: **26) VOTED**

➤ Column Variable: **93) GOVT ATTN**

➤ View: **Table**

➤ Display: **Column %**

VOTED by GOVT ATTN
Cramer's V: 0.173 **

		GOVT ATTN				
		Good deal	Some	Not much	Missing	TOTAL
VOTED	Voted	216	777	185	4	1178
		82.1%	79.4%	61.7%		76.4%
	Did not	47	201	115	9	363
		17.9%	20.6%	38.3%		23.6%
	Missing	0	0	1	252	253
	TOTAL	263	978	300	265	1541
		100.0%	100.0%	100.0%		

Here we see, as might be expected, that voting participation is higher among those who feel that the government pays attention to what the public wants.

Do patterns of voting make a difference in terms of policy? If certain types of people are less likely to vote, we might expect that their impact on public policy would be reduced. Let's examine differences between voters and nonvoters on the issue of abortion.

Data File: **NES**
Task: **Cross-tabulation**
➤ Row Variable: **58) ABORTION**
➤ Column Variable: **26) VOTED**
➤ View: **Table**
➤ Display: **Column %**

ABORTION by VOTED
Cramer's V: 0.075 *

		VOTED			
		Voted	Did not	Missing	TOTAL
ABORTION	Never	129	61	25	190
		11.2%	16.8%		12.5%
	Sometimes	526	163	101	689
		45.7%	44.9%		45.5%
	Always	496	139	118	635
		43.1%	38.3%		41.9%
	Missing	31	9	9	49
	TOTAL	1151	363	253	1514
		100.0%	100.0%		

Here there is a policy difference between voters and nonvoters: Voters are somewhat more likely to allow abortions than nonvoters are.

Your turn.

WORKSHEET

NAME:

COURSE:

DATE:

Workbook exercises and software are copyrighted. Copying is prohibited by law.

EXERCISE
8

REVIEW QUESTIONS

Based on the first part of this exercise, answer True or False to the following items:

a. Because of the increase in the average level of education, Americans are more likely to vote now than they were early in the 20th century.　　T　F

b. National surveys seldom include persons living in college dorms.　　T　F

c. Because presidential elections are held in November when the weather has gotten cold, voter turnouts are higher in the Sunbelt states.　　T　F

d. About half of Americans think it might be justified sometimes to fight with the police.　T　F

e. People who are more interested and informed about politics are more likely to vote.　T　F

f. There are no differences in the political views of voters and nonvoters.　　T　F

EXPLORIT QUESTIONS

1. Let's see what demographic characteristics affect how likely an individual is to vote.

> ➤ Data File: **NES**
> 　➤ Task: **Auto-Analyzer**
> ➤ Variable: **26) VOTED**
> 　➤ View: **Univariate**

For each demographic variable listed below, indicate whether there is any significant effect. If so, indicate which category is most likely and which is least likely to vote.

	IS THE EFFECT SIGNIFICANT?		CATEGORY MOST LIKELY TO VOTE	CATEGORY LEAST LIKELY TO VOTE
a. *View:* **Sex**	Yes	No	_____	_____
b. *View:* **Race**	Yes	No	_____	_____
c. *View:* **Pol.Party**	Yes	No	_____	_____

	IS THE EFFECT SIGNIFICANT?		CATEGORY MOST LIKELY TO VOTE	CATEGORY LEAST LIKELY TO VOTE
d. *View:* **Religion**	Yes	No	_____	_____
e. *View:* **Region**	Yes	No	_____	_____
f. *View:* **Age**	Yes	No	_____	_____
g. *View:* **Education**	Yes	No	_____	_____
h. *View:* **Income**	Yes	No	_____	_____

2. Based on the results of Question 1, describe the characteristics of those who are most likely to vote.

3. Let's look more closely at the age difference in political participation, political interest, and political knowledge.

> *Data File:* **NES**
> ➤ *Task:* **Cross-tabulation**
> ➤ *Row Variable:* **26) VOTED**
> ➤ *Column Variable:* **5) AGE**
> ➤ *View:* **Table**
> ➤ *Display:* **Column %**

	UNDER 30	30–39	40–49	50–64	65 & OVER
a. % VOTED	_____%	_____%	_____%	_____%	_____%

> *Data File:* **NES**
> *Task:* **Cross-tabulation**
> ➤ *Row Variable:* **20) INTEREST?**
> ➤ *Column Variable:* **5) AGE**
> ➤ *View:* **Table**
> ➤ *Display:* **Column %**

	UNDER 30	30–39	40–49	50–64	65 & OVER
b. %VERY MUCH	_____%	_____%	_____%	_____%	_____%

Data File: **NES**
Task: **Cross-tabulation**
➤ *Row Variable:* **21) INFORMED?**
➤ *Column Variable:* **5) AGE**
➤ *View:* **Table**
➤ *Display:* **Column %**

	UNDER 30	30–39	40–49	50–64	65 & OVER
c. % HIGH	_____%	_____%	_____%	_____%	_____%

Data File: **NES**
Task: **Cross-tabulation**
➤ *Row Variable:* **74) CONT$PARTY**
➤ *Column Variable:* **5) AGE**
➤ *View:* **Table**
➤ *Display:* **Column %**

	UNDER 30	30–39	40–49	50–64	65 & OVER
d. % YES	_____%	_____%	_____%	_____%	_____%

e. Based on these results concerning age, which of the following statements is most accurate? (Circle one.)

1. Overall, younger people have higher political interest, political knowledge, and political participation than older people do.

2. Overall, older people have higher political interest, political knowledge, and political participation than younger people do.

3. Older people have higher political participation, but younger people have higher political interest and political knowledge.

4. Older people have higher political interest and political knowledge, but younger people have higher political participation.

4. Let's examine relationships between voting participation and some political attitudes.

Data File: **NES**
Task: **Cross-tabulation**
➤ *Row Variable:* **26) VOTED**
➤ *Column Variable:* **78) PRTY DIFFS**
➤ *View:* **Table**
➤ *Display:* **Column %**

a. What is Cramer's V for this relationship?   V = _____

b. Is this relationship statistically significant?   Yes   No

c. On the basis of these results, who is more likely to vote? (Circle one.)

1. Those who think that there are important differences between what the Democrats and the Republicans stand for

2. Those who think that there are not important differences between what the Democrats and the Republicans stand for

> Data File: **NES**
> Task: **Cross-tabulation**
> Row Variable: **26) VOTED**
> ➤ Column Variable: **94) ELECT ATTN**
>   ➤ View: **Table**
>   ➤ Display: **Column %**

d. What is Cramer's V for this relationship?   V = _____

e. Is this relationship statistically significant?   Yes   No

f. On the basis of these results, which of the following statements is most accurate? (Circle one.)

1. The more that people feel that elections make the government pay attention, the more likely they are to vote.

2. The more that people feel that elections make the government pay attention, the less likely they are to vote.

3. There is no pattern here; voting participation is not related to how people view elections.

> Data File: **NES**
> Task: **Cross-tabulation**
> Row Variable: **26) VOTED**
> ➤ Column Variable: **98) GOVT WASTE**
>   ➤ View: **Table**
>   ➤ Display: **Column %**

g. What is Cramer's V for this relationship?   V = _____

h. Is this relationship statistically significant?   Yes   No

i. On the basis of these results, which of the following statements is most accurate? (Circle one.)

1. People who feel that the government is wasteful are more likely to vote.

2. People who feel that the government is wasteful are less likely to vote.

3. There is no relationship between voting participation and perception of governmental wastefulness.

5. Next we will examine differences between voters and nonvoters in terms of political issue stands.

> Data File: **NES**
> Task: **Cross-tabulation**
> ➤ Row Variable: **64) GUN CNTRL**
> ➤ Column Variable: **26) VOTED**
> ➤ View: **Table**
> ➤ Display: **Column %**

a. What is Cramer's V for this relationship?   V = _____

b. Is this relationship statistically significant?   Yes   No

c. On the basis of these results, which of the following statements is most accurate? (Circle one.)

   1. There is no difference between voters and nonvoters in terms of attitudes toward gun control.
   2. Voters favor tougher gun-control laws more than nonvoters do.
   3. Nonvoters favor tougher gun-control laws more than voters do.

> Data File: **NES**
> Task: **Cross-tabulation**
> ➤ Row Variable: **103) GOVGJOBS**
> ➤ Column Variable: **26) VOTED**
> ➤ View: **Table**
> ➤ Display: **Column %**

d. What is Cramer's V for this relationship?   V = _____

e. Is this relationship statistically significant?   Yes   No

f. On the basis of these results, which of the following statements is most accurate? (Circle one.)

   1. There is no difference between voters and nonvoters in terms of attitudes toward the government guaranteeing a standard of living for people.
   2. Voters favor a guaranteed standard of living more than nonvoters do.
   3. Nonvoters favor a guaranteed standard of living more than voters do.

> Data File: **NES**
> Task: **Cross-tabulation**
> ➤ Row Variable: **53) GOVT SPND**
> ➤ Column Variable: **26) VOTED**
> ➤ View: **Table**
> ➤ Display: **Column %**

g. What is Cramer's V for this relationship?   V = _____

h. Is this relationship statistically significant?   Yes   No

   i. On the basis of these results, which of the following statements is most accurate? (circle one)

      1. There is no difference between voters and nonvoters in terms of attitudes toward government services/spending.

      2. Voters favor an increase in governmental services/spending more than nonvoters do.

      3. Nonvoters favor an increase in governmental services/spending more than voters do.

6. Overall, on the basis of the preceding analysis of policy differences between voters and nonvoters, which of the following statements is most accurate? (Circle one.)

      a. Voters and nonvoters are virtually identical in terms of their policy preferences.

      b. There are some policy differences between voters and nonvoters, but these differences are not extremely high.

      c. Voters and nonvoters are extremely different from one another in terms of their policy preferences.

POLITICAL PARTIES

No free Country has ever been without parties,
which are a natural offspring of Freedom.
JAMES MADISON, 1787

Tasks: Mapping, Univariate, Cross-Tabulation, Scatterplot, Auto-Analyzer, Historical Trends
Data Files: NATIONS, NES, HISTORY

Political parties can be defined as organizations that sponsor candidates for political office and attempt (to a greater or lesser degree) to coordinate the actions of their elected members. Within this definition of party are three distinct groups of people, each with its important contribution.

First are the people who hold elective or appointive office or who run for office as candidates of the party. These can be identified as the *party-in-government*.

Second are the staff members and political activists who constitute the formal *party organization*. Included here are several million Americans who belong to political parties in the same way that people belong to other organizations: They contribute money, they attend meetings, and they may perform various duties such as passing out campaign literature or helping to turn out voters on election day.

Third, a party also includes all those members of the public who regard themselves as supporters of the party, and these people often are referred to as the *party-in-the-electorate*.

> ➤ *Data File:* **NATIONS**
> ➤ *Task:* **Mapping**
> ➤ *Variable 1:* **36) # PARTIES**
> ➤ *View:* **Map**

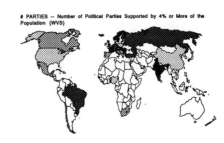

PARTIES -- Number of Political Parties Supported by 4% or More of the Population (WVS)

Nations differ a lot in their number of political parties. Some nations allow only one party and thus provide citizens with no political choices—one-party states are undemocratic and limit many freedoms people take for granted in democracies. In some nations there are two primary parties and any additional parties are too small to have any influence. But many nations have more than two major parties.

Data File:	**NATIONS**
Task:	**Mapping**
Variable 1:	**36) # PARTIES**
➤ View:	**List: Rank**

RANK	CASE NAME	VALUE
1	Slovenia	9
2	Belgium	8
3	Norway	7
3	France	7
3	Romania	7
6	India	6
6	Denmark	6
6	Hungary	6
6	Sweden	6
10	Brazil	5

Here we see that Slovenia has nine significant parties, defined as those able to attract at least 4 percent of the electorate (there are many additional smaller parties in Slovenia and elsewhere). Belgium has eight significant parties, while France, Norway, and Romania have seven each. At the bottom of the list, Ireland, Poland, and Japan have three parties, the United States and Nigeria have only two, and China allows only one.

Data File:	**NATIONS**
Task:	**Mapping**
Variable 1:	**36) # PARTIES**
➤ Variable 2:	**37) %BIG PARTY**
➤ Views:	**Map**

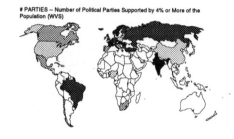

PARTIES -- Number of Political Parties Supported by 4% or More of the Population (WVS)

r = –0.467**

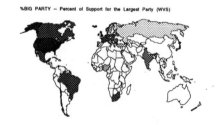

%BIG PARTY -- Percent of Support for the Largest Party (WVS)

This map shows the strength of the leading party. In each nation interviewers asked, "If there were a general election tomorrow, which party would you vote for?" Because some voters in each nation said they were undecided, only in Ireland did 50 percent support the same party. In Chile, 46 percent supported the same party, as did 45 percent of Americans. But in Slovenia and Belgium, the most popular party drew support from only 18 percent of the public and in Switzerland only 16 percent. Clearly, then, where there are many parties, each tends to be small, as is indicated by the negative correlation of –0.467**.

Nations not only differ in how many parties they have, they also differ in how easy it is to join a party. For example, in many nations (including Canada and Great Britain), parties are very tightly controlled national organizations and only candidates selected by the central party committees can run for office under the party label.

By comparison, American political parties are extremely easy to join. Even at the party-in-government level, people often run in and win party primaries without prior party participation and even in opposition to candidates backed by the party organization. For example, Dwight David Eisenhower successfully gained the Republican nomination for president in 1952, defeating Senator Robert A. Taft in primaries and in the convention, without any prior connections to the Republican Party. In fact, he had never even voted before (at that time, many military officers did not vote on the grounds that their allegiance was to the nation, not to any party). As for becoming an official member of the Republican or Democratic parties, it is pretty much a case of just showing up and joining. Even so, few Americans are actual party members (recall how few give money to a party). For most people, political parties are labels attached to candidates and political positions, and their own party "membership" is really only a preference or self-identification.

➤ *Data File:* **NES**
➤ *Task:* **Univariate**
➤ *Primary Variable:* **16) PARTY**
➤ *View:* **Pie**

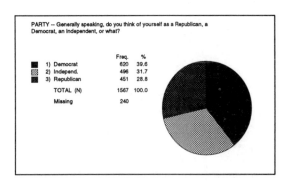

Most Americans are partisans, either Democrats or Republicans, but nearly one in three Americans calls themselves a political independent. Those naming a third party fall below 1 percent.

Partisanship influences a number of other attitudes and activities. Partisanship has a strong effect on the candidates that people support.

Data File: **NES**
➤ *Task:* **Cross-tabulation**
➤ *Row Variable:* **27) PVOTE LNG**
➤ *Column Variable:* **16) PARTY**
➤ *View:* **Table**
➤ *Display:* **Column %**

PVOTE LNG   by   PARTY
Cramer's V: 0.549 **

		PARTY				
		Democrat	Independ	Republican	Missing	TOTAL
P V O T E L N G	Gore	392	139	24	35	555
		94.0%	47.4%	7.1%		53.0%
	Bush	24	129	311	66	464
		5.8%	44.0%	92.0%		44.3%
	Buchanan	0	2	1	0	3
		0.0%	0.7%	0.3%		0.3%
	Nader	1	23	2	7	26
		0.2%	7.8%	0.6%		2.5%
	Missing	203	203	113	132	651
	TOTAL	417	293	338	240	1048
		100.0%	100.0%	100.0%		

This table clearly shows the strong influence partisanship had on voters' choices in the 2000 presidential election. Ninety-four percent of Democrats voted for Al Gore, while 92 percent of Republicans voted for George W. Bush. Independent voters split their ballots between the two major party candidates. Notice that most independents did not vote for either of the minor party candidates—Pat Buchanan of the Reform Party or Ralph Nader of the Green Party. One reason that minor party candidates have such a difficult time in gaining votes is that two-thirds of Americans are either Democrats or Republicans and tend to vote for their own party's candidate. Even independent voters are more likely to support one of the major party candidates rather than voting for a minor party candidate.

While partisanship clearly is linked to voters' choices in presidential elections, partisanship is not always as strongly linked to other political attitudes. Let's examine the relationship between partisanship and political ideology.

Data File:	**NES**	
Task:	**Cross-tabulation**	
➤ Row Variable:	**17) IDEOLOGY**	
➤ Column Variable:	**16) PARTY**	
➤ View:	**Table**	
➤ Display:	**Column %**	

IDEOLOGY   by   PARTY
Cramer's V: 0.341 **

		PARTY				
		Democrat	Independ.	Republican	Missing	TOTAL
IDEOLOGY	Liberal	98	55	12	14	165
		46.0%	28.4%	6.3%		27.6%
	Moderate	70	69	36	40	175
		32.9%	35.6%	18.8%		29.3%
	Conserv	45	70	143	21	258
		21.1%	36.1%	74.9%		43.1%
	Missing	407	302	260	165	1134
	TOTAL	213	194	191	240	598
		100.0%	100.0%	100.0%		

Republicans show the greatest consistency in their ideology. Nearly three out of four Republicans call themselves conservatives. The Democratic party is much more diverse in terms of ideology. Democrats are split between liberals and moderates. Furthermore, one in five Democrats considers themselves to be conservative.

The Democratic and Republican party organizations rely on individual American citizens to contribute money to support their activities. In the exercise on political participation, we saw that only 6 percent of Americans contribute money to a political party. Are partisans more willing to contribute money than independents?

Data File:	**NES**	
Task:	**Cross-tabulation**	
➤ Row Variable:	**74) CONT$PARTY**	
➤ Column Variable:	**16) PARTY**	
➤ View:	**Table**	
➤ Display:	**Column %**	

CONT$PARTY   by   PARTY
Cramer's V: 0.073 *

		PARTY				
		Democrat	Independ.	Republican	Missing	TOTAL
CONT$PARTY	Yes	30	24	39	6	93
		5.7%	5.6%	9.7%		6.9%
	No	496	403	363	194	1262
		94.3%	94.4%	90.3%		93.1%
	Missing	94	69	49	40	252
	TOTAL	526	427	402	240	1355
		100.0%	100.0%	100.0%		

Republicans are slightly more likely to contribute money to a political party than either Democrats or Independents. Yet, only one in ten Republicans contributes money to the party. Contributing to the political parties is a very infrequent task for all U.S. citizens.

Your turn.

WORKSHEET

NAME:

COURSE:

DATE:

EXERCISE

9

REVIEW QUESTIONS

Based on the first part of this exercise, answer True or False to the following items:

a. Most democratic nations have at least three major political parties.	T	F
b. Three-fourths of Democrats say they are liberals.	T	F
c. Nearly one-half of the American electorate considers themselves to be political independents.	T	F
d. In the 2000 presidential election, at least three-fourths of partisans supported their own party's presidential candidate.	T	F
e. Republicans are more likely than Democrats to have contributed money to a political party.	T	F

EXPLORIT QUESTIONS

1. In the opening section of this exercise, we noted that American political parties are often discussed in terms of three components: the party in government, the party in the electorate, and the party organization. Beginning with the party-in-government component, one can note that two major parties, the Democrats and the Republicans, have dominated the government over the past century. All other parties are referred to as third parties or minor parties. How many third-party candidates have been a part of the government? Let's investigate by looking at the percentage of seats in the U.S. House and Senate controlled by members of a third party or by political independents.

> *Data File:* **HISTORY**
> > *Task:* **Historical Trends**
> *Variables:* **68) HSE-OTH**
> **69) SEN-OTH**

Answer True or False to the following items:

a. The percentage of third-party members in the U.S. House often exceeds 20 percent. (Hint: Look at the scale on the left-hand side of the graph. The numbers listed are the percentages of seats held by third parties.)	T	F
b. The percentage of third-party members in the U.S. House and Senate has increased substantially in recent years.	T	F

Exercise 9: Political Parties

2. Now let's compare the percentage of seats held by the Democratic versus the Republican party in the U.S. House. The party that has the most seats is referred to as the majority party. The majority party leader becomes the Speaker of the House, and the majority party controls the chairs of all of the congressional committees. The majority party has considerable influence over the decisions made by Congress.

> Data File: **HISTORY**
> Task: **Historical Trends**
> ➤ Variables: **16) %DEM HOUSE**
> **70) %REP HOUSE**

Answer True or False to the following items:

a. The Democratic party was the majority party in the U.S. House from the middle of the 1950s to the middle of the 1990s.   T   F

b. Throughout the 20th century, the Democratic party was more likely to be the majority party in the House than was the Republican party.   T   F

3. Now let's look at the party in the electorate. Earlier we saw that partisans were no more likely than independents to contribute money to political candidates. Are partisans more likely than independents to participate in other types of political activities?

Fill in the table at the end of this question after completing each of the following analyses:

> ➤ Data File: **NES**
> ➤ Task: **Cross-tabulation**
> ➤ Row Variable: **26) VOTED**
> ➤ Column Variable: **16) PARTY**
> ➤ View: **Table**
> ➤ Display: **Column %**

> ➤ Row Variable: **20) INTEREST?**
> ➤ Column Variable: **16) PARTY**
> ➤ View: **Table**
> ➤ Display: **Column %**

> ➤ Row Variable: **21) INFORMED?**
> ➤ Column Variable: **16) PARTY**
> ➤ View: **Table**
> ➤ Display: **Column %**

(Note: V for each of these tables is statistically significant.)

NES SURVEY

	DEMOCRAT	INDEPEND.	REPUBLICAN
a. 26) VOTED % voted	_____%	_____%	_____%
b. 20) INTEREST? % very much	_____%	_____%	_____%
c. 21) INFORMED? % high	_____%	_____%	_____%

Answer True or False to the following items:

d. Democrats and Republicans are about equally likely to vote, but independents
are considerably less likely to vote.   T   F

e. Those who claim a party preference are generally less interested in politics
than are independents.   T   F

f. Democrats and Independents are about equally as well informed about politics, but
Republicans are the most informed.   T   F

4.   "Because of their keen interest in following politics, independents make their decisions on an issue-
by-issue basis and refuse to be categorized by party." Do you agree or disagree with this statement?
Why or why not? Use the information you collected in Question 3 to support your position.

5.   In Exercise 8, low voter turnouts in the United States were attributed, at least in part, to the limited
choices posed by the two-party system. Let's look at other nations to see if there is any support for
this idea.

> *Data File:* **NATIONS**
> *Task:* **Scatterplot**
> *Dependent Variable:* **38) % VOTED**
> *Independent Variable:* **36) # PARTIES**
> *View:* **Reg. Line**

Answer True or False to the following items:

a. The greater the number of political parties in a nation, the higher the percentage voting.   T   F

b. This scatterplot supports the idea that the limited choice of parties in the United States may be depressing the voter turnout rate.   T   F

6.   Let's use the AUTO-ANALYZER task to see who's most likely to be a Democrat and who's most likely to be a Republican.

> ➤ *Data File:* **NES**
> ➤ *Task:* **Auto-Analyzer**
> ➤ *Variable:* **109) DEM/REP**
> ➤ *View:* **Univariate**

For each demographic variable listed below, indicate whether there is any significant effect. If so, indicate which category is most likely and which is least likely to identify with the Democratic party.

	IS THE EFFECT SIGNIFICANT?		CATEGORY MOST LIKELY TO BE DEMOCRAT	CATEGORY LEAST LIKELY TO BE DEMOCRAT
a. *View:* **Sex**	Yes	No	_____	_____
b. *View:* **Race**	Yes	No	_____	_____
c. *View:* **Religion**	Yes	No	_____	_____
d. *View:* **Region**	Yes	No	_____	_____
e. *View:* **Education**	Yes	No	_____	_____
f. *View:* **Income**	Yes	No	_____	_____

7.   a. Based on the results in Question 6, describe the characteristics of those who are most likely to be Democrats.

b. Based on the results in Question 6, describe the characteristics of those who are least likely to be Democrats.

8. Finally, let's examine the financial standing of the two major parties. An important component of the party organization is the ability to raise money. Money is needed to fund the national headquarters, to pay staff, to conduct polling, and to assist the party's candidates. Are the two political parties on an equal financial footing? Let's examine the money raised (in millions of dollars) by the Democratic and Republican parties over recent decades.

> ➤ *Data File:* **HISTORY**
> ➤ *Task:* **Historical Trends**
> ➤ *Variables:* **71) DEM$**
> **72) REP$**

Answer True or False to the following item:

The Republican party raises more funds than the Democratic party.   T   F

ELECTIONS

Bad politicians are sent to Washington by good people who don't vote.

WILLIAM E. SIMON, 1985

Tasks: Mapping
Data Files: STATES

By law, all positions in the House of Representatives and one-third of those in the Senate are filled by an election held on the first Tuesday after the first Monday in November in every even-numbered year. Consequently, all members of the House face reelection every two years and all senators every six. In addition, every second national election is a presidential election as presidents of the United States serve a four-year term (and are limited to two elected terms by the 22nd Amendment, adopted in 1951). Unlike elections for other offices, both national and local, American presidents are elected in a somewhat unusual way.

➤ *Data File:* **STATES**
➤ *Task:* **Mapping**
➤ *Variable 1:* **178) GORE**
➤ *View:* **Map**

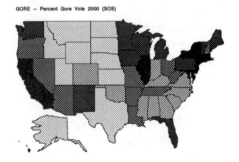

GORE -- Percent Gore Vote 2000 (SOS)

The darker the state, the higher the percentage of the vote won by Al Gore. Since these are the votes cast by individual voters, they are referred to as the **popular** vote. Combining all the votes cast nationwide in 2000, Al Gore won the popular vote, receiving approximately 500,000 more votes than George W. Bush. However, 105 million votes were cast in the 2000 presidential election, so Gore's margin of victory over Bush in the popular vote was less than 1 percent of the total votes cast. The popular vote in the 2000 presidential election was one of the closest in history. Despite winning the popular vote, Gore lost the presidential election to Bush. Let's see how this happened.

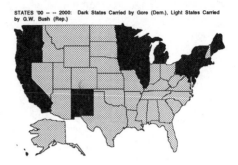

STATES '00 -- -- 2000:   Dark States Carried by Gore (Dem.), Light States Carried by G.W. Bush (Rep.)

Gore had the most votes in 20 states plus Washington D.C. George W. Bush won 30 states. Bush garnered 271 electoral college votes from those 30 states. A candidate needs to win a majority of the electoral college votes to become president. Since there are 538 electoral college votes, a candidate needs to win a minimum of 270 electoral college votes to become president. George W. Bush won the presidency with only one more electoral college vote than needed. The 2000 presidential election was indeed an extremely close race.

Electoral votes exist because the Constitution does not provide for the direct election of the president or vice president. Instead, Article II of the Constitution directs that the president and vice president shall be elected by a group known as the **electoral college**:

> Each State shall appoint, in such Manner as the Legislature thereof may direct, a Number of Electors, equal to the whole Number of Senators and Representatives to which the State may be entitled in the Congress; but no Senator or Representative, or Person holding an Office of Trust or Profit under the United States, shall be appointed an Elector.

Once appointed, each state's electors were directed to gather (thereby constituting an electoral college) whereupon each would vote for two persons—at least one of whom could not be a resident of their state—and these votes then were to be forwarded to the president of the Senate (who always is the current vice president). The votes of all electors from all states then were to be opened and counted.

The person receiving a majority of the electoral college votes was elected president. After the president was elected, the person receiving the second most votes was elected vice president. When no person received a majority, or a tie occurred, then the House of Representatives chose the president from the five highest vote getters in the electoral college. The representatives of each state voted as a state delegation and thus had one vote. The person having the majority of the votes was elected president. If there was a tie for vice president, the Senate elected the vice president. Each senator cast a vote, and it required a majority to be elected.

In 1804 the 12th Amendment made several changes in this procedure. Each elector was to cast two separate votes, one for president, the other for vice president. When no person received a majority, or a tie occurred, in the vote for president, then the House of Representatives chose the president from the three highest vote getters in the electoral college. Again, the representatives of each state voted as a state delegation and thus had one vote. The person having the majority of the votes was elected president. When no person received the majority, or a tie occurred, in the vote for vice president, the Senate elected the vice president from the top two vote getters in the electoral college. Each senator cast a vote, and it required a majority to be elected.

Because each state has the number of electors equal to its total membership in Congress, and each state is guaranteed at least one representative and two senators, no state will have fewer than three electors. The 23rd Amendment to the Constitution, which took effect in 1961, gives three electoral college votes to the residents of Washington D.C. Since the nation's capital is not part of any state, prior to that date, residents of Washington D.C. had no say in the selection of the president. The Constitution leaves it to the states *how* the electors shall be selected, and in early days they often were selected by the state legislatures. As time passed, and political parties emerged, people began to campaign to be selected as electors on the basis of their promise to vote for a specific presidential candidate. Eventually, electors were selected by the voters in each state.

Thus, we do not vote directly for the president or vice president. Instead, each party files a slate of electors committed to cast their votes (now called electoral votes) for the party's presidential and vice presidential candidates. When we mark our ballots for a particular person for president, what we really are doing is voting for the appropriate slate of electors. The winning candidate in each state, the one with the most votes whether or not these are more than half of all votes, receives *all* of that state's electoral votes because the winner's slate of electors is elected. Following each election, in December, each elector casts his or her official vote, and these are sent to the U.S. Senate where they are counted under the supervision of the vice president (of the previous administration) and reported to Congress. Once in a while an elector votes for someone other than the candidate he or she was pledged to support. In 2000, one of the electors chosen from Washington D.C. left the ballot blank, reducing Al Gore's electoral college vote from 267 to 266. The elector left the ballot blank to protest the fact that residents of Washington D.C. have no voting members in the U.S. Congress.

Although it takes a majority of electoral votes to be elected, at the state level it's winner-take-all. All of a state's electoral votes go to the candidate receiving the most votes. Maine and Nebraska use winner-take-all at the state level to assign two of their electors and winner-take-all at the congressional district to assign their remaining electors. Sometimes, candidates win a state's electors with less than a majority vote. In fact, a candidate only needs to win more votes than any other candidate on the ballot. This is winning by a **plurality** of the votes cast. Typically in U.S. presidential elections, almost all of the votes are cast for the Democratic or Republican presidential candidate. However, when a significant portion of the vote is cast for a third-party or independent candidate, a presidential candidate may win many of the electoral college votes by plurality victories in the states' popular vote. When this occurs in a number of states, the candidate winning the electoral college may have a plurality of the popular vote but not a majority of the popular vote. Presidents who receive less than half of the total popular vote are sometimes called "minority presidents." President Clinton won less than a majority of the popular vote in the 1992 and 1996 presidential elections due to the number of votes cast for third-party candidate Ross Perot.

Data File:	**STATES**
Task:	**Mapping**
➤ Variable 1:	**84) ELECTOR90**
➤ View:	**List: Rank**

RANK	CASE NAME	VALUE
1	California	54
2	New York	33
3	Texas	32
4	Florida	25
5	Pennsylvania	23
6	Illinois	22
7	Ohio	21
8	Michigan	18
9	New Jersey	15
10	North Carolina	14

Here we see the current distribution of electoral votes by state in 2000. California has 54 electoral votes, or 10 percent of the total. Next come New York (33), Texas (32), Florida (25), Pennsylvania (23), Illinois (22), and Ohio (21). In contrast, seven states have only 3 electoral votes and six have only 4. Put another way, the 13 least populous states have fewer electoral votes (45) among them than does California alone.

Every ten years, following each census, the House of Representatives is **reapportioned** as seats in the House are shifted to growing states. Reapportionment of the House automatically shifts electoral votes too. Consequently, the number of electoral votes shifts in response to shifts in the relative size of state populations.

Electoral college vote totals will change for some states by the 2004 presidential election. Results from the 2000 census show which states have gained more citizens and which states have lost citizens, or at least not have grown as fast. The 2000 census figures are used to reapportion the seats in the House of Representatives and thus adjust the electoral college votes for each state as well.

Data File: **STATES**
Task: **Mapping**
➤ Variable 1: **191) EC GAIN00**
➤ View: **Map**

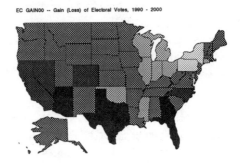

EC GAIN00 -- Gain (Loss) of Electoral Votes, 1990 - 2000

Two states, New York and Pennsylvania, will have two fewer electoral college votes in 2004 than they did in the 2000 presidential election. Eight other states, mostly in the Midwest, will lose one electoral college vote. On the other hand, four states—Arizona, Florida, Georgia, and Texas—will gain two electoral college votes, while four additional states will pick up one vote each. Once again the movement of Americans away from the "rust belt" of the Midwest and East to the Sunbelt of the South and West will alter the political clout of the states in presidential elections.

Your turn.

WORKSHEET

NAME:

COURSE:

DATE:

EXERCISE

10

REVIEW QUESTIONS

Based on the first part of this exercise, answer True or False to the following items:

a. Reapportionment is the process of adjusting seats in the House based on population shifts in the United States.   T   F

b. In case of a tie in electoral votes, the Senate selects the president.   T   F

c. No state may have fewer than three electoral votes.   T   F

d. "Minority president" refers to presidents who won because of their overwhelming support by racial and ethnic minority voters.   T   F

e. George W. Bush won the electoral college vote while losing the popular vote.   T   F

EXPLORIT QUESTIONS

1. It takes 270 electoral college votes to win an election. Although each state has at least three electoral college votes, the number of electoral college votes varies across the states.

> ➤ *Data File:* **STATES**
> ➤ *Task:* **Mapping**
> ➤ *Variable 1:* **84) ELECTOR90**
> ➤ *View:* **List: Rank**

a. How many states have 20 or more electoral college votes?   _____

b. How many states have 5 or fewer electoral college votes?   _____

2. Suppose you are the campaign manager for a presidential candidate. One of your tasks is to determine which voters you want to reach in the campaign. Remember, it is a majority vote in the electoral college, rather than a plurality victory in the popular vote, that ultimately determines the winner of the presidency. Thus, a winning campaign strategy requires a plan to garner 270 electoral college votes. One way to investigate candidate strategy is to see which states candidates visit during the fall campaign. No candidate can visit all 50 states in the crucial campaign months of September and October. Rather, candidates select states which they view as essential to an electoral college victory.

Exercise 10: Elections

> Data File: **STATES**
> Task: **Mapping**
> ➤ Variable 1:   **176) BS-VISITS**
> ➤ Variable 2:   **84) ELECTOR90**
> ➤ View: **MAP**

a. What is the Pearson's r between number of Bush visits to a state and
number of electoral college votes in a state?   r = _____

Some states consistently vote for one party's candidates in presidential elections. For example, Minnesota has voted for the Democratic presidential candidate in every presidential election since 1980. In contrast, Alabama, Alaska, and 14 other states consistently voted for the Republican party's candidate in the 1980–1996 presidential elections. Let's see if the competitiveness of a state influences presidential candidates' strategies. Variable COMPETITIV ranks the competitiveness of states based on their votes in the 1980–1996 presidential elections. States which always voted for the same party are listed as uncompetitive. States which supported one party's presidential candidate in all but one of the five elections are listed as somewhat competitive, and states which split their votes between the two parties are listed as very competitive.

> Data File: **STATES**
> Task: **Mapping**
> Variable 1:   **176) BS-VISITS**
> ➤ Variable 2:   **188) COMPETITIV**
> ➤ View: **MAP**

b. What is the Pearson's r between number of Bush visits to a state and
the competitiveness of a state?   r = _____

c. Based solely on these results, in what types of states would you advise your presidential candidate to spend a great deal of time and money campaigning? (circle one)

1. States with a large number of electoral college votes that have consistently supported your party's candidates in recent elections.

2. States with a large number of electoral college votes that have consistently supported the opposition party's candidates in recent elections.

3. States with a large number of electoral college votes that have split their support between the two parties in recent elections.

3. In 1992, Ross Perot ran as a third-party candidate for president and won almost 20 percent of the popular vote, yet he received no electoral college votes. Let's see how this happened.

> Data File: **STATES**
> Task: **Mapping**
> ➤ Variable 1:   **38) %PEROT 92**
> ➤ View: **List: Rank**

a. List Perot's top six states and the percentage he received in each state. (Ignore the third column for now.)

	STATE	PERCENT	NUMBER OF ELECTORAL COLLEGE VOTES
HIGHEST	_____	_____ %	_____
SECOND HIGHEST	_____	_____ %	_____
THIRD HIGHEST	_____	_____ %	_____
FOURTH HIGHEST	_____	_____ %	_____
FIFTH HIGHEST	_____	_____ %	_____
SIXTH HIGHEST	_____	_____ %	_____

To win a state, a candidate must win more votes than any other candidate. In a three-candidate race, the minimum total that could win a state would be 34 percent. This assumes that the two other candidates each received 33 percent of the vote. Of course, even though one candidate wins 34 percent of the vote, that candidate would still lose the state if a second candidate won more than 34 percent, for example 40 percent, while the third candidate won a smaller proportion of the vote, say 26 percent. Still, 34 percent is the minimum vote total that could win a state, so let's investigate that.

b. In how many states did Perot win at least 34 percent of the vote? _____

c. In how many states did Perot get less than 10 percent of the vote? _____

d. Which of the following statements better describes Perot's support in this election?

    1. Perot's vote was concentrated in a particular region.

    2. Perot's vote was relatively evenly spread across regions and states.

> Data File: **STATES**
> Task: **Mapping**
> ➤ Variable 1: **84) ELECTOR90**
> ➤ View: **List: Alpha**

Use this information to complete the third column of the preceding table (i.e., determine the number of electoral college votes for each of the states listed). Then answer the following two questions.

e. If Perot had won in these six states, how many electoral college votes would he have received? _____

f. Even though Perot won no electoral college votes, several analysts have argued that he had a significant impact on the outcome of the election. How is this possible?

4. In 1968, George Wallace ran as a third-party candidate for president and won 14 percent of the popular vote. He won 46 electoral college votes. Let's see how Wallace could win so many electoral college votes when Perot, with a higher percentage of the popular vote, won none.

> Data File: **STATES**
> Task: **Mapping**
> ➤ Variable 1: **54) %WALLACE68**
> ➤ View: **List: Rank**

a. List Wallace's top six states and the percentage he received in each state.

	STATE	PERCENT
HIGHEST	_____	_____ %
SECOND HIGHEST	_____	_____ %
THIRD HIGHEST	_____	_____ %
FOURTH HIGHEST	_____	_____ %
FIFTH HIGHEST	_____	_____ %
SIXTH HIGHEST	_____	_____ %

b. In how many states did Wallace win at least 34 percent of the vote? _____

c. In how many states did Wallace get less than 10 percent of the vote? _____

d. Which of the following statements better describes Wallace's support in this election?

1. Wallace's vote was concentrated in a particular region.
2. Wallace's vote was relatively evenly spread across regions and states.

Wallace won the electoral votes in his five highest states. In addition, he received one electoral college vote from North Carolina. (Remember that each electoral college vote is actually cast by an *individual* who was elected a member of a slate committed to a particular candidate. However, the individual is *legally free* to cast a vote for anyone.)

5. A third-party candidate, receiving 20 percent of the popular vote nationwide, can win electoral college votes

     a. by receiving an equal percentage of the popular vote in each state.

     b. by having support concentrated in a smaller number of states.

     c. under no circumstances.

6. Another time that a third-party vote can affect the outcome of an election is in a very close election. A third-party candidate may draw support away from one of the major party candidates to the extent that the major party candidate fails to garner enough votes in certain states to win those states' electoral college votes. In 2000, Ralph Nader, the Green Party candidate, may have played such a spoiler role against Al Gore. Of course, we cannot completely predict how Nader voters would have cast their ballots for anyone other than the Green Party. Some of Nader's voters may have simply stayed home and not voted in the presidential election. Others may have switched to another minor party candidate, and some may have preferred George W. Bush to Al Gore. Still, many commentators felt that Nader voters tended to prefer Gore to Bush. Let's first see how many states had extremely close margins of victories for one of the two major presidential candidates in 2000. The MARGINP variable gives the difference between the vote for Gore and Bush as a percent of all votes cast in a state. A low number indicates a very small margin of victory.

> *Data File:* **STATES**
> *Task:* **Mapping**
> ➤ *Variable 1:* **184) MARGINP**
> ➤ *View:* **List: Rank**

Florida had the closest margin of victory, with a listing of 0 percentage points in the data set. The official figure was 537 votes, or .009 percent of the votes cast in Florida. List the four other states where the difference in the vote margin was less than 1 percent of the votes cast.

	STATE	PERCENT
LOWEST	FLORIDA	0%
SECOND LOWEST	_____	_____%
THIRD LOWEST	_____	_____%
FOURTH LOWEST	_____	_____%
FIFTH LOWEST	_____	_____%

7. Now let's consider a scenario where all voters who cast their ballots for Ralph Nader instead voted for Al Gore. Would this have changed the outcome of the 2000 presidential election? By adding together the votes cast for Gore and Nader in each state, we can recalculate whether Gore or Bush won the plurality of the vote.

> Data File: **STATES**
> Task: **Mapping**
> ➤ Variable 1: **185) STATES '00**
> ➤ Variable 2: **189) GORENADER**
> ➤ View: **Map**

a. Two states that Bush won in 2000 would have gone to Gore if all of Nader's voters had switched to supporting Gore. Compare the light and dark states in the top map to the bottom map to see which two states could have been won by Gore.

	STATE	ELECTORAL COLLEGE VOTES
FIRST STATE	_____	_____
SECOND STATE	_____	_____

To see whether the switch of these two states to Gore would have changed the 2000 election outcome, find out the number of electoral college votes in the two states listed above.

> Data File: **STATES**
> Task: **Mapping**
> ➤ Variable 1: **84) ELECTOR90**
> ➤ View: **List: Alpha**

Add the total of the electoral college votes from these two states to the 266 electoral college votes Gore won based on his vote alone.

	ELECTORAL COLLEGE VOTES
b. TOTAL FROM TWO STATES LISTED ABOVE	_____
ORIGINAL GORE TOTAL	266
c. SUM FOR "HYPOTHETICAL GORE TOTAL"	_____

d. Would Gore have won the presidency with this hypothetical electoral
   college vote total?   Yes   No

e. How likely do you think it would have been for many of Nader's voters to have switched their
   support to Gore?

EXERCISE **11**

INTEREST GROUPS
AND PACS

*Politics has got so expensive that it takes lots of
money to even get beat with nowadays.*
                                    WILL ROGERS, 1931

Tasks: Mapping, Univariate, Cross-Tabulation
Data Files: NATIONS, GSS, HOUSE107

Quite often in politics elected public officials or candidates for political office attack "special interest groups" or "pressure groups," or they suggest that their opponents or critics are in league with such groups. What is the difference between a "special interest group," an "interest group," a "pressure group," and a "group of public-spirited citizens"? The answer a person gives to this question might very well depend on which side of an issue the person favors. People tend to view groups on the other side of an issue in negative terms, referring to them as "special interest groups" or "pressure groups." On the other hand, groups involved in political issues often tend to view themselves as citizens who are looking out for the public interest either directly or indirectly.

Here we will use the term "interest group" in a neutral fashion to refer to any group of people who share some political value and attempt to pursue that value in the political system. This shared political value might be economic (e.g., views on tax decreases, aid to education, minimum wage laws) or noneconomic (e.g., views on abortion, freedom of speech, the rights of defendants in court).

Two basic kinds of interest groups exist: *affinity groups*, which are unorganized publics sharing a particular condition or concern such as elderly people who feel that current Social Security payments are inadequate, and *organized groups* (such as the American Association of Retired Persons), which collect dues and use them to sustain professional staffs to influence both public opinion and public officials. Another example of an affinity group consists of people who share certain views about civil liberties. Not everyone who shares this set of views is part of an organized group, but an example of an organized group dealing with civil liberties is the American Civil Liberties Union.

If you think about affinity groups, you will recognize that most, if not all, Americans belong to an interest group and most of us belong to many. The problem is that we tend to define *our* interest groups as unselfish and in the general interest while opposing *other* people's interest groups as selfish and out to harm the rest of us.

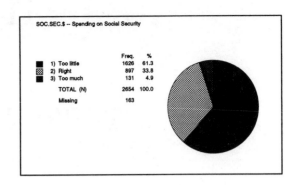

Data File:	**GSS**
➤ Task:	**Univariate**
➤ Primary Variable:	**31) SOC.SEC.$**
➤ View:	**Pie**

Here we see that over half (61.3 percent) of Americans think we are spending too little on Social Security. There can be little doubt that among those wanting an increase is an interest group that has become a favorite in political campaigning, variously referred to as "our neglected senior citizens" or as the "selfish Social Security lobby," depending on the candidate.

Data File:	**GSS**
➤ Task:	**Cross-tabulation**
➤ Row Variable:	**31) SOC.SEC.$**
➤ Column Variable:	**9) AGE**
➤ View:	**Table**
➤ Display:	**Column %**

SOC.SEC.$ by   AGE
Cramer's V: 0.086 **

		AGE					Missing	TOTAL
		Under 30	30 to 39	40 to 49	50 to 64	65 & over		
SOC.SEC.$	Too little	269	378	378	345	251	5	1621
		56.9%	66.5%	61.7%	64.6%	54.8%		61.3%
	Right	177	156	195	173	193	3	894
		37.4%	27.5%	31.8%	32.4%	42.1%		33.8%
	Too much	27	34	40	16	14	0	131
		5.7%	6.0%	6.5%	3.0%	3.1%		5.0%
	Missing	53	42	21	22	25	0	163
	TOTAL	473	568	613	534	458	8	2646
		100.0%	100.0%	100.0%	100.0%	100.0%		

Everyone knows that people on Social Security are militant about their rights and never think they are getting enough benefits. But in this case, what "everyone" knows, isn't so. People over 65 are least likely to think too little is being spent on Social Security.

Data File:	**GSS**
Task:	**Cross-tabulation**
➤ Row Variable:	**41) GUN LAW?**
➤ Column Variable:	**69) OWN GUN?**
➤ View:	**Table**
➤ Display:	**Column %**

GUN LAW?   by   OWN GUN?
Cramer's V: 0.231 **

		OWN GUN?		Missing	TOTAL
		Yes	No		
GUN LAW?	Favor	408	1057	14	1465
		69.4%	88.2%		82.0%
	Oppose	180	141	11	321
		30.6%	11.8%		18.0%
	Missing	15	33	958	1006
	TOTAL	588	1198	983	1786
		100.0%	100.0%		

Something else we all know is that gun owners bitterly oppose all gun-control legislation. But this table shows that isn't so. Here we see that 70 percent of gun owners favored a law requiring that a person obtain a police permit before buying a gun. It's not gun owners as an affinity interest group who oppose gun-control laws; rather, it is the organized interest group known as the National Rifle Association that "speaks on behalf of gun owners" in opposition to such laws.

These findings let us recognize something very important about interest groups—that organized interest groups may or may not represent the constituency for whom they claim to speak.

<table>
<tr><td colspan="2"></td><td colspan="6">GUN LAW?   by   SOC.SEC.$
Cramer's V: 0.095 **</td></tr>
</table>

Data File: **GSS**
Task: **Cross-tabulation**
Row Variable: **41) GUN LAW?**
➤ Column Variable: **31) SOC.SEC.$**
➤ View: **Table**
➤ Display: **Total %**

		SOC.SEC.$				
		Too little	Right	Too much	Missing	TOTAL
G U N L A W ?	Favor	904	438	53	84	1395
		52.8%	25.6%	3.1%		81.5%
	Oppose	171	124	22	15	317
		10.0%	7.2%	1.3%		18.5%
	Missing	551	335	56	64	1006
	TOTAL	1075	562	75	163	1712
		62.8%	32.8%	4.4%		

An extremely important point about memberships in interest groups is that the same person is usually included in a variety of such groups. Thus, a person might side with particular people on one issue and different people on another issue. Here we see that the views of people on Social Security overlap somewhat with their views on gun control (V = 0.095**). This time the instructions asked for the total percent to be listed in each cell of the table. The total percent is the number of respondents in each cell divided by the total number of respondents answering the two questions. Thus, 52.8 percent of the respondents to the 2000 GSS indicated that they wanted both tougher gun-control laws and more spending on Social Security. However, half of the sample had some other combination of answers. On another set of issues we might find that some of those who favor tougher gun-control laws might be on one side of the issue while another portion of those who favor tougher gun-control laws takes a different position on the second issue. People do not consistently line up on the same side of every issue.

This is important for the stability of a political system because it means that there are not just two permanent "sides" in political conflict. The coalitions for or against something can shift with the issue. A person who loses on one issue might win on another issue. This helps to reduce the overall conflict within society.

➤ Data File: **NATIONS**
➤ Task: **Mapping**
➤ Variable 1: **7) INTEREST G**
➤ View: **List: Rank**

RANK	CASE NAME	VALUE
1	Iceland	27
2	Netherlands	24
2	Norway	24
4	Latvia	23
4	United States	23
4	Finland	23
7	South Korea	20
8	Switzerland	18
8	Austria	18
8	Brazil	18

Organized interest groups are not peculiar to American politics. About 1 person in 4 belongs to an organized political interest group in Iceland, the Netherlands, Norway, the United States, Finland, and Latvia. That drops to 1 in 20 persons in Argentina, Spain, and Rumania, and to only 1 in 33 in Japan.

We noted earlier that organized interest groups may or may not accurately reflect the concerns and preferences of those they presume to represent. But, if this is so, why do politicians pay so much attention to organized interest groups? Because they are one of the sources of campaign funds.

A primary fact of life facing every elected official is that the next election is always just around the corner and it costs money to win elections. Since they are up for reelection every two years, many members of the House are never really able to cease campaigning, and perhaps the single most central aspect of campaigning is fund-raising.

> *Data File:* **HOUSE107**
> *Task:* **Univariate**
> *Primary Variable:* **21) CAMPAIGN $**
> *View:* **Pie**

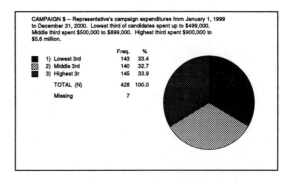

CAMPAIGN $ -- Representative's campaign expenditures from January 1, 1999 to December 31, 2000. Lowest third of candidates spent up to $499,000. Middle third spent $500,000 to $899,000. Highest third spent $900,000 to $5.6 million.

		Freq.	%
■	1) Lowest 3rd	143	33.4
▨	2) Middle 3rd	140	32.7
■	3) Highest 3r	145	33.9
	TOTAL (N)	428	100.0
	Missing	7	

More than two-thirds of the representatives spent at least $500,000 on their 2000 campaigns. The highest amount ($5.6 million) was spent by Richard Gephardt (D-MO), the minority leader in the 107th Congress. Representative William Jenkins (R-TN) spent the least amount of money on his campaign, $92,463, but he had no opponent. Representative Nick Smith (R-MI) spent the lowest amount ($152,467) for a candidate with an opponent. (His opponent, however, spent only $3,753.) On average, the typical winning candidate in the 2000 House elections spent $850,000.

> *Data File:* **HOUSE107**
> *Task:* **Univariate**
> *Primary Variable:* **27) $ PER VOTE**
> *View:* **Pie**

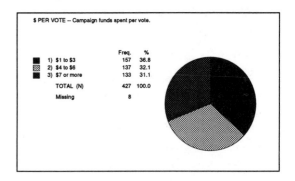

$ PER VOTE -- Campaign funds spent per vote.

		Freq.	%
■	1) $1 to $3	157	36.8
▨	2) $4 to $6	137	32.1
■	3) $7 or more	133	31.1
	TOTAL (N)	427	100.0
	Missing	8	

Another way to examine campaign spending is on the basis of the amount spent for each vote the candidate received. Nearly one-third of the representatives spent at least $7 per vote. Now let's see where all of this money comes from.

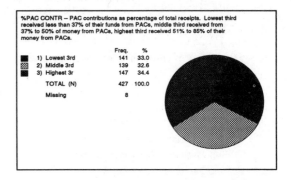

Data File: **HOUSE107**
Task: **Univariate**
➤ Primary Variable: **24) %PAC CONTR**
➤ View: **Pie**

Much of the campaign money came from political action committees—PACs. Almost any organization—a corporation, a union, a professional association, a neighborhood club, or even a bowling team—can create its own PAC and then raise funds from member contributions or even by seeking funds from nonmembers. Over a third of the members of the House received more than half of their total funding from PACs. Keep in mind that individual contributors are still the largest source of campaign funds, providing about half of all campaign funds for House races. However, PACs are the second largest source, accounting for about one-third of all campaign funds. PACs also can give larger contributions, up to $5,000 per candidate, and there are a large number of PACs, nearly 4,500.

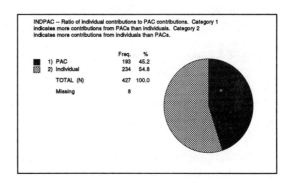

Data File: **HOUSE107**
Task: **Univariate**
➤ Primary Variable: **26) INDPAC**
➤ View: **Pie**

Here we see that 45.2 percent of the members of the 107th House received a larger proportion of their campaign funds from PACs than from individuals. Yet, 54.8 percent received a greater proportion of their campaign money from individuals than from PACs. Let's explore which representatives received a higher level of support from PACs.

Data File: **HOUSE107**
➤ Task: **Cross-tabulation**
➤ Row Variable: **24) %PAC CONTR**
➤ Column Variable: **14) INCUMBENT**
➤ View: **Table**
➤ Display: **Column %**

%PAC CONTR by INCUMBENT
Cramer's V: 0.308 **

		INCUMBENT		
		Incumbent	New rep.	TOTAL
%PAC CONTR	Lowest 3rd	109	32	141
		28.4%	74.4%	33.0%
	Middle 3rd	129	10	139
		33.6%	23.3%	32.6%
	Highest 3r	146	1	147
		38.0%	2.3%	34.4%
	Missing	1	7	8
	TOTAL	384	43	427
		100.0%	100.0%	

Representatives who have served in the House in a prior session (i.e., incumbents) received a higher proportion of their campaign funds from PACs than did new representatives. This reflects the strategy of many PACs to contribute more heavily to incumbents seeking reelection. By backing incumbents, who are mostly reelected, PACs gain greater access to representatives in the following session of Congress.

Data File:	**HOUSE107**
Task:	**Cross-tabulation**
Row Variable:	**24) %PAC CONTR**
➤ Column Variable:	**13) # TERMS**
➤ View:	**Table**
➤ Display:	**Column %**

%PAC CONTR   by   # TERMS
Cramer's V: 0.274 **

%PAC CONTR	# TERMS				
		One	2-4 terms	5 or more	Missing	TOTAL
Lowest 3rd	32	58	51	0	141
	74.4%	35.8%	23.1%		33.1%
Middle 3rd	10	65	64	0	139
	23.3%	40.1%	29.0%		32.6%
Highest 3r	1	39	106	1	146
	2.3%	24.1%	48.0%		34.3%
Missing	7	0	1	0	8
TOTAL	43	162	221	1	426
	100.0%	100.0%	100.0%		

Here we see that the PAC strategy is extended to giving greater support to more senior members of the House. Nearly half (48.0 percent) of the representatives who have served five or more terms fell into the highest third for receiving PAC contributions. In part, PACs want to contribute to these more senior members because these representatives are more likely to hold powerful positions in Congress as party leaders, committee chairs, or subcommittee chairs.

Is there a party difference between representatives in their level of PAC contributions? On the one hand, we might expect that Republican representatives received more contributions from PACs, because Republicans were the majority party in the prior Congress and held more of the powerful positions. On the other hand, we might expect that Democratic representatives received a greater proportion of their campaign fund from PACs, because the Democratic party draws a greater proportion of its support from less wealthy Americans who are less able to contribute money to candidates. In contrast, the Republican party in the electorate tends to be wealthier and more able to contribute to Republican candidates, reducing the need for Republican candidates to rely only on PAC contributions.

Data File:	**HOUSE107**
Task:	**Cross-tabulation**
Row Variable:	**24) %PAC CONTR**
➤ Column Variable:	**11) PARTY**
➤ View:	**Table**
➤ Display:	**Column %**

%PAC CONTR   by   PARTY
Cramer's V: 0.237 **

%PAC CONTR	PARTY			
		Democrat	Republican	Missing	TOTAL
Lowest 3rd	54	86	1	140
	25.8%	39.8%		32.9%
Middle 3rd	59	79	1	138
	28.2%	36.6%		32.5%
Highest 3r	96	51	0	147
	45.9%	23.6%		34.6%
Missing	2	6	0	8
TOTAL	209	216	2	425
	100.0%	100.0%		

The second hypothesis is more accurate. Democrats received a higher proportion of their campaign funds from PACs than did Republicans. While only one-quarter (23.6 percent) of Republicans fell in the group receiving the highest proportion of their funds from PACs, nearly half (45.9 percent) of Democrats did so.

<table>
<tr><td rowspan="2" align="right">Data File:</td><td>**HOUSE107**</td></tr>
</table>

Data File: **HOUSE107**
Task: **Cross-tabulation**
➤ Row Variable: **25) %IND CONTR**
➤ Column Variable: **11) PARTY**
➤ View: **Table**
➤ Display: **Column %**

%IND CONTR   by   PARTY
Cramer's V: 0.179 **

| | | PARTY | | | |
		Democrat	Republican	Missing	TOTAL
%IND CONTR	Lowest 3rd	87	54	0	141
		41.6%	24.9%		33.1%
	Middle 3rd	59	75	1	134
		28.2%	34.6%		31.5%
	Highest 3r	63	88	1	151
		30.1%	40.6%		35.4%
	Missing	2	5	0	7
	TOTAL	209	217	2	426
		100.0%	100.0%		

Finally, we see that Republican representatives received a higher proportion of their campaign funds from individual contributors.

Your turn.

NAME:

COURSE:

DATE:

REVIEW QUESTIONS

Based on the first part of this exercise, answer True or False to the following items:

a. Most gun owners oppose gun-control legislation.   T   F

b. Only a small minority of Americans belong to an affinity interest group.   T   F

c. Organized interest groups exist in only a few countries.   T   F

d. The stability of the American political system is aided by the fact that there are no permanent "sides" in political conflict—the coalition for or against something can shift with the particular issue involved.   T   F

e. Democratic representatives received a larger proportion of their campaign funds from PACs than Republican representatives did.   T   F

f. Representatives who have served more terms received a higher proportion of their campaign funds from PACs.   T   F

EXPLORIT QUESTIONS

1. As indicated before, older people constitute an affinity group. During the 2000 election campaign, both major party candidates made appeals to the elderly on the basis of Social Security issues and medical care issues. However, in the first part of this exercise, we found that contrary to what we might assume, people over 65 were the least likely to think increases in Social Security were needed. Let's now see whether older people were more likely to want the government to help with medical costs.

> ➤ *Data File:* **GSS**
> ➤ *Task:* **Cross-tabulation**
> ➤ *Row Variable:* **77) GOV.MED.**
> ➤ *Column Variable:* **9) AGE**
> ➤ *View:* **Table**
> ➤ *Display:* **Column %**

Make sure to read the variable description for GOV.MED. and then answer True or False to the following items.

    a. People 65 and older were the ones who most favored government help with medical costs.   T   F

    b. Generally, those under retirement age (65) favor government help with medical costs.   T   F

2.   Let's examine some other affinity groups, starting with the residents of big cities.

> Data File: **GSS**
> Task: **Cross-tabulation**
> ➤ Row Variable: **26) BIG CITY$**
> ➤ Column Variable: **19) URBAN?**
> ➤ View: **Table**
> ➤ Display: **Column %**

    a. The majority of big-city residents think the government is spending too little on the problems of big cities.   T   F

    b. Pretty much everyone thinks too little is being spent on big-city problems, regardless of where they live.   T   F

3.   African Americans form an affinity group.

> Data File: **GSS**
> Task: **Cross-tabulation**
> ➤ Row Variable: **27) BLACK$**
> ➤ Column Variable: **7) RACE**
> ➤ View: **Table**
> ➤ Display: **Column %**

Most African Americans think too little is being spent on improving the conditions of Blacks.   T   F

4.   There are various kinds of religious-political groups that constitute both affinity groups (e.g., those who believe in prayer in public schools versus those who don't) and organized groups (the Christian Coalition, People for the American Way, Bread for the World, American Jewish Committee, etc.). Let's see whether views on prayer and Bible reading in the public schools are affected by how religious people consider themselves to be.

> Data File: **GSS**
> Task: **Cross-tabulation**
> ➤ Row Variable: **45) SCH.PRAY**
> ➤ Column Variable: **15) RELPERSN**
> ➤ View: **Table**
> ➤ Display: **Column %**

a. People who consider themselves to be very religious are the ones who most support prayer in public schools.   T   F

b. A majority of those who are not at all religious oppose prayer in public schools.   T   F

5. Those elected to Congress often represent affinity groups within their district. Let's look at the racial/ethnic composition of congressional districts.

> ➤ *Data File:* **HOUSE107**
> ➤ *Task:* **Univariate**
> ➤ *Primary Variable:* **16) DIS AFRAM%**
> ➤ *View:* **Pie**

a. In 6 percent of the congressional districts, half the population or more is African American.   T   F

b. In over 50 percent of the congressional districts, less than 6 percent of the population is African American.   T   F

> *Data File:* **HOUSE107**
> *Task:* **Univariate**
> ➤ *Primary Variable:* **17) DIST HISP%**
> ➤ *View:* **Pie**

c. In about 4 percent of the congressional districts, half the population or more is Hispanic.   T   F

6. Now let's see to what extent congresspersons are from the same racial/ethnic groups as their constituents.

> *Data File:* **HOUSE107**
> ➤ *Task:* **Cross-tabulation**
> ➤ *Row Variable:* **5) RACE/ETHNI**
> ➤ *Column Variable:* **16) DIS AFRAM%**
> ➤ *View:* **Table**
> ➤ *Display:* **Column %**

Copy the *second row* of the percentaged table. (Just ignore the message about a potential significance problem; this is not actually a problem here since we are using all 435 representatives rather than a sample of representatives.)

	50 OR +	15%–49.9%	6%–14.9%	0–5.9%
a. %AFRICAN-AM	_____%	_____%	_____%	_____%

Data File: **HOUSE107**
Task: **Cross-tabulation**
Row Variable: **5) RACE/ETHNI**
➤ Column Variable: **17) DIST HISP%**
➤ View: **Table**
➤ Display: **Column %**

Copy the *third row* of the percentaged table.

	50% OR +	10%–49.9%	3%–9.9%	UNDER 3%
b. %HISPANIC	_____%	_____%	_____%	_____%

c. Circle the number of the statement that best summarizes the results of these two tables.

1. Congresspersons are very likely to share the race or ethnicity of their constituents.
2. The racial and ethnic composition of a district appears to have little effect on the race or ethnicity of the person elected to Congress.
3. Race/ethnicity appears to have an effect in Hispanic districts, but not in African American districts, suggesting that language differences may be more important than racial differences.

7. In addition to affinity groups, there are organized groups who work to influence public opinion and public officials. Many groups track bills in Congress that affect their constituencies and rate members of Congress based on their support of or opposition to particular bills. Let's look at one of these ratings. The American Civil Liberties Union (ACLU) rated members of Congress on their votes on several different bills.

Let's look at the effect of the person's party on this rating.

Data File: **HOUSE107**
Task: **Cross-tabulation**
➤ Row Variable: **28) ACLU RATE**
➤ Column Variable: **11) PARTY**
➤ View: **Table**
➤ Display: **Column %**

Copy the *third* row of the percentaged table.

	DEMOCRAT	REPUBLICAN
a. %HIGH	_____%	_____%

b. What is the value of V for this table? V = _____

c. Is V statistically significant? Yes   No

    d. Republican and Democratic members of Congress are equally likely to get high
       ratings from the ACLU.   T   F

8.   While the ACLU focuses on one area (civil liberties issues), some organized interest groups concern themselves with a broad spectrum of political issues. For example, on the conservative end of the spectrum, the American Conservative Union (ACU) rates members of Congress in terms of a wide variety of issues. Let's see how the political party affiliations of representatives relate to the ACU ratings.

>   *Data File:* **HOUSE107**
>   *Task:* **Cross-tabulation**
> ➤ *Row Variable:* **29) ACU RATE**
> ➤ *Column Variable:* **11) PARTY**
>   ➤ *View:* **Table**
>   ➤ *Display:* **Column %**

Make sure to read the variable description for ACU RATE and then answer the following questions.

    a. What is the value of Cramer's V for this table?   V = _____

    b. Is V statistically significant?   Yes   No

    c. Republican members of Congress are overwhelmingly conservative by the
       ACU ratings, and Democratic members are overwhelmingly liberal.   T   F

    d. The ACU ratings of representatives tend to be high (conservative) or low
       (liberal) rather than in between.   T   F

9.   Let's see whether liberals or conservatives have the advantage in attracting PAC money.

>   *Data File:* **HOUSE107**
>   *Task:* **Cross-tabulation**
> ➤ *Row Variable:* **24) %PAC CONTR**
> ➤ *Column Variable:* **29) ACU RATE**
>   ➤ *View:* **Table**
>   ➤ *Display:* **Column %**

    a. What is the value of Cramer's V for this table?   V = _____

    b. Is V statistically significant?   Yes   No

    c. Which group received the highest percentage of its campaign funds
       from PACs? (Circle one.)   Liberals

                                                 Moderates

                                         Conservatives

Part IV

INSTITUTIONS

Everyone talks about "the government." It's too big, too expensive, too conservative, too intrusive, too unresponsive—but, what *is* the government? Is it politicians, bureaucrats, judges, elected officials, or what? In the United States, it is all of these things.

The American government consists of three branches, or institutions: the legislative, the executive, and the judicial. The first consists of the Senate and the House of Representatives. The primary purpose of the legislative branch is to *enact* laws. The executive branch is headed by the president and includes all of the millions of employees who staff the government agencies. The primary purpose of the executive branch is to *administer* the laws. The judicial branch of government consists of federal courts, headed by the Supreme Court. Its primary purpose is to *interpret and apply* the laws.

In the next four exercises you will explore the institutions of our government.

THE CONGRESS

All legislative Powers herein granted shall be vested in a Congress of the United States. . .

ARTICLE I, UNITED STATES
CONSTITUTION

Tasks: Mapping, Univariate, Cross-Tabulation, Historical Trends
Data Files: STATES, HOUSE107, HISTORY, GSS

This table shows the number of members of the U.S. House of Representatives from each state beginning in 2003. California has the most, 53. Texas is second highest with 32, just barely ahead of New York with 29, followed by Florida (25), Pennsylvania (19), and Illinois (19).

➤ *Data File:* **STATES**
➤ *Task:* **Mapping**
➤ *Variable 1:* **192) HOUSE03**
➤ *View:* **List: Rank**

RANK	CASE NAME	VALUE
1	California	53
2	Texas	32
3	New York	29
4	Florida	25
5	Pennsylvania	19
5	Illinois	19
7	Ohio	18
8	Michigan	15
9	New Jersey	13
9	North Carolina	13

Membership in the House is based on population, so the more populous states have the most members. Because the number of seats in the House has been fixed at 435, and because states often grow or decline and their populations change relative to one another, seats are reapportioned every ten years. Reapportionment takes place the year after the census and goes into effect in the next election. The reapportionment from the 2000 census (listed above) starts with the 2002 elections. However, no state, no matter how small its population, may be denied at least one representative.

➤ *Data File:* **HISTORY**
➤ *Task:* **Historical Trends**
➤ *Variable:* **15) APPORTION**

Population Per Representative

In 1790, each U.S. representative represented about 34,000 people. As the nation's population grew, the number of representatives increased until it was decided that no more representatives would be added. Thus, each representative today represents about 600,000 people.

In the following discussion, we'll look at certain features of the House of Representatives and use the members of the 107th Congress (elected in November 2000) to demonstrate these features.

➤ *Data File:* **HOUSE107**
➤ *Task:* **Univariate**
➤ *Primary Variable:* **11) PARTY**
➤ *View:* **Pie**

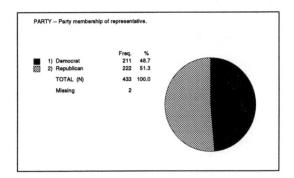

The first feature to note is that the House is currently split fairly evenly between Republicans and Democrats. Up until the 1994 election, Democrats had outnumbered Republicans in the House for 40 years—by substantial margins for most of that time. Then the 1994 election dramatically shifted power to the Republican Party. In the 104th Congress (1995–1996), Republicans outnumbered Democrats 235 to 199. In the 105th Congress (1997–1998), Republicans continued to outnumber Democrats 230 to 204. In the 106th Congress (1998–2000), Republicans continued to outnumber Democrats but only by a margin of 223 to 211. The 2000 elections resulted in a similar 222 to 211 margin.

Note that the numbers of Democrats and Republicans do not add up to 435. The 107th Congress had two independents: Bernard Sanders of Vermont and Virgil Goode of Virginia. These two representatives will be excluded from any analysis that compares political party with voting on House bills. Also, on almost any bill some representatives do not vote. Thus, the number of ayes and nays often does not add up to 435. Finally, during the two-year session of Congress a tiny number of representatives resign their position or die. New representatives are selected in special elections. The HOUSE107 data set includes the replacement representatives, who obviously did not vote on the bills considered prior to their election.

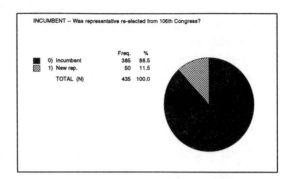

INCUMBENT -- Was representative re-elected from 106th Congress?

		Freq.	%
■	0) Incumbent	385	88.5
▨	1) New rep.	50	11.5
	TOTAL (N)	435	100.0

A second feature of Congress is the power of incumbency. We see here that 88.5 percent of the representatives in the 107th Congress were incumbents who were reelected. Thus, once a representative wins election to the House, the probability is extremely high that he or she can get reelected. This probability is even higher than it first appears, because some of the representatives in the previous Congress simply retired and did not run for reelection. In the elections of 2000, more than 400 House members chose to run for reelection and over 98 percent of them won.

Let's use the Second Congressional District in Indiana as a case study. In the November 2000 election, Mike Pence (a conservative Republican) won this congressional seat in a three-way contest against a conservative Democrat and another conservative Republican who ran as an Independent after failing to win the Republican nomination. Now that Pence has won his first election, how long will he be able to stay in Congress? He will probably stay in Congress until

- he decides to run for a different office—as did his predecessor (David McIntosh), who gave up the seat to make an unsuccessful run for the governor's office; or

- he decides to retire—as did his predecessor's predecessor (Phil Sharp); or

- he gets swept away by political events—as his predecessor's predecessor's predecessor (David Dennis) did.

Let's trace this sequence back to 1974 when David Dennis, a conservative Republican, was the representative in this area. Representative Dennis had served a number of terms and seemed destined to serve for a long time to come. However, he was swept away by national events—the Watergate scandal and his continuing defense of President Nixon long after many other Republicans in Congress decided that Nixon should resign or be impeached. Representative Dennis's opponent in 1974 was Phil Sharp, a moderate Democrat who had twice before run against Dennis. This time, Phil Sharp won—as did a number of other Democratic congressional candidates across the country whose Republican opponents were hurt by the Watergate scandal.

Despite winning initially because of Watergate, Representative Sharp won reelection nine more times before deciding to retire. How did a moderate Democrat win reelection in a fairly conservative, Republican district? First, he took moderate stands on many of the issues and conservative stands on some. Second, he provided a great number of constituency services. Third, given the short two-year term of representatives, Representative Sharp—like many representatives are forced to do—carried on a virtually constant campaign and outdid his opponents. Fourth, in campaign messages and in debates with his opponents, Sharp had the insider's advantage—knowledge of the workings of Congress, bills that had been considered, and so on.

When Sharp retired, the district again elected a conservative Republican, David McIntosh. In 1994, as indicated previously, events were sweeping away a number of incumbent Democrats (but no incumbent Republican lost in 1994). The country elected a number of additional Republicans to Congress and switched power from the Democrats to the Republicans. Representative McIntosh was easily reelected several times, but he decided in 2000 to run for governor. That's when Mike Pence (who had twice run against Representative Sharp) ran and won.

<table>
<tr><td></td><td colspan="5">EC_STIMUL by PARTY
Cramer's V: 0.953 **</td></tr>
</table>

Data File: **HOUSE107**
➤ *Task:* **Cross-tabulation**
➤ *Row Variable:* **31) EC_STIMUL**
➤ *Column Variable:* **11) PARTY**
➤ *View:* **Table**
➤ *Display:* **Column %**

EC_STIMUL		Democrat	Republican	Missing	TOTAL
	No	195	0	1	195
		95.1%	0.0%		46.4%
	Yes	10	215	1	225
		4.9%	100.0%		53.6%
	Missing	6	7	0	13
	TOTAL	205	215	2	420
		100.0%	100.0%		

Another feature of Congress is that party affiliation is a very important determinant of how representatives vote on many bills. While there are many routine, noncontroversial bills in Congress on which Republicans and Democrats are not different from one another, there is a substantial percentage of bills that find a majority of Republicans on one side and a majority of Democrats on the other side. Here we see that almost all Democrats voted against this tax bill and every Republican voted for it. The differences between Democrats and Republicans are not this sharp on most bills, but there are definite patterns. In a previous exercise, we examined American Civil Liberties Union ratings of members of Congress and we examined some American Conservative Union (ACU) ratings. Let's now examine the liberal Americans for Democratic Action (ADA) ratings of members of Congress by party.

ADA RATE by PARTY
Cramer's V: 0.929 **

Data File: **HOUSE107**
Task: **Cross-tabulation**
➤ *Row Variable:* **30) ADA RATE**
➤ *Column Variable:* **11) PARTY**
➤ *View:* **Table**
➤ *Display:* **Column %**

ADA RATE		Democrat	Republican	Missing	TOTAL
	Conservati	1	197	1	198
		0.5%	90.4%		46.3%
	Moderate	39	21	0	60
		18.6%	9.6%		14.0%
	Liberal	170	0	1	170
		81.0%	0.0%		39.7%
	Missing	1	4	0	5
	TOTAL	210	218	2	428
		100.0%	100.0%		

If you read the variable description, you see that we have categorized members of Congress in terms of ADA scores as follows. Representatives whose scores are 0 to 24 percent are classified as conservatives. Those whose scores are 25 percent to 75 percent are classified as middle of the road. Those whose scores are 76 percent to 100 percent are classified as liberals. Given this classification, we see that 80 percent of Democrats are rated as liberal and 90 percent of Republicans are rated as conservative. If we were to use the American Conservative Union ratings, the results would be similar.

		ACU RATE				
		Liberal	Moderate	Conservati	Missing	TOTAL
CAMPAIGN R	No	4	19	161	4	184
		2.5%	21.8%	93.6%		43.6%
	Yes	159	68	11	2	238
		97.5%	78.2%	6.4%		56.4%
	Missing	0	1	5	1	7
	TOTAL	163	87	172	7	422
		100.0%	100.0%	100.0%		

CAMPAIGN R   by   ACU RATE
Cramer's V: 0.849 **

Data File: **HOUSE107**
Task: **Cross-tabulation**
➤ Row Variable: **42) CAMPAIGN R**
➤ Column Variable: **29) ACU RATE**
➤ View: **Table**
➤ Display: **Column %**

Interest groups such as the ADA or the ACU base their ratings of members of Congress on how representatives vote on bills. These ratings are also highly predictive of how representatives will vote on other bills that concern the general liberal-conservative dimension. Here, for example, we see that (using categories based on the American Conservative Union ratings) almost all liberals voted for this bill reforming campaign finances and almost all conservatives voted against it.

Data File: **HOUSE107**
➤ Task: **Univariate**
➤ Primary Variable: **30) ADA RATE**
➤ View: **Bar Freq.**

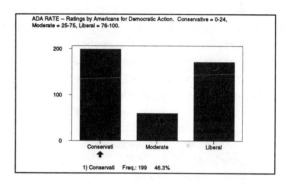

The next feature of Congress that we want to explore is whether members of Congress are more ideologically split than the general public is. We need to emphasize that we cannot directly and completely answer this question with the results used here, but we can explore it. Look at the distribution of ADA scores for all members of the House of Representatives. Even though the middle-of-the-road category includes scores from 25 percent to 75 percent, only one-fifth of the representatives are in the ideologically middle category. For exploratory comparison, we can look at the ideological self-classifications of the general public.

➤ Data File: **GSS**
➤ Task: **Univariate**
➤ Primary Variable: **23) LIB./CONS.**
➤ View: **Bar Freq.**

In the general public, we see that the biggest group is the middle group, those who classified themselves as moderates. While there are serious limitations in comparing the House results with these general public results, a look at the two distributions does support the idea that ideological differences among U.S. representatives are sharper than ideological differences within the general public.

> *Data File:* **HOUSE107**
> > *Task:* **Cross-tabulation**
> > *Row Variable:* **29) ACU RATE**
> > *Column Variable:* **4) SEX**
> > *View:* **Table**
> > *Display:* **Column %**

ACU RATE   by   SEX
Cramer's V: 0.276 **

| | | SEX | | |
		Male	Female	TOTAL
ACU RATE	Liberal	121	42	163
		32.8%	71.2%	38.1%
	Moderate	80	8	88
		21.7%	13.6%	20.6%
	Conservati	168	9	177
		45.5%	15.3%	41.4%
	Missing	7	0	7
	TOTAL	369	59	428
		100.0%	100.0%	

Another feature of Congress is that the background characteristics of representatives can also affect how they vote. So far we have good indications that members of Congress are usually either fairly liberal or fairly conservative and that these ideological differences are related to party affiliation (Democrats are liberal and Republicans are conservative). Here we see that gender is also related to how representatives vote: Female representatives are more liberal than male representatives are. Is this because women are more likely to be Democrats? Let's check.

> *Data File:* **HOUSE107**
> > *Task:* **Cross-tabulation**
> > *Row Variable:* **11) PARTY**
> > *Column Variable:* **4) SEX**
> > *View:* **Table**
> > *Display:* **Column %**

PARTY   by   SEX
Cramer's V: 0.178 **

| | | SEX | | |
		Male	Female	TOTAL
PARTY	Democrat	169	42	211
		45.2%	71.2%	48.7%
	Republican	205	17	222
		54.8%	28.8%	51.3%
	Missing	2	0	2
	TOTAL	374	59	433
		100.0%	100.0%	

We see here that a majority of women in Congress are Democrats and a majority of men are Republicans. So, the party difference might account for why women are more liberal than men in Congress. Let's see whether women are more liberal than men *within* the parties.

> *Data File:* **HOUSE107**
> > *Task:* **Cross-tabulation**
> > *Row Variable:* **29) ACU RATE**
> > *Column Variable:* **4) SEX**
> > *Control Variable:* **11) PARTY (Democrat)**
> > *View:* **Table**
> > *Display:* **Column %**

ACU RATE   by   SEX
Controls: PARTY: Democrat
Cramer's V: 0.248 **
Warning: Potential significance problem. Check row and column totals.

| | | SEX | | |
		Male	Female	TOTAL
ACU RATE	Liberal	120	41	161
		71.4%	97.6%	76.7%
	Moderate	44	1	45
		26.2%	2.4%	21.4%
	Conservati	4	0	4
		2.4%	0.0%	1.9%
	Missing	1	0	1
	TOTAL	168	42	210
		100.0%	100.0%	

The option for selecting a control variable is located on the same screen you use to select other variables. For this example, select 11) PARTY as a control variable and then click [OK] to continue as usual. Separate tables showing the relationship between the ACU ratings and gender will be shown for Democrats and Republicans.

By specifying PARTY as a control variable, we will obtain two tables: one table for Democrats and one for Republicans. The first table is for Democrats. Among Democrats, we see that 97.6 percent of women are liberals, which is higher than the 71.4 percent of men who are liberals. Now let's look at the Republican table. We do this by clicking the right arrow under the phrase "Control 1 of 2" on the left side of the screen.

Data File:	**HOUSE107**
Task:	**Cross-tabulation**
Row Variable:	**29) ACU RATE**
Column Variable:	**4) SEX**
➤ Control Variable:	**11) PARTY (Republican)**
➤ View:	**Table**
➤ Display:	**Column %**

ACU RATE   by   SEX
Controls: PARTY: Republican
Cramer's V: 0.285 **
Warning: Potential significance problem. Check row and column totals.

ACU RATE	SEX		
	Male	Female	TOTAL
Liberal	0	1	1
	0.0%	5.9%	0.5%
Moderate	36	7	43
	18.1%	41.2%	19.9%
Conservati	163	9	172
	81.9%	52.9%	79.6%
Missing	6	0	6
TOTAL	199	17	216
	100.0%	100.0%	

Among Republicans, we see that while there is only one liberal (a woman), a higher percentage of women than men are in the middle category. As a result, 81.9 percent of the male Republicans are conservatives, but only 52.9 percent of women are in the conservative category.

Thus, among both Democrats and Republicans, women in Congress are more liberal (or less conservative) than men are. Now let's examine the effects of region on voting behavior.

Data File:	**HOUSE107**
Task:	**Cross-tabulation**
➤ Row Variable:	**47) NUCLEAR**
➤ Column Variable:	**15) REGION**
➤ View:	**Table**
➤ Display:	**Column %**

NUCLEAR   by   REGION
Cramer's V: 0.370 **

NUCLEAR	REGION				
	East	Midwest	South	West	TOTAL
No	31	22	15	49	117
	36.0%	22.2%	10.2%	53.8%	27.7%
Yes	55	77	132	42	306
	64.0%	77.8%	89.8%	46.2%	72.3%
Missing	2	6	2	2	12
TOTAL	86	99	147	91	423
	100.0%	100.0%	100.0%	100.0%	

Note: Before selecting the variables for this analysis, it would be a good idea to click the [Clear All] option to clear all the previous analysis, including the control variable.

Here we see that region can affect how representatives vote on particular issues. In this situation, Southern representatives were the most supportive of storing nuclear waste in Nevada, while western representatives were the most opposed. Sometimes there has been a coalition (the "conservative coalition") of Republicans and some Southern Democrats against non-Southern Democrats. Does this coalition still exist now that Republicans control Congress? Let's examine votes on this bill broken down by three categories: Democrats, Southern Democrats, and Republicans.

Data File: **HOUSE107**
Task: **Cross-tabulation**
Row Variable: **47) NUCLEAR**
➤ *Column Variable:* **12) SOUTH DEM**
➤ *View:* **Table**
➤ *Display:* **Column %**

NUCLEAR   by   SOUTH DEM
Cramer's V: 0.577 **

| | SOUTH DEM | | | | |
	Democrat	S.Democrat	Republican	Missing	TOTAL
No	91	12	13	1	116
	62.3%	20.3%	6.0%		27.6%
Yes	55	47	203	1	305
	37.7%	79.7%	94.0%		72.4%
Missing	5	1	6	0	12
TOTAL	146	59	216	2	421
	100.0%	100.0%	100.0%		

A strong majority of Southern Democrats (79.7 percent) and a strong majority of Republicans (94.0 percent) supported this bill while a majority of non-Southern Democrats (62.3 percent) opposed the bill. Thus, the "conservative coalition" is still very much alive in Congress.

Politics concerns making decisions about matters over which there is conflict and disagreement. Thus, many bills in Congress are passed with a majority of Democrats on one side and a majority of Republicans on the other side. However, a final feature of Congress that we want to stress is that the members of Congress sometimes reach a consensus or nearly a consensus. There are several bills included in the HOUSE107 file in which substantial majorities of both parties voted together. Let's finish by looking at the distribution of votes on a bill, taken after the terrorist attacks of 9/11, to allow public schools to post the words "God Bless America."

Data File: **HOUSE107**
➤ *Task:* **Univariate**
➤ *Primary Variable:* **40) GOD BLESS**
➤ *View:* **Pie**

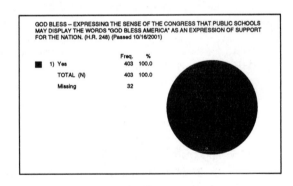

GOD BLESS -- EXPRESSING THE SENSE OF THE CONGRESS THAT PUBLIC SCHOOLS MAY DISPLAY THE WORDS "GOD BLESS AMERICA" AS AN EXPRESSION OF SUPPORT FOR THE NATION. (H.R. 248) (Passed 10/16/2001)

	Freq.	%
■ 1) Yes	403	100.0
TOTAL (N)	403	100.0
Missing	32	

How's that for a concensus? Every representative who voted on this bill voted for it.

Your turn.

Part IV: Institutions

NAME:

COURSE:

DATE:

REVIEW QUESTIONS

Based on the first part of this exercise, answer True or False to the following items:

a. In the earlier history of the United States, as the population increased the number of members in the House of Representatives increased.   T   F

b. Republicans have outnumbered Democrats in the House since the elections of 1952.   T   F

c. In the 107th Congress (2001– 2002), Republicans outnumber Democrats in the House.   T   F

d. If a person gets elected to Congress, the probability is roughly 90 percent that he or she will get reelected the next time.   T   F

e. Political party affiliation is only weakly related to how members vote on bills in the House of Representatives.   T   F

f. Democratic members of Congress are very likely to be liberal, and Republican members are very likely to be conservative.   T   F

g. In the House of Representatives, women are more conservative than men are.   T   F

h. The "conservative coalition" in Congress consists of Republicans and Southern Democrats.   T   F

EXPLORIT QUESTIONS

1. You have seen that incumbents have a powerful advantage in getting reelected. Does incumbency also affect the margin by which the representative wins?

▷ Data File: **HOUSE107**
▷ Task: **Cross-tabulation**
▷ Row Variable: **20) % OF VOTE**
▷ Column Variable: **14) INCUMBENT**
▷ View: **Table**
▷ Display: **Column %**

a. Fill in the percentages in the following table.

	INCUMBENT	NEW REP.
UNDER 55%	_____%	_____%
55% TO 65%	_____%	_____%
OVER 65%	_____%	_____%

b. Write in the value of Cramer's V.   V = _____

c. Is this relationship between incumbency and percentage of the vote
   statistically significant?   Yes   No

d. Incumbents are much more likely to receive over 65 percent of the vote than
   nonincumbents are.   T   F

e. Nearly half of the new representatives won by less than 55 percent of the vote.   T   F

2. Let's compare the religious preferences of U.S. representatives with those of the general public. Using information from the General Social Survey, the following table presents the percentages of the public who are Catholic, liberal Protestant, conservative Protestant, Jewish, and all others.

The All Others category includes a variety of religious orientations such as Hindus, Buddhists, Muslims, and some Protestants who could not be classified in the liberal or conservative category. Also, the All Others category includes the 14.2 percent who selected the No Religion option. We cannot compare the No Religion category in the general public with the results for representatives, because candidates who want to win elections in the United States must at least give the appearance of being religious. Therefore, what we can compare here are the percentages of the general public and representatives who are Catholic, liberal Protestant, conservative Protestant, or Jewish. Please do the following analysis and fill in the percentages for the representatives in the table.

> Data File: **HOUSE107**
> ➤ Task: **Univariate**
> ➤ Primary Variable: **7) RELIGION**
> ➤ View: **Pie**

	GENERAL PUBLIC	107TH CONGRESS
a. CATHOLIC	25.2%	_____%
LIB.PROT.	20.8%	_____%
CON.PROT.	28.9%	_____%
JEWISH	1.8%	_____%
ALL OTHERS	23.3%	_____%

b. The largest group in the general public is conservative Protestants, but the largest group in Congress is liberal Protestants.   T   F

c. Catholics and Jews are underrepresented in Congress relative to their percentages in the general public.   T   F

3. Let's compare the educational levels of the general public and members of Congress. The following table includes information for the general public. Do the following analysis and fill in the information for members of Congress.

> Data File: **HOUSE107**
> Task: **Univariate**
> ➤ Primary Variable: **8) EDUCATION**
> ➤ View: **Pie**

	GENERAL PUBLIC	107TH CONGRESS
a. NO COLLEGE	47.4%	_____%
SOME COLL	27.2%	_____%
COLL. GRAD	14.6%	_____%
GRAD SCH.	10.8%	_____%

b. The education level of U.S. representatives is substantially higher than that of the general public.   T   F

c. Approximately one-third of U.S. representatives do not have a college degree.   T   F

4. In the preceding analysis, we saw that members of Congress have different educational and religious distributions than the general public. Does this make any difference on the voting behavior of representatives? Let's look at the effects of religion and education on a bill to ban human cloning. We'll also compare these effects to those of party.

> Data File: **HOUSE107**
> ➤ Task: **Cross-tabulation**
> ➤ Row Variable: **37) CLONING**
> ➤ Column Variable: **7) RELIGION**
> ➤ View: **Table**
> ➤ Display: **Column %**

Fill in the percentages for the second row (*Yes* votes) below.

	CATHOLIC	LIB. PROT.	CONS. PROT	JEWISH	OTHER
a. %YES	_____%	_____%	_____%	_____%	_____%

b. What is Cramer's V for this table?   V = _____

c. Is Cramer's V statistically significant?   Yes   No

d. Jewish representatives are the least likely to support this ban.   T   F

e. Protestant representatives are less likely than Catholics to support this ban.   T   F

           Data File: **HOUSE107**
              Task: **Cross-tabulation**
     Row Variable: **37) CLONING**
➤ Column Variable: **8) EDUCATION**
         ➤ View: **Table**
     ➤ Display: **Column %**

	NO COLLEGE	SOME COLL	COLL. GRAD	GRAD SCH.
f. %YES	_____%	_____%	_____%	_____%

g. What is Cramer's V for this table?   V = _____

h. Is Cramer's V statistically significant?   Yes   No

i. Representatives with the least education were the most likely to support the
   ban on human cloning.   T   F

j. A majority of representatives in all educational categories supported a ban on
   human cloning.   T   F

           Data File: **HOUSE107**
              Task: **Cross-tabulation**
     Row Variable: **37) CLONING**
➤ Column Variable: **11) PARTY**
         ➤ View: **Table**
     ➤ Display: **Column %**

	DEMOCRAT	REPUBLICAN
k. %YES	_____%	_____%

l. What is Cramer's V for this table?   V = _____

m. Is Cramer's V statistically significant?   Yes   No

n. Republicans were more unified (casting more votes on the same side) than Democrats were on this issue.   T   F

o. A majority of Democrats opposed a ban on human cloning while a majority of Republicans supported the ban.   T   F

p. Which factor had the greatest effect on how representatives voted? (Circle one.)

   1. Religion

   2. Education

   3. Party

5. Each representative's constituency has a set of characteristics. Some House members represent districts with a large number of African Americans or Latino residents. Some representatives come from wealthier districts, and of course, House members represent different states from different regions of the country. Let's begin with an analysis comparing the percentage of African Americans in a representative's district and his or her voting record. We'll use ADA (Americans for Democratic Action) ratings of how liberal representatives voted to explore this question.

Data File:	**HOUSE107**
Task:	**Cross-tabulation**
➤ *Row Variable:*	**30) ADA RATE**
➤ *Column Variable:*	**16) DIS AFRAM%**
➤ *View:*	**Table**
➤ *Display:*	**Column %**

a. What is Cramer's V for this table?   V = _____

b. Is Cramer's V statistically significant?   Yes   No

Fill in the percentages from the third row (liberal) in the following table:

	50% OR +	15%–49.9%	6%–14.9%	0%–5.9%
c. %LIBERAL	_____%	_____%	_____%	_____%

d. Representatives whose districts contain higher percentages of African Americans are more liberal.   T   F

6. Let's do the same type of analysis but use the percentage of the district that is Hispanic.

Data File:	**HOUSE107**
Task:	**Cross-tabulation**
Row Variable:	**30) ADA RATE**
➤ *Column Variable:*	**17) DIST HISP%**
➤ *View:*	**Table**
➤ *Display:*	**Column %**

a. What is Cramer's V for this table?

V = _____

b. Is Cramer's V statistically significant?

Yes   No

	50% OR +	10%–49.9%	3%–9.9%	UNDER 3%
c. %LIBERAL	_____%	_____%	_____%	_____%

d. Representatives whose districts contain higher percentages of Hispanics are more liberal.

T   F

7. Let's compare the effect of a wealthier versus poorer district, as measured by the median (i.e., average) family income.

> Data File: **HOUSE107**
> Task: **Cross-tabulation**
> Row Variable: **30) ADA RATE**
> ➤ Column Variable: **18) DIS FAM$**
> ➤ View: **Table**
> ➤ Display: **Column %**

	LOWEST 3RD	MIDDLE 3RD	HIGHEST 3RD
a. %LIBERAL	_____%	_____%	_____%

b. What is Cramer's V for this table?

V = _____

c. Is Cramer's V statistically significant?

Yes   No

d. Representatives from wealthier districts are less liberal.

T   F

8. Finally, let's look at the influence of region on the liberalness of a representative.

> Data File: **HOUSE107**
> Task: **Cross-tabulation**
> Row Variable: **30) ADA RATE**
> ➤ Column Variable: **15) REGION**
> ➤ View: **Table**
> ➤ Display: **Column %**

	EAST	MIDWEST	SOUTH	WEST
a. %LIBERAL	_____%	_____%	_____%	_____%

b. What is Cramer's V for this table?

V = _____

c. Is Cramer's V statistically significant?

Yes   No

d. Representatives from the East and West tend to be more liberal.

T   F

THE PRESIDENCY

[S]hould my administration prove to be a very wicked one, or what is more probable, a very foolish one, if you, the people, are but true to yourselves and to the Constitution, there is but little harm I can do, thank God!

ABRAHAM LINCOLN, 1861

Tasks: Mapping, Univariate, Cross-Tabulation
Data Files: STATES, USPRES

The American presidency was invented by the Constitutional Convention. Never before had a nation been led by a freely elected chief executive with powers independent of the legislative branch of government. In all other democracies at that time, and nearly all of them since, executive power was vested in the leader of the legislature; if we were to adopt that system, the Speaker of the House of Representatives would be the chief executive. Only a handful of nations, all of them in North and South America, follow the American model of an elected, independent executive who is in charge of the entire executive branch of government.

Because the American presidency has so much authority and so many independent resources, the delegates at the Constitutional Convention were very worried about the wrong sort of person gaining office. That's why they created the electoral college. They never meant for presidents to be elected by popular vote. Instead, they wanted presidents to be selected by a few of the nation's most informed and concerned leaders. Thus, Alexander Hamilton explained in 1788 that the process of selection by the electoral college "affords a moral certainty, that the office of president will never fall to the lot of any man who is not in an eminent degree endowed with the requisite qualifications."

While vestiges of the electoral college remain, these days the popular vote pretty much decides who becomes president, with the 2000 election being a major exception. Over the previous 100 years, the electoral college vote mirrored the popular vote, but even when this occurred, the electoral college still had subtle effects on who became president. So, let's see how well the system has worked.

➤ *Data File:* **STATES**
  ➤ *Task:* **Mapping**
➤ *Variable 1:* **88) PRESIDENTS**
    ➤ *View:* **List: Rank**

RANK	CASE NAME	VALUE
1	New York	7
1	Ohio	7
3	Virginia	5
4	Massachusetts	4
5	Texas	3
5	California	3
5	Tennessee	3
8	Pennsylvania	1
8	Louisiana	1
8	Kansas	1

Here we see the home states of each of the 43 presidents, from George Washington to George W. Bush (although Bush was the 42nd person to hold the office, the record books refer to him as the 43rd president because they count Grover Cleveland twice since his two terms of office were not consecutive).

The eastern bias is clear. More than half of all presidents have come from four states: Ohio (7), New York (7), Virginia (5), and Massachusetts (4). Eleven states have had only one president, and 32 have had none. Two major factors have played a role: population size and when states entered the union. In the beginning, only a few states *could* produce presidents because there were only 14 states. Thus, New York, Virginia, and Massachusetts were electing presidents long before most other states existed. Moreover, even in the days when the electoral college actually met and chose a president, population size mattered a lot since each state's votes were proportionate to its population. In 1790 Virginia was by far the most populous state being twice as large as second-place Pennsylvania, hence its many presidents—including George Washington and Thomas Jefferson. New York's many presidents can be traced to the fact that it too was one of the original states and soon became by far the most populous state (it was not until the early 1960s that California had more people than New York, and Texas did not pass New York until the 1990s).

That leaves Ohio. How did it elect seven presidents? There are three factors: age, population, and location. Ohio is an old state, having entered the union in 1803, and it soon became one of the most populous states, ranking fourth largest in the latter 19th century. But of even greater importance is location. Ohio is the most eastern state of the Midwest, so its politicians often mediated conflicts between the East and the more westerly areas, which was an advantage for its presidential candidates. They were acceptable to all regions—so much so that in the 1920 election the winner was the Republican senator from Ohio (Harding) and the loser was the governor of Ohio (Cox).

Data File: **STATES**
    Task: **Mapping**
Variable 1: **88) PRESIDENTS**
➤ *Variable 2:* **2) POPULATION**
    ➤ *Views:* **Map**

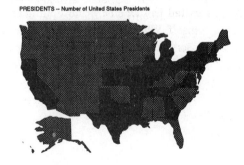

PRESIDENTS -- Number of United States Presidents

r = 0.560**

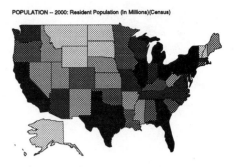

POPULATION -- 2000: Resident Population (In Millions)(Census)

Even though populations have changed a lot through the decades, there still is a strong and significant correlation between the number of presidents a state has produced and its population.

Now, let's see what sorts of people have been president. For one thing, they all have been males. A woman ran for vice president in 1984, but as yet no woman has been nominated for president by a major party. But what about other features of the American presidency?

> *Data File:* **USPRES**
> *Task:* **Univariate**
> *Primary Variable:* **6) PARTY**
> *View:* **Pie**

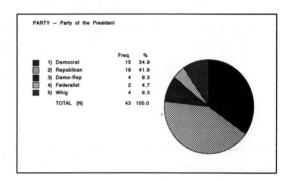

This data file consists of the 43 presidents. Here we see their party affiliations. There have been 15 Democrats and 18 Republicans. But that leaves 10 others. The Federalists were an antiparty party. The name was applied to the opponents of political parties as divisive "factions," including George Washington, who devoted much of his farewell address to condemning parties: "Let me . . . warn you in the most solemn manner against the baneful effects of the spirit of party, generally."

The Federalist name was adopted by Alexander Hamilton to clarify opposition to the party formed by Thomas Jefferson, who was as ardently in favor of parties as Washington was against them. Jefferson's party was called the Democratic-Republicans and they elected four early presidents, including Jefferson himself. When Andrew Jackson became a presidential candidate, the party shortened its name to the Democratic Party. Meanwhile, the name Federalist disappeared; the new opposition party came to be known as the Whigs, and they elected four presidents. During the 1850s the issue of slavery split both the Whigs and the Democrats, and the antislavery factions of each withdrew to form the Republican Party, whose first successful presidential candidate was Abraham Lincoln. Since 1853, all U.S. presidents have been either Democrats or Republicans.

Data File: **USPRES**
Task: **Univariate**
➤ Primary Variable: **17) YRS IN OFF**
➤ View: **Pie**

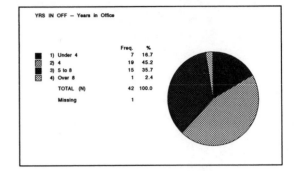

A presidential term in office is four years. Here we see that seven presidents served fewer than four years. These were either presidents who died in office or vice presidents who succeeded and then did not serve a term of their own. Nineteen presidents served but a single term, and 15 more began a second term (and most completed it). For 150 years no president ever sought a third term, modeling themselves on George Washington, who declined a third term. Indeed, as the Democratic Party platform put it in 1896, "We declare it to be the unwritten law of this Republic, established by custom and usage of 100 years . . . that no man should be eligible for a third term of the Presidential office."

After Franklin D. Roosevelt ran for and won third and fourth terms, the 22nd Amendment to the Constitution was adopted:

> No person shall be elected to the office of the President more than twice, and no person who has held the office of President, or acted as President, for more than two years of a term to which some other person was elected President shall be elected to the office of President more than once.

Presidents have many formal and informal powers. One of their formal powers is the ability to veto legislation passed by Congress. President Washington vetoed only two pieces of legislation during his two terms in office. President Franklin Delano Roosevelt cast the most vetoes—at 635. He, however, was president for 14 years. Dividing 635 by 14 reveals that Roosevelt cast an average of 45 vetoes for each year in office.

Data File: **USPRES**
Task: **Univariate**
➤ Primary Variable: **18) VETOES**
➤ View: **Pie**

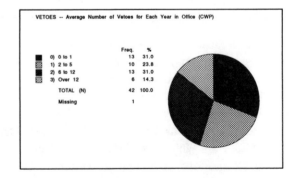

Here we see that about one-third of the presidents cast no more than one veto for each year in office, one-quarter of the presidents cast between two and five vetoes each year, another third vetoed six to twelve pieces of legislation each year, and 14 percent vetoed twelve or more bills for every year in office.

Data File: **USPRES**
➤ Task: **Cross-tabulation**
➤ Row Variable: **18) VETOES**
➤ Column Variable: **35) ERA**
➤ View: **Table**
➤ Display: **Column %**

VETOES   by   ERA
Cramer's V: 0.815 **
Warning: Potential significance problem. Check row and column totals.

VETOES	ERA		
	Pre CW	Post CW	TOTAL
0 to 1	12	1	13
	75.0%	3.8%	31.0%
2 to 5	4	6	10
	25.0%	23.1%	23.8%
6 to 12	0	13	13
	0.0%	50.0%	31.0%
Over 12	0	6	6
	0.0%	23.1%	14.3%
Missing	0	1	1
TOTAL	16	26	42
	100.0%	100.0%	

Presidents up until the time of the Civil War were quite reluctant to use the veto power. As mentioned previously, George Washington cast only two vetoes. John Adams, Thomas Jefferson, John Quincy Adams, William Harrison, Zachary Taylor, and Millard Fillmore did not veto any legislation. Three-quarters of the pre–Civil War presidents cast either no vetoes or less than one veto for each year in office. None of these presidents averaged more than five vetoes per year. Since the Civil War, half of the presidents have cast between six and twelve vetoes for each year in office.

Presidential vetoes may be considered a sign of a strong presidency or a weak presidency. Franklin Delano Roosevelt was one of the strongest presidents in U.S. history, convincing Congress to pass his New Deal programs. Yet, Roosevelt often resorted to using vetoes as well. Thus, some great presidents use the veto power to further increase their influence. On the other hand, vetoes also may be a sign of presidential weakness. A stronger president should be able to influence Congress during the early stages of the legislative process, such that bills the president finds objectionable do not pass Congress. Gerald Ford succeeded to the presidency after the resignation of President Richard Nixon. Ford was never elected president and thus could not claim a popular mandate. He also faced a Congress controlled by the opposition party. Ford had little influence over Congress and used the presidential veto 66 times. Many of Ford's vetoes, additionally, were overturned by Congress.

Congress can vacate a presidential veto with two-thirds votes in both the U.S. House of Representatives and the Senate. With a super-majority vote required in both houses of Congress, overrides of presidential vetoes are rare. Less than 5 percent of vetoes are overturned by Congress. Perhaps a surer sign of presidential weakness is the percent of vetoes overridden by Congress.

Data File: **USPRES**
➤ Task: **Univariate**
➤ Primary Variable: **29) OVERRIDE**
➤ View: **Pie**

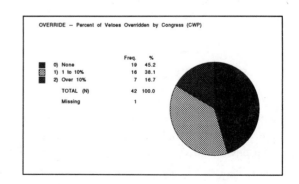

OVERRIDE -- Percent of Vetoes Overridden by Congress (CWP)

	Freq.	%
0) None	19	45.2
1) 1 to 10%	16	38.1
2) Over 10%	7	16.7
TOTAL (N)	42	100.0
Missing	1	

This chart shows that nearly half (45 percent) of presidents have had no vetoes overridden. But remember that a number of early presidents cast no vetoes and therefore could have no vetoes overridden. A more appropriate chart would examine only presidents from the post–Civil War era, when vetoes, and overrides of vetoes, are more common.

Data File: **USPRES**
Task: **Univariate**
Primary Variable: **29) OVERRIDE**
➤ *Subset Variable:* **35) ERA**
➤ *Subset Categories:* **Include: 1) Post CW**
➤ *View:* **Pie**

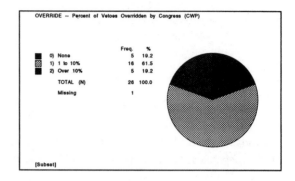

Looking only at presidents since the Civil War, we see that presidents can expect that between 1 and 10 percent of their vetoes will be overridden by Congress. Only five presidents have been able to sustain all of their vetoes, while five other presidents have seen more than 10 percent overturned.

Presidents attempt to influence the legislative process by proposing legislation, molding the national agenda, and signing or vetoing legislation. They influence the judicial branch through their appointment of judges. Presidents nominate potential judges, and the Senate typically confirms these nominees. Presidents nominate judges both to the Supreme Court and for all other federal courts. Once confirmed, these judges serve lifetime appointments. Thus, one of the legacies of any president is in the number of judges appointed. Let's first look at Supreme Court appointments.

Data File: **USPRES**
Task: **Univariate**
➤ *Primary Variable:* **25) SUP CT**
➤ *View:* **Pie**

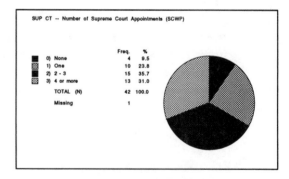

If you are replicating this pie chart, be sure to delete the subset variable from the previous example.

Four presidents were unable to appoint any Supreme Court judges, because no vacancies occurred on the Court during that president's term in office. President Jimmy Carter was one of these presidents who never had the opportunity to appoint a Supreme Court justice. Of the nine justices on the Supreme Court in June 2002, President Reagan appointed four, Presidents George H. Bush and Bill Clinton each appointed two, and one was appointed by President Ford. As the pie chart shows, most presidents can expect to appoint between one and three Supreme Court justices, but one-third of the presidents have been able to appoint four or more justices.

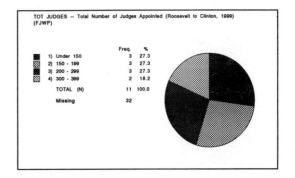

Data File: **USPRES**
Task: **Univariate**
➤ Primary Variable: **26) TOT JUDGES**
➤ View: **Pie**

Presidents make many more judicial appointments to federal district courts or to the federal court of appeals. The pie chart above indicates the total number of judges appointed by presidents since Franklin Delano Roosevelt's presidency. As shown, presidents make hundreds of judicial appointments. Because presidents tend to appoint judges from their own political party, these presidential appointments shape the future decision making of the judicial branch.

Your turn.

WORKSHEET

NAME:

COURSE:

DATE:

EXERCISE

13

REVIEW QUESTIONS

Based on the first part of this exercise, answer True or False to the following items:

a. More presidents are from California than from any other state.　　　　T　F

b. Most democracies have copied the American institution of the presidency.　　　　T　F

c. The 22nd Amendment limits presidents to two terms.　　　　T　F

d. Abraham Lincoln was the first Republican to be elected president.　　　　T　F

e. Most presidents can expect that over 10 percent of their vetoes will be overridden by Congress.　　　　T　F

f. Every president has been able to appoint at least one Supreme Court justice.　　　　T　F

EXPLORIT QUESTIONS

1. Everyone knows that there has never been an African American, Asian, or female president. However, what is really surprising is how few ethnicities have been represented among the presidents. In the table on the following page, the second column shows the approximate percentages of the 1990 U.S. population with each racial and ethnic descent. These percentages are only approximate since many people don't know the ethnicity of their ancestors.

    Let's look at the race and ethnicity of presidents.

    > *Data File:* **USPRES**
    > *Task:* **Cross-tabulation**
    > *Row Variable:* **20) ETHNICITY**
    > *Column Variable:* **27) CENTURY**
    > *View:* **Table**
    > *Display:* **Column %**

    a. Use these results to complete the following table including the total column at the far right. (Note: If a category listed in the table does not appear on the screen, that means no president has been of that race or ethnicity. Hence, many of the percentages in these columns will be zero.)

PRESIDENTS

RACE/ETHNICITY	% U.S. POPULATION, 1990	18TH, 19TH	20TH, 21ST	TOTAL
Black	12%	_____ %	_____ %	_____ %
Asian	3%	_____ %	_____ %	_____ %
Hispanic	9%	_____ %	_____ %	_____ %
German	23%	_____ %	_____ %	_____ %
Irish	15%	_____ %	_____ %	_____ %
Italian	6%	_____ %	_____ %	_____ %
Dutch	2%	_____ %	_____ %	_____ %
British	18%	_____ %	_____ %	_____ %
Eastern European	8%	_____ %	_____ %	_____ %

Answer True or False to the following items:

b. There has never been a president of Italian or Eastern European descent.   T   F

c. Over 80 percent of the presidents have been of British ancestry.   T   F

d. In this table, African Americans stand out from other racial/ethnic groups because of their underrepresentation in the presidency.   T   F

e. The ancestry of American presidents closely matches the ancestry of the population as a whole.   T   F

f. The ancestry of American presidents has been more varied in the 20th and 21st centuries than in the 18th and 19th centuries.   T   F

2. In 2000, Joseph Lieberman became the first Jewish American to be nominated by a major party for the office of vice president. No Jewish American has been president, and John Kennedy has been the only Catholic president.

Let's now look at the distribution of religion across presidents and compare this to the distribution in the population today. Again the column of percentages of each religious denomination in the general population has already been provided.

> Data File: **USPRES**
> ➤ Task: **Univariate**
> ➤ Primary Variable: **15) RELIGION**
> ➤ View: **Statistics (Summary)**

Note: Select the [Statistics (Summary)] option and use the second column on the screen to answer this question.

a. Use the percentages to complete the following table:

RELIGIOUS DENOMINATION	POPULATION	% U.S. PRESIDENTS
Non-denom.	9.0%	_____%
Episcop.	1.8%	_____%
Congreg.	0.4%	_____%
Presby.	3.0%	_____%
Baptist	19.6%	_____%
Methodist	8.2%	_____%
Dutch Ref.	0.2%	_____%
Quaker	0.2%	_____%
Unitar.	0.3%	_____%
Rom.Cath.	25.2%	_____%
Disciples	0.1%	_____%
Jewish	2.3%	_____%

Answer True or False to the following items:

b. No religious denomination is overrepresented among American presidents.   T   F

c. The Jewish faith is the only religious category underrepresented among U.S. presidents.   T   F

d. More than 90 percent of the U.S. presidents have been Protestants.   T   F

3. The experience and background of a candidate becomes an issue in every presidential election. Vice presidents, such as Al Gore, benefit, or suffer, based on the public's view of the current administration. Governors, such as George W. Bush, and others with no experience in Washington D.C., may benefit from being outsiders, but may also be accused of lacking experience in national and international affairs. Candidates from appointed positions or nongovernment positions, such as Elizabeth Dole, may be attacked for not having served in an elective office, but may benefit from having broad experience in cabinet, diplomatic, or other nongovernment positions.

Let's see if past presidents shared common backgrounds.

Data File: **USPRES**
Task: **Univariate**
➤ *Primary Variable:* **21) GOV?**
➤ *View:* **Pie**

a. What percentage of past presidents had been governors?   _____%

Data File: **USPRES**
Task: **Univariate**
➤ *Primary Variable:* **22) SEN?**
➤ *View:* **Pie**

b. What percentage of past presidents had been senators?   _____%

Data File: **USPRES**
Task: **Univariate**
➤ *Primary Variable:* **23) VEEP?**
➤ *View:* **Pie**

c. What percentage of past presidents had been vice presidents?   _____%

4. In Exercise 10, the term "minority" president was introduced. Rather than referring to the ethnic or racial background of a president, this term referred to presidents who were elected by less than 50 percent of the popular vote. President George W. Bush is a minority president, since he lost the popular vote to Democratic candidate Al Gore, but won the presidency with a majority of the electoral college vote. President Bill Clinton also was a minority president, because the strong showing of third-party candidate Ross Perot split the popular vote three ways, leaving Clinton to win the presidency with 43 percent (1992) and 49 percent (1996) of the popular vote. How many U.S. presidents have been minority presidents, elected with less than 50 percent of the popular vote? (The ten missing cases in the pie chart occur because no popular vote was recorded for the first five presidents and five presidents succeeded to the office from the vice presidency and never won the presidency on their own.)

Data File: **USPRES**
Task: **Univariate**
➤ *Primary Variable:* **34) MINOR**
➤ *View:* **Pie**

Nearly half of the U.S. presidents have been minority presidents, receiving less than half of the popular vote.   T   F

5. In the opening section of this exercise, we saw that the rate at which presidents veto legislation varied. Early presidents rarely vetoed legislation. Since the Civil War, some presidents have cast many vetoes, while others have vetoed very little legislation. Let's see if we can uncover any patterns in the use of the veto power by presidents.

Since the veto power was not used frequently by presidents prior to the Civil War, we will use the subsetting facility of MicroCase to look only at post–Civil War presidents. Once you select 35) ERA as the subset variable, a menu will appear with categories to select. Use your mouse to check off the category for post–Civil War presidents. Make sure that the option of "Include Selected Categories" has a black dot in the circle. If this option is not selected, click on it with your mouse. The remainder of the questions in this exercise will use only post–Civil War presidents. Once you have selected this subset of cases, it will remain in force as long as you use the arrow key (rather than the menu key) to return to the cross-tabulation menu.

Another factor to keep in mind when looking at post–Civil War presidents is that there are only 26 people who have been the nation's chief executive during this time period. With so few cases, patterns in the data have to be very strong before we can assume that these patterns have not occurred by random chance. Thus, differences in percentages across categories will need to be very large to reach statistical significance. However, if we find patterns which are statistically significant, they also will be substantively important. Let's first examine whether Democratic or Republican presidents have cast more vetoes.

Data File:	**USPRES**
➤ Task:	**Cross-tabulation**
➤ Row Variable:	**18) VETOES**
➤ Column Variable:	**6) PARTY**
➤ Subset Variable:	**35) ERA**
➤ Subset Categories:	**Include: 1) Post CW**
➤ View:	**Table**
➤ Display:	**Column %**

a. What is the value of V for this table?   V = _____

b. Is V statistically significant?   Yes   No

c. The pattern in this table is strong enough to exceed random chance, and thus
   we can conclude that Republican presidents cast more vetoes than Democratic
   presidents.   T   F

Presidential success with Congress may depend on the strength of the presidential party in Congress. A Republican president will have more natural allies, who would vote to sustain the president's vetoes, if the Republican party was the majority party in Congress. Variable 28) PTY-CONG measures the strength of the president's party in Congress by the number of years the president's party is the majority party in one or both houses of Congress. Does the strength of the president's party in Congress influence the rate at which presidents veto legislation?

Data File:	**USPRES**
Task:	**Cross-tabulation**
Row Variable:	**18) VETOES**
➤ Column Variable:	**28) PTY-CONG**
➤ Subset Variable:	**35) ERA**
➤ Subset Categories:	**Include: 1) Post CW**
➤ View:	**Table**
➤ Display:	**Column %**

Exercise 13: The Presidency

d. What is the value of V for this table?   V = _____

e. Is V statistically significant?   Yes   No

f. We can be certain, beyond a reasonable doubt, that when the president's
party is stronger in Congress the president will cast fewer vetoes.   T   F

Do "minority" presidents, elected by less than 50 percent of the popular vote, have less influence over Congress and thus need to resort to casting more presidential vetoes?

> Data File: **USPRES**
> Task: **Cross-tabulation**
> Row Variable: **18) VETOES**
> ➤ Column Variable: **34) MINOR**
> ➤ Subset Variable: **35) ERA**
> ➤ Subset Categories: **Include: 1) Post CW**
> ➤ View: **Table**
> ➤ Display: **Column %**

g. What is the value of V for this table?   V = _____

h. Is V statistically significant?   Yes   No

i. We can be certain, beyond a reasonable doubt, that presidents elected by
less than a majority of the popular vote will cast more vetoes.   T   F

We might expect that presidents who served as senators may better understand Congress and thus have to resort to a veto less often, whereas presidents who served as governors may be less acquainted with the ways of Washington D.C. and have to cast more vetoes.

> Data File: **USPRES**
> Task: **Cross-tabulation**
> Row Variable: **18) VETOES**
> ➤ Column Variable: **22) SEN?**
> ➤ Subset Variable: **35) ERA**
> ➤ Subset Categories: **Include: 1) Post CW**
> ➤ View: **Table**
> ➤ Display: **Column %**

j. What is the value of V for this table?   V = _____

k. Is V statistically significant?   Yes   No

l. We can be certain, beyond a reasonable doubt, that presidents who
previously served in the Senate will cast fewer vetoes.   T   F

Data File: **USPRES**
Task: **Cross-tabulation**
Row Variable: **18) VETOES**
➤ Column Variable: **21) GOV?**
➤ Subset Variable: **35) ERA**
➤ Subset Categories: **Include: 1) Post CW**
➤ View: **Table**
➤ Display: **Column %**

m. What is the value of V for this table?   V = _____

n. Is V statistically significant?   Yes   No

o. We can be certain, beyond a reasonable doubt, that presidents who
   previously served as governors will cast more vetoes.   T   F

6. George W. Bush is a Republican president elected by less than a majority of the popular vote. He
   served as the governor of Texas but was never a senator. Also, consider the strength of the
   Republican party in Congress. Given these background characteristics, what can we predict about
   Bush's use of the presidential veto? (Circle one.)

   a. Bush will cast many vetoes.

   b. Bush will cast few vetoes.

   c. We cannot predict how many vetoes Bush will cast.

7. In the beginning of this exercise, we also saw that presidents vary in their success in sustaining their
   vetoes. While few vetoes are overridden by Congress, some presidents had none of their vetoes overturned; other presidents have more than 10 percent overridden by Congress. Once again, we will confine
   our analysis to post–Civil War presidents, who have been more likely to issue vetoes and thus have presented Congress with more opportunities to overturn these vetoes. Do Democratic or Republican presidents have more of their vetoes overridden by Congress?

Data File: **USPRES**
Task: **Cross-tabulation**
➤ Row Variable: **29) OVERRIDE**
➤ Column Variable: **6) PARTY**
➤ Subset Variable: **35) ERA**
➤ Subset Categories: **Include: 1) Post CW**
➤ View: **Table**
➤ Display: **Column %**

a. What is the value of V for this table?   V = _____

b. Is V statistically significant?   Yes   No

c. The pattern in this table exceeds random chance; thus we can conclude that
   Republican presidents have more of their vetoes overridden by Congress.   T   F

Exercise 13: The Presidency   207

Next let's test whether the strength of the president's party in Congress influences the rate at which presidential vetoes are overridden.

Data File:	**USPRES**
Task:	**Cross-tabulation**
Row Variable:	**29) OVERRIDE**
➤ *Column Variable:*	**28) PTY-CONG**
➤ *Subset Variable:*	**35) ERA**
➤ *Subset Categories:*	**Include: 1) Post CW**
➤ *View:*	**Table**
➤ *Display:*	**Column %**

d. What is the value of V for this table?   V = _____

e. Is V statistically significant?   Yes   No

f. The pattern in this table exceeds random chance; thus we can conclude
   that when the presidential party is stronger in Congress, presidential
   vetoes are overturned less often.   T   F

Next let's once again examine the effect of winning the presidency with less than a majority of the popular vote.

Data File:	**USPRES**
Task:	**Cross-tabulation**
Row Variable:	**29) OVERRIDE**
➤ *Column Variable:*	**34) MINOR**
➤ *Subset Variable:*	**35) ERA**
➤ *Subset Categories:*	**Include: 1) Post CW**
➤ *View:*	**Table**
➤ *Display:*	**Column %**

g. What is the value of V for this table?   V = _____

h. Is V statistically significant?   Yes   No

i. The pattern in this table exceeds random chance; thus we can conclude
   that presidents elected with less than a majority of the popular vote will
   see more of their vetoes overturned by Congress.   T   F

Let's return to prior service as senators versus governors to see if either is more successful in sustaining their vetoes.

Data File:	**USPRES**
Task:	**Cross-tabulation**
Row Variable:	**29) OVERRIDE**
➤ *Column Variable:*	**22) SEN?**
➤ *Subset Variable:*	**35) ERA**
➤ *Subset Categories:*	**Include: 1) Post CW**
➤ *View:*	**Table**
➤ *Display:*	**Column %**

j. What is the value of V for this table? V = _____

k. Is V statistically significant? Yes   No

l. The pattern in this table exceeds random chance; thus we can conclude that presidents with prior service in the Senate have their vetoes overridden less often by Congress. T   F

Data File:	**USPRES**
Task:	**Cross-tabulation**
Row Variable:	**29) OVERRIDE**
➤ *Column Variable:*	**21) GOV?**
➤ *Subset Variable:*	**35) ERA**
➤ *Subset Categories:*	**Include: 1) Post CW**
➤ *View:*	**Table**
➤ *Display:*	**Column %**

m. What is the value of V for this table? V = _____

n. Is V statistically significant? Yes   No

o. The pattern in this table exceeds random chance; thus we can conclude that presidents with prior service as governors have their vetoes overridden more often by Congress. T   F

8. Answer True or False to the following items:

a. Because George W. Bush was not a U.S. Senator, we might expect him to have more of his vetoes overridden by Congress. T   F

b. If the Republican party greatly outnumbers the Democratic party in Congress, we might expect fewer of President Bush's vetoes to be overridden. T   F

c. Because President Bush is a minority president, we might expect more of his vetoes to be overridden by Congress. T   F

d. Because President Bush is a Republican, we might expect more of his vetoes to be overridden by Congress. T   F

THE BUREAUCRACY

*The President ... may require the Opinion, in writing,
of the principal Officer in each of the executive
Departments, upon any Subject relating to the Duties
of their respective Offices ... and by and with the
Advice and Consent of the Senate, shall appoint
Ambassadors, other public Ministers and Consuls,
Judges of the supreme Court, and all other Officers of
the United States, whose Appointments are not herein
otherwise provided for, and which shall be established
by Law; but the Congress may by Law vest the
Appointment of such inferior Officers, as they think
proper, in the President alone, in the Courts of Law, or
in the Heads of Departments.*

SECTION 2, ARTICLE II, UNITED
STATES CONSTITUTION

Tasks: Mapping, Univariate, Cross-Tabulation, Historical Trends, Scatterplot
Data Files: STATES, GSS, NES, HISTORY, NATIONS

The section of the Constitution quoted above is *everything* the founders bothered to say about the executive branch of government, aside from the presidency. Nothing is said about a cabinet, about a State Department, or about any of the thousands of agencies that today constitute the federal government and often are referred to collectively as the bureaucracy. The reason the Constitution said so little about this aspect of government is that in those days the government was so little.

In traditional agrarian societies, such as those in Europe during medieval times, the government was nothing more than the king's or queen's household and court. Needed functionaries such as clerks, accountants, and tax collectors were servants of the crown, equal in status to the cooks, grooms, and butlers making up the royal household. When the ruler needed a general, an advisor, a chief justice, or an administrator of the treasury, one of the noble members of the court was asked to do the job. The nobles did not regard a government post as an occupation or even a full-time activity. Often they had no special qualifications beyond their noble birth and their social graces.

This system worked because governments in those days did very little. Beyond extracting taxes from the populace, maintaining a minimum of public order, and defending the realm against invaders, there was little to do. After all, more than 90 percent of the population led quiet rural lives without schools, post offices, roads, hospitals, or fire departments. Laws were simple. There were no regulatory agencies, no inspectors, and no *paperwork*—tax collectors used carts, not forms.

As the world became modern, this system could not suffice. With rapidly growing populations and the rise of industry, the demands on government grew. As a result, governments got much larger. And, as more and more people were needed to staff the government, the old selection methods became obsolete.

When George Washington took office as the first president of the United States, his first task was to appoint people to fill all of the jobs in the federal government including postmasters to manage all the local post offices. In making these appointments, Washington *personally* evaluated each person. How could he? Easily, there being fewer than 700 of them! For years, each time the political party in control of the American government changed, nearly all government employees were discharged and replaced with supporters of the new administration. Thus, when Thomas Jefferson took office, he fired hundreds of Federalists appointed by Presidents Washington and Adams and replaced them with his supporters. This practice was known as the **spoils system**: the spoils (or benefits) of public office go to the supporters of winning politicians. This system reached its height in American history when Andrew Jackson was elected and thousands of government employees were terminated.

Aside from corruption and other abuses, the spoils system was undesirable because it meant that many technical or otherwise complex jobs were continually being turned over to beginners. Eventually, the civil service system was introduced whereby people are hired and promoted on the basis of merit, not political connections, and they may be terminated only for sufficient cause.

Today, governments, like all *large organizations*, are **bureaucracies**. All bureaucracies have certain key features. They consist of a set of positions, each with very specific and often very specialized duties. These positions are administered on the basis of clearly specified lines of authority. Hiring and promotion are done on the basis of qualifications and training. Finally, and very important, careful, written records are kept of all communications and transactions.

Bureaucracies exist because they are the most efficient solution to the problems of coordinating and controlling the actions of large numbers of people involved in some common enterprise, whether it be managing General Motors or running the Department of Commerce.

The problem is that bureaucracies often develop goals of their own, and these may put them in conflict with the purposes for which the organization was created or with the interests of those whom it was intended to serve. This is why the words *bureaucrat* and *bureaucracy* carry unpleasant connotations, suggesting meddlesome people and muddled organizations. This is especially true when people speak of government bureaucracies. From all parties and nearly all candidates, complaints are directed toward government agencies and their millions of employees—the bureaucracy. It is too big, too wasteful, too arrogant, too powerful, and too inefficient.

Let's pursue some of these concerns.

RANK	CASE NAME	VALUE
1	Maryland	2740
2	Virginia	2562
3	Alaska	2550
4	Hawaii	2239
5	Utah	2034
6	New Mexico	1695
7	Colorado	1583
8	Oklahoma	1427
9	Montana	1406
10	Alabama	1385

➤ *Data File:* **STATES**
➤ *Task:* **Mapping**
➤ *Variable 1:* **18) FED.EMPLOY**
➤ *View:* **List: Rank**

Here we see that the federal bureaucracy is not confined to Washington D.C. Among the states, Maryland and Virginia have the highest proportions of federal employees because so many agencies have moved to suburbs near Washington. Their employees often become residents of these two states which surround the District. However, many other states far from Washington are high in federal employees. One reason is that they have many military installations. Members of the armed forces are not counted in these personnel figures, but military bases always employ a lot of civilians.

Obviously, the federal payroll has grown incredibly since the days of George Washington. Every state has many times more federal employees than made up the total number in 1789. Let's examine this growth.

➤ *Data File:* **HISTORY**
➤ *Task:* **Historical Trends**
➤ *Variables:* **53) NON-D EMP**

Non-defense executive branch employees per 1000 population

In 1900 there were slightly over 2 government employees per 1,000 population. Since the mid-sixties, this rate has been about 8 per 1,000. (Those employed in national defense are not included in these numbers.)

➤ *Data File:* **GSS**
➤ *Task:* **Univariate**
➤ *Primary Variable:* **52) FED.GOV'T?**
➤ *View:* **Pie**

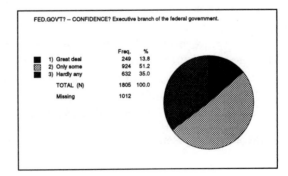

Here we see that although a third (35.0 percent) of Americans say they have only a low level of confidence in the executive branch of the federal government, a majority of Americans (51.2 percent) say they have at least some confidence—but only 13.8 percent say they have a "great deal" of confidence. That is not a very powerful vote of confidence. What about public evaluations of other branches of government?

	Data File:	**GSS**
	➤ Task:	**Cross-tabulation**
	➤ Row Variable:	**52) FED.GOV'T?**
	➤ Column Variable:	**55) SUP.COURT?**
	➤ View:	**Table**
	➤ Display:	**Total %**

FED.GOV'T? by SUP.COURT?
Cramer's V: 0.273 **

	SUP.COURT?				
		Great deal	Only some	Hardly any	Missing	TOTAL
FED.GOV'T?	Great deal	155	73	9	12	237
		9.0%	4.2%	0.5%		13.7%
	Only some	299	536	60	29	895
		17.3%	31.0%	3.5%		51.7%
	Hardly any	128	308	162	34	598
		7.4%	17.8%	9.4%		34.6%
	Missing	19	15	8	970	1012
	TOTAL	582	917	231	1045	1730
		33.6%	53.0%	13.4%		

Clearly, people who lack confidence in the Supreme Court also tend to lack confidence in the executive branch. Only 9 percent of Americans have a great deal of confidence in both the executive branch and the Supreme Court. (Notice that the instructions asked for total percents to be listed.) One-third of Americans (31.0 percent) have only some confidence in both branches of the government, while 9.4 percent have hardly any confidence in these institutions. By looking at the total row, one can see that about one-third of Americans (33.6 percent) had a great deal of confidence in the Supreme Court, while only one in ten (13.7 percent in the total column) had a great deal of confidence in the executive branch. Thus, while opinions on the two branches overlap somewhat, Americans generally have a more favorable opinion of the Supreme Court than of the executive branch.

	Data File:	**GSS**
	Task:	**Cross-tabulation**
	Row Variable:	**52) FED.GOV'T?**
	➤ Column Variable:	**57) CONGRESS?**
	➤ View:	**Table**
	➤ Display:	**Total %**

FED.GOV'T? by CONGRESS?
Cramer's V: 0.401 **

	CONGRESS?				
		Great deal	Only some	Hardly any	Missing	TOTAL
FED.GOV'T?	Great deal	114	105	23	7	242
		6.5%	6.0%	1.3%		13.8%
	Only some	84	662	158	20	904
		4.8%	37.7%	9.0%		51.5%
	Hardly any	22	252	337	21	611
		1.3%	14.3%	19.2%		34.8%
	Missing	7	25	14	966	1012
	TOTAL	220	1019	518	1014	1757
		12.5%	58.0%	29.5%		

Americans are more likely to hold a similar evaluation of the executive branch and Congress, since Cramer's V = 0.401**. This is a stronger value than the 0.273** correlation between evaluations of the executive branch and the Supreme Court as shown in the previous table. Nearly one in five Americans (19.2 percent) has hardly any confidence in both the executive and legislative branches of the government, while less than one in ten (6.5 percent) has a great deal of confidence in both institutions.

Americans have been losing confidence in their government over the past 40 years.

➤ *Data File:* **HISTORY**
    ➤ *Task:* **Historical Trends**
➤ *Variables:* **34) TRUST GOV**

Percent who say they trust the government in Washington to do
what is right most of the time (survey data)

One might suppose that if people lack confidence in their government, they may become apathetic and cease to take part in politics. But it could be argued with equal plausibility that people who lack confidence will be more likely to vote because they want change.

➤ *Data File:* **NES**
    ➤ *Task:* **Cross-tabulation**
➤ *Row Variable:* **26) VOTED**
➤ *Column Variable:* **87) TRUST GOV**
    ➤ *View:* **Table**
    ➤ *Display:* **Column %**

VOTED   by   TRUST GOV
Cramer's V: 0.029

		TRUST GOV			
		Always/mst	Some/never	Missing	TOTAL
VOTED	Voted	527	652	3	1179
		77.7%	75.3%		76.4%
	Did not	151	214	7	365
		22.3%	24.7%		23.6%
	Missing	1	0	252	253
	TOTAL	678	866	262	1544
		100.0%	100.0%		

Here we see that trust in the federal government is unrelated to having voted in the 2000 presidential election—perhaps apathy and anger are cancelling one another out.

Your turn.

REVIEW QUESTIONS

Based on the first part of this exercise, answer True or False to the following items:

a. The civil service system also is called the spoils system. T F

b. The secretary of agriculture is the only cabinet member mentioned in the
Constitution. T F

c. Thomas Jefferson participated in the spoils system. T F

d. The principal defect of bureaucracies is that promotion usually is based on who
you know. T F

e. Large business organizations manage not to become bureaucracies. T F

EXPLORIT QUESTIONS

1. According to the preliminary discussion, a sizable proportion of federal employees are used to staff
military installations. Let's look at the relationship between the per capita Defense Department
expenditures and the federal employment rate across states.

➤ Data File: **STATES**
➤ Task: **Scatterplot**
➤ Dependent Variable: **18) FED.EMPLOY**
➤ Independent Variable: **19) DEFENSE $**
➤ View: **Reg. Line**

a. What is the value of the Pearson correlation coefficient? r = _____

b. Is the relationship statistically significant? Yes No

c. This result fails to support the idea that the greater the military presence in a state,
the higher the federal employment rate. T F

Exercise 14: The Bureaucracy

2. Many people are concerned about the growth of government. Let's look at government growth in more detail.

> ➤ *Data File:* **HISTORY**
>   ➤ *Task:* **Historical Trends**
> ➤ *Variables:* **49) FED EMP RT**

a. Government employment seems to

1. have increased at a relatively constant rate.
2. have spikes at certain short periods.
3. have had little change over time.

b. Scrolling through the events listed at the bottom, which of the following events seem to have had the greatest impact on the government employment rate?

1. presidential elections
2. wars
3. new inventions
4. constitutional amendments

3. Let's separate defense employment from nondefense government employment.

> *Data File:* **HISTORY**
>   *Task:* **Historical Trends**
> ➤ *Variables:* **50) DEF EMP RT**
>   **53) NON-D EMP**

a. Wars affect defense employment but have relatively little impact on other types of government employment.   T   F

b. Since the Vietnam War ended in 1974, the defense employment rate has slowly declined.   T   F

c. The nondefense government employment rate has remained fairly constant since the mid-sixties.   T   F

d. Except for wartime, nondefense employment is higher than defense employment.   T   F

4. Government outlays over time also reflect the relative growth of various segments of government.

> *Data File:* **HISTORY**
>   *Task:* **Historical Trends**
> ➤ *Variables:* **54) DEF$/POP**
>   **55) HR$/POP**

a. What is the description of 54) DEF$/POP?

_____

_____

b. What is the description of 55) HR$/POP?

_____

_____

c. Spending on human resources has been growing since the late sixties.   T   F

d. Since the mid-eighties, spending on national defense has been fairly stable.   T   F

5. Let's look at a finer breakdown on the human resources expenditures. These are some of the categories that are included in human resources:

> Data File: **HISTORY**
> Task: **Historical Trends**
> ➤ Variables: **56) S.S.$/POP**
> **57) I.S.$/POP**
> **58) MED$/POP**

a. What is the description of 56) S.S.$/POP?

_____

_____

b. What is the description of 57) I.S.$/POP?

_____

_____

c. What is the description of 58) MED$/POP?

_____

_____

Answer True or False to the following items:

d. Federal spending has increased on Social Security, income security, and
   Medicare since the 1970s.   T   F

e. The federal government spends more money on Medicare than on Social Security.   T   F

6. The federal government is not the only level of government that has bureaucracies. State and local governments also have bureaucracies and provide many complementary services to the federal government. Both levels of government have agencies responsible for schools, transportation, crime prevention, and a host of other government functions. Let's examine health care spending by the 50 state governments. The specific variable in the STATES file looks at health care spending per capita, that is the dollar amount spent per state resident.

> ➤ *Data File:* **STATES**
> ➤ *Task:* **Mapping**
> ➤ *Variable 1:* **109) HLTH$/CAP**
> ➤ *View:* **List: Rank**

	STATE	DOLLARS
a. State that spends the highest dollar amount per state resident.	_____	_____
b. State that spends the lowest dollar amount per state resident.	_____	_____

One reason states may vary in health expenditures is the types of preferences found in the population. In general, Democrats tend to prefer more government spending on social welfare programs, whereas Republicans tend to prefer less government spending on such programs. Let's add a measure of the partisanship of each state's residents to see if this can explain variations in state expenditures on health programs.

> *Data File:* **STATES**
> *Task:* **Mapping**
> *Variable 1:* **109) HLTH$/CAP**
> ➤ *Variable 2:* **171) POP-DEM**
> ➤ *View:* **Map**

c. What is the correlation between Democratic citizenry and state spending on health programs? $r = $ _____

d. Is it statistically significant? Yes   No

7. Nations also vary in their level of government support for health care. Many of the industrialized nations provide their citizens with health insurance. In the United States health insurance is privately funded. Let's see how the United States compares to other industrial countries in total spending (both private and government spending) per capita on health care.

> ➤ *Data File:* **NATIONS**
> ➤ *Task:* **Mapping**
> ➤ *Variable 1:* **41) HEALTH**
> ➤ *View:* **List: Rank**

RANK

    a. U.S. ranking on total (private and public) spending on health care as a percentage of GDP (gross domestic product)

         _____

Now let's look at how the United States ranks on government spending on health care. The variable in the NATIONS data set calculates the percentage of total health care spending which comes from government sources.

>   *Data File:* **NATIONS**
>   *Task:* **Mapping**
> ➤ *Variable 1:* **42) GOVT-HLT**
> ➤   *View:* **List: Rank**

RANK

    b. U.S. ranking on government spending on health care

         _____

    c. Describe government spending on health care in the United States at the federal and state levels and how it compares to that in other industrial countries.

8.   Now let's return to public attitudes toward the government. First let's see if Democrats and Republicans differ in their opinion of the government.

> ➤   *Data File:* **NES**
> ➤   *Task:* **Cross-tabulation**
> ➤   *Row Variable:* **87) TRUST GOV**
> ➤ *Column Variable:* **16) PARTY**
> ➤   *View:* **Table**
> ➤   *Display:* **Column %**

Opinions on trust of the government:

	DEMOCRAT	INDEPENDENT	REPUBLICAN
a. %ALWAYS/MST	_____%	_____%	_____%

    b. What is the value of V for this table?   V = _____

c. Is V statistically significant?   Yes   No

> ➤ *Data File:* **GSS**
> ➤ *Task:* **Cross-tabulation**
> ➤ *Row Variable:* **52) FED.GOV'T?**
> ➤ *Column Variable:* **21) PARTY**
> ➤ *View:* **Table**
> ➤ *Display:* **Column %**

Opinions on confidence in the federal government:

	DEMOCRAT	INDEPENDENT	REPUBLICAN
d. % GREAT DEAL	_____%	_____%	_____%

e. What is the value of V for this table?   V = _____

f. Is V statistically significant?   Yes   No

g. Circle the number of the statement that provides the best summary of these two tables.

1. Democrats have more confidence in the federal government and are more likely to think that the government can be trusted.

2. Democrats have more confidence in the federal government; party has no effect on trust in the government.

3. Democrats have less confidence in the federal government and are more likely to think that the government can be trusted.

4. Democrats have less confidence in the federal government; party has no effect on trust in the government.

5. Democrats and Republicans are pretty much the same in their views of the federal government.

9. Finally, let's see if there is a "gender gap" in evaluations of the government.

> ➤ *Data File:* **NES**
> ➤ *Task:* **Cross-tabulation**
> ➤ *Row Variable:* **87) TRUST GOV**
> ➤ *Column Variable:* **3) SEX**
> ➤ *View:* **Table**
> ➤ *Display:* **Column %**

Opinions on trust of the government:

	MEN	WOMEN
a. %ALWAYS/MST	_____%	_____%

b. What is the value of V for this table?   V = _____

c. Is V statistically significant?   Yes   No

> *Data File:* **GSS**
> *Task:* **Cross-tabulation**
> *Row Variable:* **52) FED.GOV'T?**
> *Column Variable:* **6) SEX**
> *View:* **Table**
> *Display:* **Column %**

Opinions on confidence in the federal government:

	MEN	WOMEN
d. % GREAT DEAL	_____%	_____%

e. What is the value of V for this table?   V = _____

f. Is V statistically significant?   Yes   No

g. Is there a gender gap in confidence in and trust of the federal government?   Yes   No

THE COURTS

The judicial Power of the United States shall be vested in one supreme Court, and in such inferior Courts as the Congress may from time to time ordain and establish. The Judges, both of the supreme and inferior Courts, shall hold their Offices during good Behaviour, and shall, at stated Times, receive for their Services, a Compensation, which shall not be diminished during their Continuance in Office.

ARTICLE III, UNITED STATES
CONSTITUTION

Tasks: Mapping, Univariate, Cross-Tabulation, Historical Trends, Auto-Analyzer
Data Files: STATES, GSS, NES, HISTORY

The Supreme Court consists of nine justices, one of whom serves as chief justice. Justices are nominated by the president, and their appointment is confirmed (or rejected) by the Senate. Because all federal judges are appointed for life, the average term on the Court is quite long. Since the first justices were appointed in 1789, only 106 men and 2 women have served on the Court (Sandra Day O'Connor was appointed to the Court in 1981 by President Ronald Reagan, and Ruth Bader Ginsburg was appointed in 1993 by President Bill Clinton) and William Rehnquist is only the 15th chief justice.[1] Lifetime appointments also result in a relatively older Court—the average age was nearly 67 in 2002.

➤ *Data File:* **STATES**
➤ *Task:* **Mapping**
➤ *Variable 1:* **92) # S. COURT**
➤ *View:* **List: Rank**

RANK	CASE NAME	VALUE
1	New York	14
2	Ohio	9
2	Massachusetts	9
4	Virginia	8
5	Tennessee	6
5	Pennsylvania	6
7	Kentucky	5
8	Georgia	4
8	Maryland	4
8	California	4

---

[1] In 1975, John Rutledge served for four months while Congress recessed. The Senate rejected his nomination when Congress reconvened. Thus, some scholars say Rehnquist is the 16th chief justice.

Here we see the number of justices from each state. Understandably, the oldest states have more justices since they have had much greater opportunity. Nevertheless, the South has been somewhat overrepresented on the Court, five of the top twelve states being southern or border states. A total of 19 states never have had a justice.

The Constitution says nothing about the courts having the power to overrule Congress and to reject laws as unconstitutional. Rather, those who wrote the Constitution assumed that the courts would confine themselves to applying existing law to specific cases, and they never anticipated judges asserting new "laws" or discarding old ones. Thus, in *The Federalist Papers*, Alexander Hamilton characterized the courts as the "least dangerous" and "the weakest" branch of government. However, in deciding a case in 1803, Chief Justice of the Supreme Court John Marshall asserted the right of the courts "to say what the law is." He further claimed that "a law repugnant to the Constitution is void." This position went unchallenged in Congress at that time and soon became the accepted view of Court power. This has resulted in frequent and often bitter conflicts between the Supreme Court, Congress, and the President. For example, President Franklin D. Roosevelt became so frustrated with rulings prohibiting many of his New Deal programs that in 1937 he proposed to "pack" the Court with new appointees. He asked Congress for legislation that would allow him to name an additional justice for every current member of the Court over age 70 (up to a total Court membership of 15), unless that judge retired, thus permitting appointment of a replacement. Since there were then six justices over 70, Roosevelt would have been able to appoint six new justices, giving his New Deal control of the Court. The bill did not pass and became irrelevant when a current justice switched to Roosevelt's side on issues.

Roosevelt was hardly alone in his antagonism toward the Supreme Court. Through the years the Supreme Court often has stirred up controversy by making decisions that many feel usurped the powers of Congress.

➤ *Data File:* **GSS**
➤ *Task:* **Univariate**
➤ *Primary Variable:* **45) SCH.PRAY**
➤ *View:* **Pie**

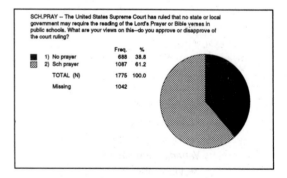

Although it has been more than 40 years since the Supreme Court prohibited prayer in the public schools, in 1962, this decision still has not gained general public acceptance. A large majority (61.2 percent) favor prayer in public schools. This is true even though the wording of the survey question maximizes support for the Court position since it does not deal with *allowing* prayer or Bible reading, but rather with laws *requiring* prayer or Bible reading.

Among the most controversial rulings are those interpreted by many as favoring the rights of criminals over those of victims of crimes. These concerns are not limited to the Supreme Court but are directed against the court system in general.

Data File: **GSS**
        Task: **Univariate**
➤ *Primary Variable:* **42) COURTS?**
        ➤ *View:* **Pie**

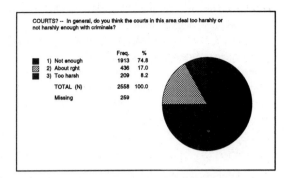

Americans overwhelmingly accuse the courts of not being sufficiently harsh in their treatment of criminals.

        Data File: **GSS**
        Task: **Univariate**
➤ *Primary Variable:* **55) SUP.COURT?**
        ➤ *View:* **Pie**

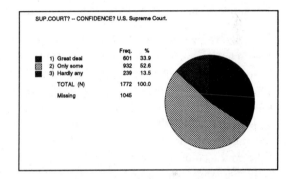

Given these results, it is not surprising that Americans are somewhat ambivalent about the Supreme Court. While about one in three expresses a great deal of confidence in the Court, more than half (52.6 percent) say they have "only some" confidence and 13.5 percent say they have "hardly any" confidence in the Court.

But, whatever they feel about the Court, what do Americans actually *know* about it? For example, how many even know the name of the chief justice?

➤ *Data File:* **NES**
        ➤ *Task:* **Univariate**
➤ *Primary Variable:* **84) CHIEF J.ID**
        ➤ *View:* **Pie**

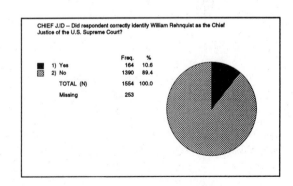

When asked to name the job or political office held by William Rehnquist, only about one in ten could correctly identify him as the chief justice of the Supreme Court, thus revealing him to be one of the least-known major public officials.

Data File: **NES**
➤ Task: **Cross-tabulation**
➤ Row Variable: **84) CHIEF J.ID**
➤ Column Variable: **24) NEWS TYPE**
➤ View: **Table**
➤ Display: **Column %**

CHIEF J.ID   by   NEWS TYPE
Cramer's V: 0.140 **

		NEWS TYPE					
		TV & paper	Paper	TV	Neither	Missing	TOTAL
CHIEF J.ID	Yes	40	49	20	55	0	164
		17.7%	15.3%	8.8%	7.1%		10.6%
	No	186	271	207	723	3	1387
		82.3%	84.7%	91.2%	92.9%		89.4%
	Missing	22	42	40	149	0	253
	TOTAL	226	320	227	778	3	1551
		100.0%	100.0%	100.0%	100.0%		

How do we learn the names of public officials? Obviously it's from the news media. Here we see a clear example of the differential impact of TV and newspapers in informing citizens. People who read newspapers every day, but do not watch TV news that often, are twice as likely to have correctly identified William Rehnquist than are those who rely only on TV for their daily news. And those who rely on both TV and newspapers are as likely to know Rehnquist as those who rely entirely on printed news.

A very plausible reason for the failure of TV to inform the public on many matters is that it is well known that TV scrimps on coverage of events for which it has no video and gives extra coverage, even to rather unimportant events, if it has good video. There is no video of the Supreme Court, so TV cannot let us see Rehnquist or other Court members in their official roles. Instead, important Supreme Court decisions usually are reported on TV by a reporter standing on the steps of the Court building and summarizing what the Court has done. Further, TV reports always are much shorter than the coverage given the same stories in newspapers—news stories usually contain many times more words than do the equivalent TV stories. As a result, the names of judges are mentioned far less often on TV than the names of other important officials.

The U.S. Supreme Court has many powers. It interprets laws and, occasionally, declares laws unconstitutional. But before the Supreme Court can issue a ruling on a case, it must first decide to hear that case. The Supreme Court selects to hear only a few cases from the thousands of cases appealed to it each year. Foremost the Supreme Court justices have time to hear only a select number of cases, as each case involves a number of stages from oral arguments, to preliminary discussion of decisions, to a final written opinion. By selecting among cases, the Court also demonstrates its power to decide what are the most important legal questions facing the nation. Let's examine both the number of cases appealed to the Supreme Court and the number of cases that conclude with a written opinion.

➤ Data File: **HISTORY**
➤ Task: **Historical Trends**
➤ Variables: **61) #CASE,S.CT**
             67) #S.C.DEC

• Number of cases filed in the Supreme Court

✘ Number of Supreme Court cases decided by signed opinions

As you can see, the number of cases appealed to the Supreme Court has risen dramatically over the years, from slightly less than 1,000 in the 1940s to between 7,000 and 8,000 in the past decade. Yet, the number of cases on which the Supreme Court issues a written opinion has varied only from 81 to 199. The Supreme Court simply refuses to hear more than 95 percent of the cases appealed to it. Since 1993, the Supreme Court has issued fewer than 100 written opinions each year, exercising even more control over its docket.

Your turn.

NAME:

COURSE:

DATE:

REVIEW QUESTIONS

Based on the first part of this exercise, answer True or False to the following items:

a. There are 12 justices on the Supreme Court.   T   F

b. Bill Clinton was the first president to appoint a woman to the Court.   T   F

c. President Ronald Reagan became so angry about Supreme Court decisions that he asked Congress to let him "pack" the Court.   T   F

d. Federal judges are appointed for life.   T   F

e. Most Americans oppose prayer in public schools.   T   F

f. The Supreme Court issues a written opinion on 95 percent of the cases appealed to it.   T   F

EXPLORIT QUESTIONS

1. Questions about confidence in various institutions have been asked in the GSS since 1972. Let's see how confidence in the Supreme Court compares with confidence in Congress and in the government in general. Let's also include confidence in medicine, an institution outside of government, for a different perspective.

> *Data File:* **HISTORY**
> *Task:* **Historical Trends**
> *Variables:* **38) CONF CONG**
> **39) CONF COURT**
> **40) CONF GOV**
> **41) CONF MED**

Note that these are survey data so that the values are only estimates of the population values—changes or differences of less than 10 percent are probably not important.

Answer True or False to each of the following items:

a. People have more confidence in the medical profession than they do in the Supreme Court or Congress.   T   F

b. People have more confidence in Congress than they do in the Supreme Court.   T   F

c. Relative confidence in these institutions (medicine, Congress, the Supreme Court) fluctuates a great deal over time, so sometimes people have the most confidence in medicine, sometimes in Congress, and sometimes in the Supreme Court.   T   F

2. Using the AUTO-ANALYZER task, let's see what demographic characteristics affect confidence in the Supreme Court.

> *Data File:* **GSS**
>> *Task:* **Auto-Analyzer**
> *Variable:* **55) SUP.COURT?**

For each demographic variable listed below, indicate whether there is any significant effect. If so, indicate which category is most likely and which is least likely to have a great deal of confidence in the Supreme Court.

	IS THE EFFECT SIGNIFICANT?		CATEGORY MOST LIKELY TO HAVE A GREAT DEAL OF CONFIDENCE	CATEGORY LEAST LIKELY TO HAVE A GREAT DEAL OF CONFIDENCE
a. *View:* **Race**	Yes	No	_____	_____
b. *View:* **Religion**	Yes	No	_____	_____
c. *View:* **Education**	Yes	No	_____	_____

d. What are the characteristics of those most likely to have a great deal of confidence in the Court?

e. What are the characteristics of those least likely to have a great deal of confidence in the Court?

3. The Supreme Court has ruled on many controversial issues, and the ruling of the Court is not always popular. Perhaps an individual's attitude on these issues affects his or her confidence in the Court.

> Data File: **GSS**
> ➤ Task: **Cross-tabulation**
> ➤ Row Variable: **55) SUP.COURT?**
> ➤ Column Variable: **45) SCH.PRAY**
> ➤ View: **Table**
> ➤ Display: **Column %**

Copy the *third* row of the percentaged table.

	NO PRAYER	SCH PRAY
a. %HARDLY ANY	_____%	_____%

b. What is the value of V for this table?   V = _____

c. Is V statistically significant?   Yes   No

d. One's attitude toward school prayer has an effect on one's confidence in the
   Supreme Court.   T   F

> Data File: **GSS**
> Task: **Cross-tabulation**
> Row Variable: **55) SUP.COURT?**
> ➤ Column Variable: **62) ABORT ANY**
> ➤ View: **Table**
> ➤ Display: **Column %**

Copy the *third* row of the percentaged table.

	YES	NO
e. %HARDLY ANY	_____%	_____%

f. What is the value of V for this table?   V = _____

g. Is V statistically significant?   Yes   No

h. One's attitude toward abortion has an effect on one's confidence in the
   Supreme Court.   T   F

Data File: **GSS**
Task: **Cross-tabulation**
Row Variable: **55) SUP.COURT?**
➤ Column Variable: **40) EXECUTE?**
➤ View: **Table**
➤ Display: **Column %**

Copy the *third* row of the percentaged table.

	FAVOR	OPPOSE
i. %HARDLY ANY	_____%	_____%

j. What is the value of V for this table?   V = _____

k. Is V statistically significant?   Yes   No

l. One's attitude toward the death penalty has an effect on one's confidence in
   the Supreme Court.   T   F

m. Taken together, these results suggest that confidence in the Supreme Court
   is generally based on more than one issue.   T   F

4. Let's see if one's basic attitudes, such as partisanship and ideology, influence attitudes toward the
    Supreme Court.

Data File: **GSS**
Task: **Cross-tabulation**
Row Variable: **55) SUP.COURT?**
➤ Column Variable: **21) PARTY**
➤ View: **Table**
➤ Display: **Column %**

	DEMOCRAT	INDEPEND	REPUBLICAN
a. %HARDLY ANY	_____%	_____%	_____%

b. What is the value of V for this table?   V = _____

c. Is V statistically significant?   Yes   No

d. Independents are the least likely to have confidence in the Supreme Court.   T   F

Data File: **GSS**
Task: **Cross-tabulation**
Row Variable: **55) SUP.COURT?**
➤ *Column Variable:* **23) LIB./CONS.**
➤ *View:* **Table**
➤ *Display:* **Column %**

	LIBERAL	MODERATE	CONSERV
e. %HARDLY ANY	_____%	_____%	_____%

f. What is the value of V for this table?   V = _____

g. Is V statistically significant?   Yes   No

h. Moderates are the least likely to have confidence in the Supreme Court.   T   F

i. Basic attitudes, such as partisanship and ideology, strongly influence one's opinion of the Supreme Court.   T   F

5. In the opening section of this exercise, we saw how the number of cases appealed to the Supreme Court has risen dramatically over the years. The Supreme Court, however, has control over its docket and can select to hear only a small fraction of these cases. The lowest level of the federal court system, the federal district court, does not have such discretionary control over the cases it hears. District courts are the starting point for criminal cases involving the violation of federal laws, though most criminal cases are heard in state courts. Federal district courts also hear civil cases, where one private party (e.g., an individual or a business) sues another private party for damages. Civil cases are heard in federal court if they involve parties from different states and seek damages over $75,000. Let's examine the number of criminal and civil cases heard in federal district court in the past 60 years.

➤ *Data File:* **HISTORY**
➤ *Task:* **Historical Trends**
➤ *Variables:* **64) #CIV COM**
65) #CRIM COM

a. The workload (combined total of criminal and civil cases) before the federal district court has risen dramatically over the past 60 years.   T   F

b. The change in the workload of the federal district court is due mainly to a large change in the number of criminal cases.   T   F

APPENDIX: VARIABLE NAMES AND SOURCES

◆ DATA FILE: COLONIAL ◆

1) CASE ID
2) POP 1790
3) %BRITISH
4) % PROT.
5) # SLAVES
6) %SLAVES 90
7) #FREE AFR.

8) % FREE
9) # AFRI.-AM
10) %BLACK 90
11) CHURCHED76
12) WHITE CH76
13) %R CATH 76
14) %ENGLISH90

15) %SCOTCH 90
16) %P.IRISH 90
17) %C.IRISH90
18) %GERMAN90
19) %DUTCH 90
20) %FRENCH 90
21) %SWEDISH90

◆ DATA FILE: COUNTY ◆

1) NAME
2) POPULATION
3) %WHITE
4) %BLACK
5) %HISPANIC
6) %HISPANIC2
7) %MEXICAN
8) %MEXICAN2
9) %AMER.IND
10) %AMER.IND2
11) %ASIAN

12) %ASIAN2
13) %NORWEG
14) %IRISH
15) %GERMAN
16) %FOREIGN
17) %FOREIGN2
18) %NON-ENGL
19) %POOR
20) MED.FAM$
21) FARM %
22) MANUFACT%

23) %NO MOVE
24) %<5 90
25) %>64 90
26) DEATH 88
27) CHLD MRT88
28) %EMERG.90
29) CHLD POR89
30) H.S.GRAD90
31) COL.DEGR90

◆ DATA FILE: GSS ◆

1) MARITAL
2) # CHILDREN
3) EDUCATION
4) DAD EDUC.
5) MOM EDUC.
6) SEX
7) RACE
8) RACE LG
9) AGE
10) PAR. BORN
11) INCOME
12) EVER UNEMP
13) UNIONIZED?
14) RELIGION
15) RELPERSN
16) ATTEND
17) PRAY
18) BIBLE

19) URBAN?
20) REGION
21) PARTY
22) DEM/REP
23) LIB./CONS.
24) VOTED 96
25) WHO IN 96?
26) BIG CITY$
27) BLACK$
28) DEFENSE$
29) FOR. AID$
30) WELFARE $
31) SOC.SEC.$
32) MASS TRAN$
33) POOR $
34) EQUALIZE$
35) TAXES?
36) ATHEIST SP

37) RACIST SP
38) COMMUN.SP
39) FR.SPEECH
40) EXECUTE?
41) GUN LAW?
42) COURTS?
43) GRASS?
44) WAR
45) SCH.PRAY
46) INTERMAR.?
47) AFFRM. ACT
48) HAPPY?
49) BIG BIZ?
50) RELIGION?
51) EDUCATION?
52) FED.GOV'T?
53) LABOR?
54) PRESS?

◆ DATA FILE: GSS (cont'd) ◆

55) SUP.COURT?
56) SCIENCE?
57) CONGRESS?
58) MILITARY?
59) MEN BETTER
60) ABORT.WANT
61) ABORT.HLTH
62) ABORT ANY
63) SEX ED?
64) PREM.SEX
65) HOMO.SEX
66) PORN.LAW?
67) EUTHANASIA
68) SUIC.WISH
69) OWN GUN?
70) HUNT?
71) NEWSPAPER?

72) WATCH TV
73) MOTH.WORK?
74) WIFE@HOME
75) HELP POOR?
76) MUCH GOVNT
77) GOV.MED.
78) GOV.BLACK
79) MELTING.POT
80) IMMIGRANTS
81) DISC MAN
82) DISC WOMAN
83) GOVT EQUAL
84) ANIM.TESTS
85) NATURE GOD
86) EVOLUTION
87) CARS ENVIR
88) GREEN HSE

89) RECYCLE
90) SEX OF SEX
91) ENGL OFFIC
92) NO BILING
93) ENGL VOTE
94) SAT DEMOC?
95) FREE PRESS
96) GCROP DANG
97) USTERROR
98) FRTERROR
99) NUCLRWAR
100) USE WEB?
101) CHAT POL
102) WEB POL
103) REV.DISCRM

◆ DATA FILE: HOUSE107 ◆

1) NAME
2) STATE
3) DISTRICT#
4) SEX
5) RACE/ETHNI
6) AGE
7) RELIGION
8) EDUCATION
9) MARITAL
10) LAWYER?
11) PARTY
12) SOUTH DEM
13) # TERMS
14) INCUMBENT
15) REGION
16) DIS AFRAM%

17) DIST HISP%
18) DIS FAM$
19) DIS HOUSE$
20) % OF VOTE
21) CAMPAIGN $
22) OPPONENT $
23) CANOPP
24) %PAC CONTR
25) %IND CONTR
26) INDPAC
27) $ PER VOTE
28) ACLU RATE
29) ACU RATE
30) ADA RATE
31) EC_STIMUL
32) MARR_PEN

33) DEATH TAX
34) EC_GRWTH
35) EDUCAT BIL
36) PAC SALMON
37) CLONING
38) ENERGY
39) TERRORISM
40) GOD BLESS
41) AIRPORT
42) CAMPAIGN R
43) CHILD PROT
44) PENSION
45) ABORT CONS
46) ACC REFORM
47) NUCLEAR

◆ DATA FILE: USPRES ◆

1) namyear
2) NAME
3) YEAR
4) ELECTVOTE
5) POPVOTE

6) PARTY
7) EARLY
8) PRESNUMBER
9) ELECT AGE
10) HEIGHT

11) EDUCATION
12) LAWYER
13) MILITARY
14) MIL FAME
15) RELIGION

Appendix: Variable Names and Sources

◆ DATA FILE: USPRES (cont'd) ◆

16) HOW RELIG
17) YRS IN OFF
18) VETOES
19) ASSASSIN
20) ETHNICITY
21) GOV?
22) SEN?

23) VEEP?
24) RATING
25) SUP CT
26) TOT JUDGES
27) CENTURY
28) PTY-CONG
29) OVERRIDE

30) UNELECT
31) # VPRES
32) SEC ELEC C
33) SEC POP VT
34) MINOR
35) ERA

◆ DATA FILE: NATIONS ◆

1) COUNTRY
2) POP98
3) P.INTEREST
4) TALK POL.
5) PERSUASION
6) PETITION?
7) INTEREST G
8) SIT-INS
9) REVOLUTION
10) LEFT/RIGHT
11) ANTI-RACE
12) ANTI-FORGN
13) ANTI-JEW
14) ANTI-GAY
15) %FEM LEGIS

16) %FEM HEADS
17) WOMEN WANT
18) DEMOCRACY
19) CIVIL LIBS
20) VERY HAPPY
21) NATL PRIDE
22) PRESS?
23) PARLIAMENT
24) UNIONS?
25) WORK PRIDE
26) CHEAT TAX
27) TAKE BRIBE
28) CARS/CAP
29) % URBAN
30) NEWSPAPERS

31) TELEVISION
32) LITERACY
33) ABRT.UNWED
34) A.UNWANT
35) GDP/CAP
36) # PARTIES
37) %BIG PARTY
38) % VOTED
39) FIGHT COPS
40) EDUC EXPTD
41) HEALTH
42) GOVT-HLT
43) MIL-GNP
44) MIL-PC

◆ DATA FILE: NES ◆

1) REGION
2) POPULATION
3) SEX
4) EDUCATION
5) AGE
6) INCOME
7) RACE
8) HISPANIC
9) MARITAL
10) UNION
11) CHURCH
12) RELIGION
13) BIBLE
14) PRAY
15) RELIG IMP

16) PARTY
17) IDEOLOGY
18) GORE IDEO
19) BUSH IDEO
20) INTEREST?
21) INFORMED?
22) READ PAPER
23) TV NEWS?
24) NEWS TYPE
25) TALK RADIO
26) VOTED
27) PVOTE LNG
28) PREVOTE
29) KNOW HOUSE
30) VOTE HOUSE

31) VOTE SEN
32) HSE TYPE
33) SENTYPE
34) PRES 96
35) CLINT APP
36) CONG APP
37) INCUM APP
38) GORE KNOW
39) BRAD. KNOW
40) CLIN THERM
41) GOTE THERM
42) BUSH THERM
43) BUCH THERM
44) NADR THERM
45) MCCN THERM

◆ DATA FILE: NES (cont'd) ◆

46) BRDL THERM
47) LBRM THERM
48) CHNY THERM
49) DIVGOV PR
50) IMMIGRATE
51) IMPORTS
52) ISOLAT
53) GOVT SPND
54) DEMS GVSP
55) REPS GVSP
56) INSURANCE
57) AFFIRM.ACT
58) ABORTION
59) GORE ABRT
60) BUSH ABRT
61) ABORT PAR
62) PBIRTH
63) GAYMIL
64) GUN CNTRL
65) SCHVCHR
66) GAY ADOPT
67) DEATH PEN

68) ECON 92
69) POL DISC
70) PRTY TALK
71) TALK POL?
72) BUTTON
73) CONTRIBUTE
74) CONT$PARTY
75) ELECT FAIR
76) GEN INT
77) JURY DUTY
78) PRTY DIFFS
79) VOLUNTR
80) GAY JOB
81) CAMP FING
82) CONTACT
83) LOTT ID
84) CHIEF J.ID
85) BRITISH ID
86) RENO ID
87) TRUST GOV
88) EQL SOCIE
89) ECON PRTY

90) PEACE PRT
91) PARTIES
92) FAMILY VAL
93) GOVT ATTN
94) ELECT ATTN
95) COMPLICATE
96) DON'T CARE
97) CROOKED?
98) GOVT WASTE
99) BIG INTERS
100) VOTE COUNT
101) MEDIA TRST
102) EQL ROLE
103) GOVGJOBS
104) ENVRG
105) GORE ER
106) BUSH ER
107) ENGLISH
108) CRIME
109) DEM/REP

◆ DATA FILE: STATES ◆

1) STATE NAME
2) POPULATION
3) BIG REGION
4) URBAN00
5) URBAN1900
6) SUNBELT
7) THE WEST
8) THE SOUTH
9) SLAVE/FREE
10) UNION/CONF
11) STATES1860
12) MOBILE HOM
13) FAMILY $
14) HIGH $
15) %POOR
16) FED$ RATIO
17) %FED LAND
18) FED.EMPLOY
19) DEFENSE $
20) INCOME TAX
21) STATE DEBT

22) %FOREIGN
23) % WHITE
24) %AFRIC.AM
25) % ASIAN
26) %HISPANIC
27) %SPAN.SPK
28) POP GROW
29) NEW HOMES
30) MALE HOMES
31) N.R./NAT.
32) %FEMALE LG
33) % VOTED'92
34) %REGIST.92
35) STATES '92
36) CLINTON'92
37) %BUSH '92
38) %PEROT 92
39) STATES '88
40) %BUSH '88
41) STATES '84
42) %REAGAN 84

43) STATES '80
44) %REAGAN'80
45) %CARTER'80
46) %ANDERSON
47) STATES '76
48) %CARTER 76
49) STATES '72
50) %NIXON '72
51) STATES '68
52) % NIXON'68
53) %HUMPH.'68
54) %WALLACE68
55) STATES '64
56) %JOHNSON64
57) STATES '60
58) %KENNEDY60
59) STATES '56
60) IKE '56
61) STATES '52
62) %IKE '52
63) STATES'48

64) %TRUMAN
65) %DEWEY'48
66) %THURMD'48
67) %WALLACE48
68) STATES '44
69) % FDR '44
70) STATES '40
71) % FDR '40
72) STATES '36
73) FDR '36
74) STATES '32
75) FDR '32
76) STATES '28
77) %HOOVER'28
78) STATES '24
79) %COOL '24
80) %LAFOLL.24
81) STATES '20
82) %HARDING20
83) % LEFT '20
84) ELECTOR90
85) ELECTOR60
86) ELECTOR40
87) EC GAIN60
88) PRESIDENTS
89) UN/CONF SL
90) %SLAV ST
91) HOUSE93
92) # S. COURT
93) %CLINTON96
94) %DOLE 96
95) %PEROT96
96) STATES '96
97) %VOTED 96
98) %REGIST.96
99) DEBT$/CAP
100) POP GO
101) DIF.ST.
102) SPEEDING
103) WELFARE
104) TOUGH LOVE
105) $ HI ED.
106) %HI EDUC $
107) STA EX/CAP
108) EDUC$/CAP
109) HLTH$/CAP

110) WELF$/CAP
111) HGHWYS$/CA
112) CORR$/CAP
113) FED$/CAP
114) PROP.TAX
115) VIOL.CRIME
116) MURDER
117) POP 98
118) RAPE
119) ROBBERY
120) ASSAULT
121) BURGLARY
122) LARCENY
123) PROP CRIME
124) HEALTH INS
125) %COLLEGE
126) %HIGH SCH
127) HATECRIMES
128) POLICE
129) #SOC.SEC
130) SS BENEFIT
131) %SOCSEC
132) UNEMP $
133) AVG ENEMP$
134) UNEMP$/CAP
135) AVG PAY
136) PER CAP$
137) STATE TAX
138) EXPENDITUR
139) TANF FAM#
140) TANF FAM
141) ABORTRATE
142) $PER PUPIL
143) TOXIC
144) LOC$/CAP
145) LOCEX$/CAP
146) FEDFUNDS
147) FDAID-CHFM
148) FDAID-HOUS
149) MED AGE
150) UNEMPLOY
151) % UNION
152) CIG TAX
153) %FOODSTAMP
154) DEM LEGIS
155) REPUB LEGI

156) DEM-REPS
157) REPUB-REPS
158) DEM-SENS
159) REPUB-SENS
160) DEM CONG
161) REPUB-CONG
162) PCOMP-CONG
163) PCOMP-LEG
164) MOTOR VTR
165) POP GROW2
166) DTH OPIN
167) DTH LAW
168) LIBERAL
169) MODERATE
170) CONSER
171) POP-DEM
172) POP-IND
173) POP-REP
174) PROCHOICE
175) PROLIFE
176) BS-VISITS
177) GR-VISITS
178) GORE
179) GWBUSH
180) NADER
181) BUCHANAN
182) THIRDPTY
183) MARGIN
184) MARGINP
185) STATES '00
186) GWB-ECVOTE
187) GORE-ECVOT
188) COMPETITIV
189) GORENADER
190) ELECTOR00
191) EC GAIN00
192) HOUSE03
193) %AMER.IN00
194) IMMIGRAN00
195) FEM.HEAD00
196) BLK.OFF 99
197) HSP.OFF 00
198) %VOTED 00
199) %REGIST.00
200) LOTTERY?
201) LTTD P/C $

◆ TREND FILE: HISTORY ◆

1) DATE
2) POPULATION
3) %<5
4) %65&OVER
5) % URBAN
6) %HS
7) %COLLEGE
8) %NO HS
9) LAWYER/CAP
10) DOCTOR/CAP
11) CPI(1967)
12) VOTER PART
13) % DEM
14) % REP
15) APPORTION
16) %DEM HOUSE
17) D.PRES %
18) M.D.PRES %
19) F.D.PRES %
20) W.D.PRES %
21) B.D.PRES %
22) %HH TELE
23) TV VIEW
24) READ PAPER

25) NEWS/100
26) TV/100HH
27) SOUTH.DEM
28) CIVLIB INX
29) %FEM PRES
30) %M F.PRES
31) %F F.PRES
32) % BLK PRES
33) GOV.CROOK?
34) TRUST GOV
35) WASTE TAX
36) CONF.TV
37) CONF.PRESS
38) CONF CONG
39) CONF COURT
40) CONF GOV
41) CONF MED
42) CONF MIL
43) ENVIR $
44) DEFENSE $
45) WELF $
46) HEALTH $
47) BLACK $
48) DRUG $

49) FED EMP RT
50) DEF EMP RT
51) LEG EMP RT
52) JUDG EMP R
53) NON-D EMP
54) DEF$/POP
55) HR$/POP
56) S.S.$/POP
57) I.S.$/POP
58) MED$/POP
59) HEAL$/POP
60) ED$/POP
61) #CASE,S.CT
62) #CASE COMM
63) #CRIM CASE
64) #CIV COM
65) #CRIM COM
66) RACE SEG
67) #S.C.DEC
68) HSE-OTH
69) SEN-OTH
70) %REP HOUSE
71) DEM$
72) REP$

SOURCES

NES–National Election Study, 2000

The NES data file is based on selected variables from the 2000 American National Election Study provided by the National Election Studies, Institute for Social Research at the University of Michigan and the Inter-university Consortium for Political and Social Research. The principal investigators are Nancy Burns, Donald R. Kinder, Steven J. Rosenstone, Virginia Sapiro, and the National Election Studies.

GSS–General Social Survey

The GSS data file is based on selected variables from the National Opinion Research Center (University of Chicago) General Social Surveys for 2000, distributed by The Roper Center and the Inter-university Consortium for Political and Social Research. The principal investigators are James A. Davis and Tom W. Smith.

STATES–The Fifty States of the U.S.

The data in the STATES file are from a variety of sources. The variable description for each variable uses the following abbreviations to indicate the source.

ABC: *Blue Book*, Audit Bureau of Circulation
CENSUS: The summary volumes of the 1990 U.S. Census
CHRON.: *The Chronicle of Higher Education Almanac*
DES: *Digest of Education Statistics*, U.S. Dept. of Education
FEC: Federal Election Commission
HCSR: Health Care State Rankings, Morgan Quitno
HIGHWAY: Highway Statistics, Federal Highway Administration, U.S. Dept. of Transportation
KOSMIN: Kosmin, Barry A. 1991. *Research Report: The National Survey of Religious Identification*. New York: CUNY Graduate Center.
SMAD: *State and Metropolitan Area Data Book*, 1991, U.S. Dept. of Commerce
SOS: Secretary of State or Election Board web pages
S.P.R.: State Policy Reference
S.R.: State Rankings, Morgan Quitno
UCR: *Uniform Crime Reports*, U.S. Dept. of Justice

NATIONS–Nations of the World

The data in the NATIONS file are from a variety of sources. The variable description for each variable uses the following abbreviations to indicate the source.

ABC: *Blue Book*, Audit Bureau of Circulation
DES: *Digest of Education Statistics*, U.S. Dept. of Education
ES: Electoral Studies
FITW: *Freedom in the World*, 1995, Freedom House
HDR: *Human Development Reports*, United Nations Development Program
PRB: *World Population Data Sheet*, 1994, Population Research Council
SA: *Statistical Abstract of the United States*
TWF: *The World Fact Book, 1994–1995*, Central Intelligence Agency

WABF: *The World Almanac and Book of Facts,* 1995

WVS: World Values Survey, Institute for Social Research, Inter-University Consortium for Political and Social Research

USPRES—Presidents of the United States

The data in the USPRES file are from a variety of readily available sources, such as a world almanac or an encyclopedia, the U.S. Census, or other government publications. The variable description for each variable uses the following abbreviations to indicate the source.

NARA: National Archives and Records Administration "Electoral College Box Scores" on Web page.

CWP: Congressional Web Pages, Gary L. Galemore, "Presidential Vetoes, 1789–1996: A Summary Overview," CRS Report for Congress, htttp://www.house.gov/rules/97–163.htm. Updated with Bill Summary & Status, 105th Congress, Vetoed Bills, House Webpages. "Political Divisions of the House of Representatives, 1789–present," http://clerkweb.house.gov/histrecs/househist/lists/divisionh.htm. "Senate Statistics: Majority and Minority Parties," http://www.senate.gov/learning/stat_13.htm.

FWP: Federal Judiciary Web Pages, "Judgeship Appointments by Presidents," http://www.uscourts.gov/history/table1.pdf.

COLONIAL—The Thirteen Colonies plus Georgia and Maine

The data in the COLONIAL file are from a variety of readily available sources, such as a world almanac or encyclopedia, the U.S. Census, or other government publications.

HOUSE107

The data in the HOUSE107 file are from a variety of readily available sources, such as a world almanac or an encyclopedia, the U.S. Census, the Thomas Web site (http://thomas.loc.gov), or other government publications.

ACLU RATE: Courtesy of the American Civil Liberties Union, The National Freedom Scorecard/ACLU Scorecard for the 107th Congress, http://scorecard.aclu.org/, 2002.

ACU RATE: Courtesy of the American Conservative Union, http://www.acuratings.com/, 2002.

ADA RATE: Courtesy of the Americans for Democratic Action, http://adaction.org/2001voting.html, 2002.